Critical Muslim

Educational Reform

Critical Muslim is published quarterly by C. Hurst & Co. (Publishers) Ltd. on behalf of and in conjunction with Critical Muslim Ltd. and the Muslim Institute, London.

All correspondence to Muslim Institute, CAN Mezzanine, 49-51 East Road, London N1 6AH, United Kingdom

e-mail for editorial: editorial@criticalmuslim.com

The editors do not necessarily agree with the opinions expressed by the contributors. We reserve the right to make such editorial changes as may be necessary to make submissions to Critical Muslim suitable for publication.

C. Hurst & Co. (Publishers) Ltd., 41 Great Russell Street, London WC1B 3PL

ISBN: 978-1-84904-542-1 ISSN: 2048-8475

To subscribe or place an order by credit/debit card or cheque (pound sterling only) please contact Kathleen May at the Hurst address above or e-mail kathleen@hurstpub.co.uk

Tel: 020 7255 2201

A one year subscription, inclusive of postage (four issues), costs £50 (UK), £65 (Europe) and £75 (rest of the world).

IIT PUBLICATIONS

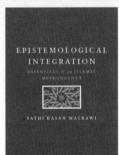

APOSTASY IN ISLAM: A HISTORICAL AND SCRIPTURAL ANALYSIS • Taha J. Alalwani

Pb: ISBN 978-1-56564-363-5 Hb: ISBN 978-1-56564-364-2
• September 2011

The Qur'an and the Sunnah promote freedom of belief. The author shows there is no evidence whatsoever for the death or any penalty in Islam for exiting the Faith.

EPISTEMOLOGICAL INTEGRATION: ESSENTIALS OF AN ISLAMIC METHODOLOGY
Fathi H. Malkawi

The work makes the case that fundamental to any Muslim recovery is laying the foundations of sound thinking and values that integrate the two main sources of knowledge: Revelation and Reality under the umbrella of Tawhid.

ISBN 978-1-56564-557-8 pb
ISBN 978-1-56564-569-1 hb
2014

Marketing Manager, IIT (USA)
Tel: 703 471 1133 ext. 108 | Fax: 703 471 3922
E-mail: sales@iiit.org | Website: www.iiit.org

Kube Publishing Ltd, United Kingdom
Tel: 01530 249 230 | Fax: 01530 249 656
E-mail: info@kubepublishing.com | Website: www.kubepublishing.com

HALAL FOOD FOUNDATION

Halal Is Much More Than Food

The Halal Food Foundation (HFF) is a registered charity that aims to make the concept of halal more accessible and mainstream. We want people to know that halal does not just pertain to food – halal is a lifestyle.

The Foundation pursues its goals through downloadable resources, events, social networking, school visits, pursuing and funding scientific research on issues of food and health, and its monthly newsletter. We work for the community and aim at the gradual formation of a consumer association. We aim to educate and inform; and are fast becoming the first port of call on queries about halal issues. We do not talk at people, we listen to them.

If you have any queries, comments, ideas, or would just like to voice your opinion - please get in contact with us.

Halal Food Foundation

109 Fulham Palace Road,
Hammersmith, London, W6 8JA
Charity number: 1139457
Website: www.halalfoodfoundation.co.uk
E-mail: info@halalfoodfoundation.co.uk

 @HFF_UK

 Halal Food Foundation

The Barbary Figs

by

Rashid Boudjedra

Translated by
André Naffis-Sahely

Buy a copy of Rashid Boudjedra's *The Barbary Figs* at
www.hauspublishing.com or by calling +44(0)20 7838 9055
and a recieve a copy of Khaled al-Berry's memoir
Life is More Beautiful than Paradise free.

RASHID AND OMAR are cousins who find themselves side by side on a flight from Algiers to Constantine. During the hour-long journey, the pair will exhume their past, their boyhood in French Algeria during the 1940s and their teenage years fighting in the bush during the revolution. Rashid, the narrator, has always resented Omar, who despite all his worldly successes, has been on the run from the ghosts of his past, ghosts that Rashid has set himself the task of exorcising. Rashid peppers his account with chilling episodes from Algerian history, from the savageries of the French invasion in the 1830s, to the repressive regime that is in place today.

RASHID BOUDJEDRA has routinely been called one of North Africa's leading writers since his debut, *La Répudiation*, was published in 1969, earning the author the first of many fatwas. While he wrote his first six novels in French, Boudjedra switched to Arabic in 1982 and wrote another six novels in the language before returning to French in 1994. *The Barbary Figs* was awarded the Prix du Roman Arabe 2010.

CM15

July–September 2015

CONTENTS

EDUCATIONAL REFORM

ARTS AND LETTERS

REVIEWS

Illustration by Sofia Niazi

Subscribe to Critical Muslim

Now in its third year, *Critical Muslim* is the only publication of its kind, giving voice to the diversity and plurality of Muslim reporting, creative writing, poetry and scholarship.

Subscribe now to receive each issue of Critical Muslim direct to your door and save money on the cover price of each issue.

Subscriptions are available at the following prices, inclusive of postage. Subscribe for two years and save 10%!

	ONE YEAR (4 Issues)	TWO YEARS (8 Issues)
UK	£50	£90
Europe	£65	£117
Rest of World	£75	£135

TO SUBSCRIBE:

CRITICALMUSLIM.HURSTPUBLISHERS.COM

41 GREAT RUSSELL ST, LONDON WC1B 3PL
WWW.HURSTPUBLISHERS.COM
WWW.FBOOK.COM/HURSTPUBLISHERS
020 7255 2201

EDUCATIONAL REFORM

INTRODUCTION
THE INTEGRATION WE SEEK

Jeremy Henzell-Thomas

What route should we take through the landscape of higher education, in particular within Muslim societies? As a keen country walker, given to long-distance trekking in a range of 'wilderness' environments, I might suggest that we approach this task as another arduous trek, setting out to cover as much ground as possible in all weathers and take in every conceivable vista on the way.

As such, I might attempt a survey, ranging over as many views and perspectives as we could hope to encompass, taking in and trying to synthesise as much evidence and analysis as possible. One could begin, for example, with an exploration of the evolution of 'Universities in Muslim Contexts' as presented by Marodsilton Muborakshoeva. 'The early Muslims', she writes, 'actively sought to harmonise the message of Islam not only with their existing cultures but also with earlier civilisations'. The institutions of higher learning that developed in the classical period, such as Al-Azhar in Cairo, Al-Qarawiyin in Fez, and Al-Zaytuna in Tunis, had 'unique architecture, funding structure and organisation of knowledge and also introduced degrees (*ijaza*) and academic rankings'. Their approach to knowledge was holistic; and they became 'the prototypes on which the Christians of Europe modelled their own universities'. But that is history. Modern universities in the Muslim world, Muborakshoeva notes, 'lack creative and original approaches to knowledge acquisition and production, and 'have very little to contribute either in the field of scientific and technological advancement or in cultural and religious studies'. A point emphasised by Martin Rose in his meticulous survey of universities in North Africa. Egypt, Libya, Algeria, Tunisia and Morocco 'have been amongst the biggest spenders in the world, fairly consistently putting some

5 per cent of GDP and about 20 per cent of government spending into education over the last half-century'. Yet, the returns, laments Rose, are 'slender'. Or I could venture into the controversial territory of the madrasas. As the symposium on *What is a Madrasa?* by Ebrahim Moosa shows, the landscape has changed drastically and is now overwhelmed by undergrowth, bogs and perilous situations on and off the path. I might wail at the desolate panorama before me and take this as incontrovertible evidence of the urgent need for reform, as urged by Abdelwahab El-Affendi. Or I could critically examine the competing models and paradigms which purport to define the nature and purpose of a university education.

All of this is invaluable. The contributors to this issue of *Critical Muslim* provide us with a wealth of analysis and insights, shine a torch on their varied findings, and furnish us with facts and arguments about what is wrong and what ought to be done to get out of the forest of decay and degeneration. Here, I want to approach this task not as a surveyor charting the territory, nor even as a trekker with his eye on the map seeking a way out of the quagmire, but as an explorer searching for new vistas.

So let me begin with a story. By a useful coincidence, both Ziauddin Sardar and I have converged on the same story by different routes, and come to very similar conclusions. Both of us are involved in 'The Reform of Higher Education in Muslim Societies', an initiative of the International Institute of Islamic Thought (IIIT). It is an attempt to give a new shape and direction to IIIT's famous 'Islamisation of Knowledge' project. Based on the late Ismail Raji al-Faruqi's *Islamisation of Knowledge: General Principles and Work Plan*, and launched in the early 1980s, it was a major, world-wide enterprise that captured the imagination of Muslim scholars, thinkers and intellectuals – and led to the establishment of some noted 'Islamic universities'. Over the last few years, IIIT has convened a number of symposiums, conferences and meetings, in Washington, London and Istanbul, to explore what lessons can be drawn from the 'Islamisation of Knowledge' project and how, in a changed and changing context, we can move towards much needed reforms in higher education in the Muslim world. Numerous reports and background papers have been presented at these gatherings; and this issue of *Critical Muslim* is a contribution to that on-going debate and discussion. Sardar was entrusted with the task of producing a 'synthesis paper' that summarised the arguments and findings and charted a way forward. The end result was 'Reinventing Ourselves: From Islamisation of Knowledge to Integration of Knowledge', which envisages a new project based on 'holistic education' in a 'universal sense'. Sardar opens the paper with this story.

On 17 June, 1744, the commissioners from Maryland and Virginia negotiated a treaty with the Indians of the Six Nations at Lancaster, Pennsylvania. The Indians were invited to send boys to William and Mary College where they would be provided for and educated in the ways of the modern world. The next day they declined the offer:

> We know that you highly esteem the type of learning taught in those colleges, and that the maintenance of our young men while with you, would be very expensive to you. We are convinced that you mean to do us good by your proposal; and we thank you heartily. But you, who are wise, must know that different nations have different conceptions of things and you will therefore not take it amiss if our ideas of this kind of education happen not to be the same as yours. We have had some experience in it. Several of our young people were formerly brought up at the colleges of the Northern Provinces; they were instructed in all of your sciences; but when they came back to us, they were bad runners, ignorant of every means of living in the woods – not fit for hunters, warriors, nor counsellors, they were totally good for nothing. We are, however, not the less obliged by your kind offer, though we decline accepting it; and to show our grateful sense of it, if the gentlemen of Virginia will send us a dozen of their sons, we will take care of their education, instruct them in all we know, and make men of them.

In his study of the Native American worldview, physicist F. David Peat maintains that the natural tendency in Western culture is to warn, help, teach, instruct and improve instead of allowing people to learn from their experience. Under the heading 'A Story about Knowledge and Knowing', he relates a story told by Joe Couture, a therapist and traditional healer, which explores the implications of these two ways of knowing and the clash between a Western education and his own Blackfoot background. The story shows how traditional people teach by telling stories rooted in their concrete experiences rather than by imparting facts or applying abstract logical reasoning. In this case a Native Elder, describing the experience of his grandson at a local school, felt no need to analyse the school's educational philosophy nor discuss the comparative value of different worldviews. He simply told a story which brought into focus some of the things that people were sensing and feeling about the impact of the school on the local community.

The story the Elder told was about the time when he was a boy and had to make a long trip along the Yukon River to Dawson City. His old pickup truck had broken down and he had faced an arduous journey of over a hundred miles in adverse conditions. In the end he had made it through. The old man said that his grandson could now read and write, but he had no doubt that if the boy were to attempt the same journey alone he would never make it back.

As an immediate reaction, and without proper regard for evidence of this kind, we might easily dismiss both stories as largely irrelevant. After all, you might say, what need is there in the modern world for the preservation of a culture so dependent on the manly skills of running, living in the woods, and fighting, even if we might agree that the other skill so prized by the Indians of the Six Nations – that of counselling – is very much in demand, especially in modern societies beset with increasingly prevalent and pressing mental health problems. And how often is the need going to arise for the skills which require a boy to travel a hundred miles in rugged country in adverse conditions in order to get home? These days, children rarely even walk to school, so perilous do their parents consider such a journey.

Sardar's commentary on the Six Nations anecdote encapsulates the underlying paradox which forms the crux of the problem before us, not only in the specific domain of education, but also in the wider field of paradigm change and its impact on the rise and fall of civilisations.

> Different nations have different conceptions of things. It is through education that a nation, a society, or a civilisation, consciously passes on the accumulated skills, knowledge and wisdom of the past to future generations. Education not only preserves the cultural identity and historical legacy of a society but ensures its survival as a distinct entity. It furnishes a worldview within which the society seeks to solve its problems, delineates it social relations and economic activity, makes sense of itself, pushes the frontiers of knowledge, and continues as a living entity. The Indians realised that the education offered by the Government of Virginia did not equip their young with the skills and

knowledge they needed to survive; worse, it threatened the very existence of their culture and society.

A society without its own sophisticated education system, designed to preserve and transmit the values and cultural traits that ensure its survival, will either be colonised or lose the distinct elements of its worldview. Both the individual and society suffer from the absence of appropriate educational institutions. The individual is denied the social instrument through which a positive sense of religious values and cultural identity can be developed. The society is deprived of its human capital with the result that almost all spheres – from values and skills to governance, law, commerce, finance, industry and cultural production – go into irreparable decline. Thus, education is not simply a process through which knowledge is imparted; it is also, in the shape of higher education, the mechanism through which knowledge is actually generated. Even if Muslim societies have values to share, without a thriving education system, as Abdelwahab El-Affendi notes, they have very little knowledge to share. This is the crisis that has confronted Muslim societies since the seventeenth century onwards when "almost all the knowledge Muslims possessed became worthless overnight in terms of worldly value". But it was not simply worldly knowledge that evaporated from Muslim societies. The decline of great Muslim educational institutions, described so aptly by George Makdisi in *The Rise of Colleges*, also eroded the appreciation of Muslim heritage and legacy, and led to the erosion of Muslim norms and values, and the perversion of religious knowledge.

But, as Sardar contends, the Six Nations anecdote also points towards a predicament. While the Indians were right to judge that the new ways of knowing were not appropriate for their society at the time, this choice did nothing to preserve their cultures or save them from catastrophic decline. The Indians, like the Muslims who followed a similar path later on, did themselves no service by remaining ignorant for the power differential cemented by colonialism 'drove the former to extinction and the latter to subjugation'. In order to confront this fundamental paradox, asserts Sardar, we need to balance the other side of the equation and face up to the fact that our spiritual and ethical values cannot survive without the power to protect our societies from subjugation. And he comes to the inescapable conclusion that it is therefore incumbent on Muslim societies 'to appreciate and achieve a degree of excellence in contemporary knowledge'.

The analysis highlights the pivotal concepts that guide us to the new vista we need to open up. It needs to be a view which can take in both a broad panoramic vision, seeing on all sides and far into the distance, and a depth of field which gives us sharp focus when we need it. To do so, we need, above all, to understand that there are different though complementary levels of description in a multi-layered and multi-faceted reality where the diversity of forms is infinite and ever-changing, but which, nevertheless, has an origin and a centre, an immutable essence which is the source of everything and where all diversity and multiplicity find ultimate unity and reconciliation.

To encompass this unity in diversity within the field of education, we need to critically examine (and, ideally, clear away) the massive impediment caused by the human tendency to divide reality into competing and mutually exclusive ideas, approaches, and paradigms of thought which generate and sustain adversarial positions. Of course, this tendency is ingrained in us in the domain of duality, for, as the Qur'an tells us, 'everything have We created in pairs' (51:49). In an essay on the power of education in the previous issue of *Critical Muslim*, I suggested that binary thinking and dichotomisation are embedded in us as one of the chief features of the simple 'narrative' or 'script' which gives us the means to judge and act quickly and decisively. 'Us' and 'them' is a powerful call to incite action, judgement, and hostility. By contrast, the armchair philosopher who scrutinises the logical minutiae of every proposition, absorbs every qualification, respects every position, seeks out every iota of evidence, and agonises over every minor dissonance and nuance may never get out of his chair. This paralysis of indecision is of course the extreme of one end of the spectrum, just as the conditioned reflex of the instant opinion or ingrained prejudice lies at the other extreme, reflecting as it does our propensity for the 'narrative fallacy', the simple story that makes comforting sense of an increasingly complex world. It is well known, for example, that in times of economic stress, social decay, or wider civilisational decline, people will often blame 'immigrants' as the source of the endemic problems within their own society. Blaming the 'other' is a characteristically simple explanation which obviates the need for any serious self-examination.

But the dilemma represented by these two types of thinking is not confined to the extremes. The simplistic doctrine of the 'Clash of Civilisations', for example, is not generally perceived as extreme. On the contrary, despite Fred Halliday's description of it as 'pernicious' and typical of the 'broad-sweep' approach which is 'careless with facts, ignorant of history and indifferent to the whole range of social theory that has, with due care, looked at such issues as culture, socialisation and tradition', its central fallacies are tenaciously clung to within a broad swathe of public opinion, the political and thinktank culture, and the media. All of these give us regular object lessons that demonstrate how vulnerable we are to rapid thinking, and how the dichotomisation which is so often a key feature of such thinking can so easily tend to the norm and become habitual and mainstream.

It is worth examining the terms 'dichotomisation' and 'dialectic'. While the former is often marshalled to divide reality by adopting a polarised and oppositional posture which rejects the 'other' and can find no commonality or convergence between competing positions, the latter ideally seeks to refine an existing position and advance knowledge and civilisation through critical engagement with a range of evidence and a plurality of alternative perspectives, and through open and respectful dialogue and polylogue with a wider community of interlocutors. I say, 'ideally' because 'discussion' in general is clearly a continuum. At one end, there is the polarised 'debate' in which each 'side' seeks to defend its 'position', proposing or opposing a 'motion', and relying as much (or more) on rhetoric as reasoned argument and evidence. As such, 'debate' may do little more than bolster the preference for dichotomisation and cement an existing hypothesis or narrative. At the other end of the continuum lies an advanced mode of thought, the committed endeavour of 'dialectic', at once rigorously logical and openly relational.

The appeal of simple stories is also only too clear in the popularity and influence of the ethnocentric polemics of Samuel Huntington, Niall Ferguson and Dinesh D'Souza in which any dissenting voice is dismissed as an agent of 'cultural relativism'. 'Relativism' is a useful bugbear of traditionalist ideologues and cultural supremacists suggesting both chronic disorientation and moral laxity. As Jacques Barzun has pointed out in his monumental survey of modern Western civilisation, the bogey word relativism has become 'a cliché that stands for the cause of every laxity', and 'a slippery slope of cunning justifications and satanic whisperings, taking us further and further away from the certainty of eternal truths and absolute values'. But the root of the word 'relativism' might be more usefully seen as a continuum ranging from a value-free 'anything goes' mentality which may indeed be rootless in a negative sense, to a very positive ability to form 'relationship', whether with ideas or with people. A book about 'Civilisation' which has the subtitle 'The West and the Rest' clearly occupies a position which is unable to disentangle the semantics of 'relativism' from that of 'relationship'.

Another topical example of muddling different shades of meanings of the same word or its root is the use of the word 'multiculturalism'. The word might refer to at least three different notions: first, the existence of plurality or diversity ('multiculturality'); second, the model of multiculturalism which promotes tolerance between separate communities within plural societies (sometimes referred to as 'plural monoculturalism'); and third, pluralism as an active process of constructive engagement between different communities (sometimes called 'interculturalism'). While some might legitimately argue that social cohesion and the building of a shared narrative is not facilitated by mere tolerance between isolated encampments within society, it is profoundly misleading to suggest that multiculturalism in its critically important sense of active intercultural engagement is dead. Lack of care in distinguishing such concepts can have profoundly negative consequences not only for minority communities but also for wider society. It is also important to distinguish pluralism in its most creative sense (as an active truth-seeking encounter) from the syncretism which cobbles together bits and pieces of different traditions, promotes a kind of wishy-washy universalism, or serves up comforting platitudes about common ground at an interfaith breakfast.

Also of relevance is the problematic nature of the term modernity and the tendency of the 'traditionalist' outlook to apply a pejorative sense to everything modern. This conflation is often carried further in the equation of modernity with the so-called 'myth of progress' and the concomitant association of the 'secular' and 'relative' with the denial of immutable truths and absolute values. The term 'secular' comes from the Latin *saeculum*, which means 'this age' or 'the present time', and the concept refers to the condition of the world at this particular time or period or age. In early Christian texts it was used to refer to the temporal, as opposed to the spiritual, world.

It can be argued, however, that it is precisely by recognising and understanding the condition of the world at this particular time that we can meet the challenge of religious and cultural pluralism. This is not to give precedence to the temporal world over the spiritual world, nor to set one against the other, but to understand that human minds are conditioned differently in each age, and that tradition must be dynamically self-renewing and responsive to new conditions and new questions if it is to remain a living tradition. In other words, time, place and people cannot be ignored in the development of human understanding.

In discussing the need for clear distinctions in the use of terminology, I introduced the phrase 'integral perspective' in considering how we might transform apparent opposition into complementarity and I would like to take the term 'integral' (and its relations 'integration' and 'integrity') as the key pointers to the new vista we need to open up. These words come from Latin *integer*, 'whole, complete, entire', and clearly relate also to the idea of 'holism' and its diverse realisations in the field of 'holistic education'. There is also an obvious connection with the principle of Divine Unity or Oneness (*tawhid*), and with the attempts to realise this principle in the domain of education through the 'Islamisation of Knowledge'.

The work of the philosopher Jean Gebser in describing the structural changes or transformations in human consciousness over time is instructive. Basing his conclusions on evidence form a wide-ranging study of human endeavour, Gebser believed that humanity is at the stage of transition from the 'Mental' to the 'Integral' structure of consciousness. He described the deficient form of the 'Mental' structure as the value-free ontology of rational materialism, but upheld that this moribund structure could not be renewed through a return to 'values'; rather, a transition was needed to an 'Integral' mode of consciousness which was not fixated on dualistically opposed categories, one-sided perspectives, fixed frames, competing paradigms, and the like.

There is a clear intersection here between Gebser's 'Integral' mode of consciousness and the process of dialectic. Some development psychologists have described dialectic as the highest stage of cognitive development, encompassing the ability to accept contradictions, constructive confrontations, paradoxes, and asynchronies. This is not a process of compromise, loose relativism or evasive fudging of difficult issues, but one of creative tension which ultimately transforms contradictions into complementarities, releasing the open-minded thinker from ingrained habits and conditioned patterns of thought, established affiliations, fear of change and instability, false certainties, and reluctance to approach anything which may be threatening to one's sense of self.

Yet, the convergence between the dialectical process as an advanced mode of human thought and the idea of an emerging integral mode of consciousness is only partial. So in what sense is the idea of an integral perspective as an 'emerging consciousness' or, in Gebser's terms, transition to a new 'mental structure', different in important respects from dialectic? Let us take dialectic in its sense of a discourse between two or more people holding different points of view about a subject who wish to persuade others of the truth of their position or refine that truth through reasoned arguments and critical engagement with the arguments of others. This is the Socratic ideal which upholds dialectic as a means of persuasion which is immeasurably superior to the rhetoric that manipulates emotionally or the sophistry that seduces by elevating oratory to an art form. This ideal has come down to us as one of the founding principles of Western civilisation, and also converges in many ways with the culture of intellectual inquiry and knowledge exchange which distinguished Islam at the height of its cultural vigour. That culture provided a vehicle for the rediscovery and transmission of classical civilisation, but it was of course much more than that. Indeed, as Muhammad Asad eloquently reminds us, it was the higher intellectual and spiritual impulse derived from the divinely revealed teachings of the Qu'ran which ignited that 'spirit of intellectual curiosity and independent inquiry', and which in turn 'penetrated in countless ways and by-ways into the mind of medieval Europe and gave rise to that revival of Western culture which we call the Renaissance, and thus became in the course of time largely responsible for the birth of what is described as the age of science: the age in which we are now living'.

No one need deny the benefits the 'age of science' has brought us (provided we distinguish it from scientism), nor the cumulative advancement of knowledge derived from rational argument, dialectic, critical thinking, logical analysis, intellectual inquiry and cross-cultural exchange. But the question remains as to the way in which any putative emerging 'integral' mode of consciousness can carry further the degree of synthesis which can be attained through a methodology based largely on analytical tools.

I suggest that the answer already lies in the concept of *tawhid*, and in what Sardar has described as the 'basic axioms of the worldview of Islam'. Referring to the 'Islamisation of Knowledge' project he describes how, starting from the Unity of Allah, 'the first principle of Islam' in the *Work Plan* 'systematically leads us to the unity of creation (the cosmic order, and the interconnection of everything), the unity of knowledge, the unity of life (human existence as a sacred trust, *amanah*, from God, and the human being as trustee, *khalifah*, of the abode of our terrestrial journey), the unity of humanity, and finally the complementary nature of revelation and reason. Collectively, these axioms offer us an excellent framework both for the pursuit of knowledge and for the reform of Muslim education.'

But, as Sardar goes on to say, the way forward within this overarching framework of unity, is the 'reinvention' of the task, taking it forward from the 'Islamisation' to the 'Integration' of knowledge'. As he argued so succinctly in an earlier critique of Islamisation, 'Islamising disciplines already infused with a materialistic metaphysics and western, secularist ethics is tantamount to a cosmetic epistemological face-lift and nothing more. At best, it would perpetuate the dichotomy of secular and Islamic knowledge' that the project was so keen to avoid.

With this fundamentally creative shift from Islamisation to integration, and its implications for a truly holistic education, I wholeheartedly concur, whether we describe it as 'reform', 'reinvention', or in other terms which have been used in recent literature, such as 'reconfiguration', 'revitalisation', 'revivification', 're-envisioning', 'regeneration', 'transformation' or even 'revolution'. The need to 'reinvent' the task is a pressing one, because, as Sardar explains, any attempt at knowledge production that begins with the unifying axioms in the *Work Plan*, 'even though they are rooted in Islamic thought and worldview, is intrinsically universal. The first principles do not focus solely on Muslims or Muslim societies but on the whole of humanity.' In 'Beyond Single Narratives', Farid Panjwani reminds us that, while retaining their ideals and values, Muslims have worked with people of other faiths and cultures to engage with problems of their times, yet 'much of the literature on Islamic education contributes to widening the gap between Islam and the West. In depicting Western civilisation as deeply problematic, and an exclusivist "Islamic" approach as the solution, it creates dichotomies and mirrors the doctrine of the clash of civilisations'. Abdulkader Tayob takes up the insights of Rumi on the 'self and the other' to argue that it is 'time that Islamic education reform locates itself more clearly in comparative perspective'. Richard Pring, asking the question 'What is a University?' refers to John Henry Newman's vision of a university as 'a place of teaching universal knowledge' and John Stuart Mill's contention that a university was not essentially a place of professional education 'teaching the knowledge required to fit men for some special mode of gaining their livelihood' but a place for creating 'capable and cultivated human beings'. Looking back to the early universities of the Muslim world in the tenth and eleventh centuries, Pring refers to the work of Muborakshoeva in describing their orientation towards 'universal knowledge' and 'the formulation of a world-view with a pluralistic concept of knowledge and epistemology, yet within the overall framework of revelation'.

The fourteenth century Andalusian philosopher and jurist Al-Shatibi, responding to the changing realities of his society in which power was shifting markedly from Muslims to Christians, taught that although individuals and communities may come from different cultures which have been shaped by particular and specific historical experiences, they all share certain universal and supra-historical principles and moral values which are not the sole property of any religion or cultural group. Nevertheless, specific formulation of such universal principles and values does not take place in a vacuum but is inevitably affected by the context provided by our particular experiences as historical beings. As a result, there is a constant need to challenge and examine the way such principles are formulated (and formalised), particularly when people with different customs continue to meet and interact.

In identifying the 'natural corollary' of the axioms underlying the *Work Plan*, Sardar contends that 'human society and individuality cannot be properly understood in terms of modernity, postmodernism, secularism, positivism, reductionism, formalism and naturalism and numerous other "isms" that have brought us to the edge of chaos in the first place. Human beings are purposeful. We create social, economic, political and cultural institutions not just to meet certain needs, achieve certain objectives, but also to realise certain values. We pursue knowledge not only to acquire greater understanding and more effective action in the real world but also to promote certain principles that integrate knowledge with our cherished values, emphasise the interdependence of creation, unite humanity, promote equity and justice, and preserve and enhance life.'

So let us return to the pressing question: in what sense, then, can an integral perspective take us further than the remedies which are so often advanced for the reform of higher education in Muslim societies? How can we expand our view beyond the dichotomy of seeing either 'Westernisation' or 'Islamisation' as a panacea? How can we go beyond the 'lame-duck' mentality which frames the answer only in terms of 'catching up' with Western models of knowledge production, professionalism, quality assurance, critical thinking, research, liberal arts, and all the other factors which seem to ensure the dominance of Western universities in global rankings? At the same time, how can we avoid the 'cosy corner' mentality which prefers to occupy a parochial corner in which everything which is not explicitly 'Islamicised' is seen as threatening or deviant? We need to be constantly on our guard against what might be called 'terminological entropy', that degradation and running down of meaning within conceptual vocabularies. Islamisation, for example, is reduced and exteriorised to the idea that there should be 'Islamic bicycles', 'Islamic trains' or the like. I have encountered this mentality many times in my advocacy work for the greater involvement of Muslims in outdoor pursuits and the natural world, having been asked on more than one occasion where Muslims can participate in 'Islamic walking' as if this is some special type of walking distinct from the way in which other human beings walk. Ultimately, how can we create an educational culture which is a beacon of excellence for all humanity? At best, Muslim educators will do what catching up is needed, and this is no mean task, but at the same time, they will be fully aware of a more pressing and more sublime mission. Islamic civilisation has more to offer the world than apologetic imitations of the worst aspects of utilitarian education systems, even if the best aspects of any system can serve to remind Muslims of what made their own civilisation a great one. We need to have the humility to realise that we can indeed reclaim and revive forgotten or stagnant aspects of Islamic tradition through dynamic contact with other intellectual and pedagogic traditions which have partially carried the underlying Qur'anic spirit of inquiry into the modern age.

But this 'reclamation' must be a truly creative process, and not the tedious harking back to the achievements of the golden age of Islamic civilisation, that backward-looking nostalgia as an illusory compensation for the dearth of new ideas which Malik Bennabi saw as a sign of 'civilisational bankruptcy'. It must examine how the values and principles which gave rise to such a civilisation can be renewed, re-interpreted and applied in the contemporary world. Bennabi's analysis concurs to some degree with the finding of Arnold Toynbee in his monumental study of history that 'archaism' (persistent idealisation of past glories) is one of the key signs of civilisational decay. As Panjwani so succinctly states in his conclusion, 'tradition cannot be inherited passively. Each generation must acquire it afresh and with labour'. While this renewal needs to tread carefully in avoiding the 'spectre of interpretive relativism', it must, above all, embrace relationship – with texts, non-fiction as well as fiction as Ruqayyah Kareem argues and Naomi Foyle shows so eloquently, with all humanity and human knowledge, with all creation and the cosmic order, and with God.

The Qur'an tells us, 'We have made you into nations and tribes so that you may come to know one another' (49:13).

And it is that saving grace of 'relationship' which is, for me, the heart of the matter. As we reach for an integral perspective, whether we conceive of it as an emerging consciousness, a shift to a new 'mental structure', or simply as a new paradigm, we need to see that this requires the totality of human faculties, 'the hearing, sight and hearts', which, as the Qur'an repeatedly reminds us, we have been endowed, and for which we have 'cause to be grateful' (16:78, 23:78, 46:26, 67:23). The stupendous range of our faculties encompasses all that makes us human: at the very least, the senses which enable us to learn by direct observation and experience; the language-based deliberative or rational faculties which enable us to think, inquire, analyse, define, discriminate, conceptualise, theorise, and argue *(fikr, 'aql)*; our capacity for memory; and the moral faculties which provide a criterion *(furqan)* for distinguishing truth from falsehood and right from wrong. These alone, without yet attempting to explore the affective dimension of feeling, 'emotional intelligence' and empathy, nor those 'higher' faculties associated with spiritual consciousness, point to many of the key objectives of the educational process, including the incorporation of both knowledge and values.

Awareness of the totality of human faculties enables us to embark on a balanced critique of the state of higher education in all societies. Let us take a typical dichotomy, the idea that if knowledge is at risk in Muslim societies, so values are at risk in Western ones. Yet, there is no shortage of voices to tell us that both knowledge and values are being undermined in Western universities, despite the dominance of Anglophone institutions of higher learning in global rankings. Henry Giroux, for instance, contends that 'higher education in America has been hijacked by the corporate elite'. He laments that 'public spheres that once offered at least the glimmer of progressive ideas, enlightened social policies, non-commodified values, and critical dialogue and exchange have been increasingly commercialised – or replaced by private spaces and corporate settings whose ultimate fidelity is to increasing profit margins.' At this time, he pleads, 'it is more crucial than ever to believe that the university is both a public trust and social good. At best, it is a critical institution infused with the promise of cultivating intellectual insight, the imagination, inquisitiveness, risk-taking, social responsibility and the struggle for justice.' Giroux's concerns are echoed by Harry Lewis, the former Dean of Harvard College, whose robust critique of Harvard is mirrored in the judgement of many scholars and experts that higher education in America is in crisis. According to Lewis, colleges in America (Harvard included) have forgotten that the fundamental goal of a university education should be is to 'turn teenagers into adults, to help them grow up, to learn who they are, to search for a larger purpose for their lives, and to leave college as better human beings'. Lewis believes that because colleges have failed to offer students reasons for education – which forces them to wrestle with deeper questions of meaning and purpose – they are failing students and a country that desperately needs a well-educated citizenry. 'The old ideal of a liberal education', he writes, 'lives on in name only. No longer does Harvard teach the things that will free the human mind and spirit.' And it is not difficult to see this decline as the extension of a profound educational crisis within the wider educational system in the West.

The very concept of qualitative education designed to nurture the full extent of human potential has been usurped by dumbed-down, uninspiring, utilitarian regimes shackled to a narrow range of prescribed content and obsessed with quantitative evaluative approaches derived from an oppressive culture of target-driven managerialism which reduces human beings to conforming and performing cogs in the industrial machine. There is an array of faculties and virtues which it ought to be the business of universities to nurture and inspire, but which are being neglected even in universities which occupy the top echelon in global rankings. As Paul Ashwin shows, the ranking of a university has little relevance to the quality of education the students receive. Indeed, the very 'notion of improving quality is silent about what quality should be'.

How then can we extend the function of a university as a 'critical institution' to the cultivation not only of those conventional analytical tools of rationality or 'critical thinking' (and their application in professional development) but also far beyond a pragmatic and utilitarian focus to the igniting of all those capacities and virtues envisioned by so many contemporary educationalists and social and cultural critics whose passionate voices seem often to be crying in the wilderness? Let us repeat them: 'intellectual insight, the imagination, inquisitiveness, risk-taking, social responsibility and the struggle for justice' as well as the liberation of the human mind and spirit, the search for deeper meaning and purpose, and a vision of what it means to be a fully human being. And let us add creativity, independent thinking, and, of course, that expansiveness and receptivity of the open heart and mind which can listen as well as talk and reaches out with real interest and deep courtesy to the 'other' not only through dialogue and discussion, but also through transforming love. To them we might add Ronald Barnett's insight that a genuine higher learning is 'unsettling' in the sense of 'subverting the student's taken-for-granted world', and 'disturbing because, ultimately, the student comes to see that things could always be other than they are. A higher education experience is not complete unless the student realises that, no matter how much effort is put in, or how much library research, there are no final answers.' And Richard Pring takes this necessary subversion a stage further, asking whether higher education must also confront and subvert 'the taken-for-granted world of others – parents, governments and other stakeholders, and 'the settled perceptions of those of us responsible for delivering it'.

I deliberately include the 'heart and mind' in my approach to the extended range of faculties (and hence a truly integral perspective) because it is the composite organ of 'mind-heart' (*fu'ad*) which is indicated by those Qur'anic verses which exhort us to be grateful for the faculties with which we have been endowed. Muhammad Asad explains that this concept encompasses both intellect and feeling, and gives various translations of the term in different verses as 'minds', 'hearts' and 'knowledgeable hearts'. In the same way, the faculty of *'aql* (intellect) though often used to mean 'reason' in the sense of logical thinking is a multi-layered concept which, as Cyril Glassé points out, corresponds in its highest and metaphysical sense, as used in Islamic philosophy, to the Intellect or nous, as understood in Platonism and Neoplatonism. This is the transcendent Intellect, through which man is capable of the recognition of Reality. In the tradition of Orthodox Christianity it is the highest faculty in man, and through it, man knows God or the inner essence or principles (*logoi*) of created things by means of direct apprehension or spiritual perception. It dwells in the depth of the soul and constitutes the innermost aspect of the Heart, the organ of contemplation. Rumi distinguishes between the two senses in his typically concrete and metaphorical language by describing the 'intellect' as the 'husk' and the 'Intellect of the intellect' as the 'kernel'.

It is important also to realise that the multi-levelled conception of *'aql* not only encompasses both reason and spiritual intelligence, or rationality and intellection, but also includes a moral dimension, in much the same way as the conception of 'excellence' expressed in the Arabic word *husn* goes far beyond the sense of personal mastery or achievement in skill or knowledge but embraces virtue and goodness. Karim Crow has shown that one of the key components of the concept of 'intelligence' expressed by the term *'aql* was 'ethical-spiritual, teaching how to rectify one's integrity and to cause one's human impulses, faculties and latent powers to flourish, with the purified emotions promoting the operation of a higher intelligence'. Such an analysis converges usefully with modern advances in the field of cognitive psychology which question the conventional reduction of human intelligence to a single unitary or g factor for 'general intelligence' as measured by IQ tests, and point instead to 'multiple intelligences'. Gardner identifies seven of these: linguistic, visual-spatial, logico-mathematical, body-kinesthetic, musical-rhythmic, interpersonal and intrapersonal. According to Crow, the combination of knowledge and understanding, and of emotional, social and moral intelligence, is also traditionally suggested by the term 'wisdom' and is manifested in 'personal integrity, conscience and effective behaviour'. Guy Claxton reports the case of people who work as handicappers at American racecourses who 'are able to make calculations, based on a highly intricate model involving as many as seven different variables, yet their ability to do so is completely unrelated to their IQ scores'.

The fact that it is the linguistic and logico-mathematical intelligences that are most prized in Western education systems partly reflects the dominant influence of Jean Piaget in the field of developmental psychology. Piaget effectively demoted the intuitive, practical intelligence to the infantile level of 'sensorimotor intelligence' which is dominant during the first two years of life, to be superseded and transformed in due course by more powerful, abstract, intellectual ways of knowing – notably, the 'formal operations' of hypothetico-deductive thinking and theory construction. Claxton points out that there is an implicit assumption in Piaget's 'stage theory' of development that the highest form of intelligence is the operation of reason and logic, and his influence on several generations of educators has ensured that 'schools, even primary schools and kindergartens, saw their job as weaning children off their reliance on their senses and their intuition, and encouraging them to become deliberators and explainers as fast as possible.' Claxton labels this type of thinking as 'd-mode', that type of deliberate conscious thinking which works well when the problem it is facing is easily subject to generalisation and neat conceptualisation; is much more interested in finding unequivocal answers and solutions than in examining the presuppositions behind the questions, which may imply awkward complexities; assumes that the way it sees the situation is the way it is and does not easily see the fault may be in the way the situation is perceived or 'framed'; seeks and prefers clarity and precision through literal and explicit language, and neither likes nor values confusion or ambiguity; is purposeful and effortful rather than playful and operates with a sense of urgency and impatience; and works well when tackling problems which can be treated as an assemblage of nameable parts and are therefore accessible to the function of language in atomising, segmenting and analysing.

In reclaiming its higher purposes from corporatisation or any other corruption of its ideals, a higher education might embrace some of those advanced critical faculties and socially responsible virtues identified by Giroux and others, but how, for example is one to develop spiritual aspiration, even if the related faculties of will, intention and decision may be more typically associated with the 'effort' which is indispensable for intellectual development? How is one to teach contemplative reflection, or pondering the signs in creation which point (through the 'creative imagination' in its deepest sense) to the existence of the Creator, or spiritual attentiveness, by which one watches over and take care of one's soul or spiritual heart, a state of presence with God in which the aspirant leaves behind all other thoughts and concerns? How is one to teach *taqwa*, in its deepest sense of 'consciousness of God', or spiritual intuition, or spiritual insight? Some of this might be on the curriculum in the form of 'meditation' in some schools (though even then often reduced to a 'tool' for relaxation, calmness, happiness, mindfulness for greater effectiveness, or some other 'useful' objective), or it might be touched on or evoked in receptive souls through 'nature education', or other holistic or creative activities, but how is it to be embedded in the specialised subject matter of a university course? Is it not something which might rather be nurtured through the totality of *tarbiyah*, that multi-faceted educational process which includes not only formal education but also what is learnt through family, friends, mentors, supplementary education, recreational activities, culture, and travel (even unto China)? Yet, it can also be argued that a good teacher should be not only a *mu'allim*, a transmitter of knowledge but also a *murabbi*, a nurturer of souls and developer of character.

But let us return to earth from the stratosphere, and to the vista we might hope to reach through educational reform founded on integration of knowledge and values and the transforming power of relationship. Abdulkader Tayob points the way in his commentary on one of the discourses of Rumi, in which Mevlana turns his attention again and again to the pain and hurt felt in the encounter between the 'self and the other' and the breakdown in relations between them. As Tayob comments, Rumi turns away from 'a self that is antagonistic or set apart from the other' and 'directs the self to unity and union with the other'. This is not to deny the pain, 'the feeling of alienation and dependency that has struck a deep chord' in those engaged in Islamic educational reform in modern times. And as Tayob asserts, that pain should certainly 'not be replaced with an uncomplicated feeling of unity and universality. The pain of colonialism, the destruction of communities and livelihoods through rampant capitalism, and other dysfunctional systems in the modern world, cannot be denied'.

Yet Rumi's appreciation of both unity and multiplicity in the world, and his profound perception that 'the road to the self passes through the other,' opens a path to modern educational reform which can transcend the attachment to distinction and difference we can see in the three major 'dispositions' identified by Tayob. Attachment to dichotomisation is only too evident in the dispositions of anti-Western 'rejectionism' and the 'bifurcation' which led to the disconnection between religious and secular education, but Tayob also contends that it is also present in the third disposition represented chiefly by the 'Islamisation' movement. Though ostensibly 'integrationist', this 'takes one step in the direction of universality and unity' only to 'retreat as quickly with another step towards distinction and difference'. In such a way, the approach of Islamisation might be characterised as a false dawn, or a cul de sac which purports to lead to integration but which ultimately focuses only on the self and does not learn any lessons from the way in which 'the Other provides a perfect reflection of the self'. A point also indirectly made by Mohammad Nejatullah Siddiqi, who after spending a life time working and researching 'Islamic economics', now concludes that both the 'theory and practice of Islamic economics and banking is flawed, full of anomalies, and have basically failed as projects. All we can do is to congratulate ourselves on having re-invented capitalism by using Islamic jurisprudence!' To claim that Muslims are somehow immune from 'secularism, individualism, and ethical malaise' is to be in a state of denial, for the problems of politics, society and ethics clearly evident in the West, in the Other, 'call for serious examination in the self' and such problems offer a real starting point for educational reform. In the same way, and perhaps more pointedly, it is also an illusion for Muslims to claim that they are immune from the 'triviality, desolation and dysfunctionality' which the former Archbishop of Canterbury, Rowan Williams, sees as increasingly evident in contemporary British society. And we might add here the searing question of Jesus in his Sermon on the Mount, asking why we behold the mote (speck) in our brother's eye but do not consider the beam in our own eye (Matthew 7:1-5). Also known as the 'Discourse on Judgmentalism', its succinct metaphor about the inter-relationship between self and other is also expressed in the language of modern 'depth' psychology in the concepts of 'shadow' and 'projection'. In denying the beam in our own eye, we unconsciously project it onto the other, in the same way as we project the ills of our own society onto immigrants, scapegoating and even demonising the 'alien'. In such a way, the other is perceived as 'dark', a projection of our own 'shadow', that nether region of the psyche which we fail to recognise in ourselves as part of our 'identity'. Numerous malignant outcomes of this unconsciousness might be mentioned, including the murderous rampages of Boko Haram and Anders Breivik, discussed by Sindre Bangstad in his article on Islamophobia in Norway, in their respective demonisation either of the 'West' (Boko = Western books) or the 'multiculturalism' which raises for the xenophobes the hideous spectre of the 'Islamification' of Europe.

Tayob's conclusion that 'values' must take precedence over 'identity' in steering a new course towards the 'radical unity' needed for educational reform appears to contradict Gebser's belief that the 'moribund "Mental" structure' cannot be renewed through a return to 'values', but only through a transition to an 'Integral' mode of consciousness. But both these insights are immensely valuable, and one way to move towards a resolution of any seeming contradictions is to take 'radical' in its sense of relating to the 'root' or origin, and not in its later subsidiary sense as referring to political activism or innovative reform and change. It is only too evident how terminological entropy has further truncated the term in its sense of 'radicalisation' applied to extremists.

Being 'radical' in the sense of turning to one's origin is to avoid tunnel vision, neither facing narrowly to the front (seduced by the 'progressivism' which rejects all tradition) nor to the rear (incarcerated in regressive dogmatism or drowning in nostalgia for past times) but facing always to the Centre, which is the 'original point' indicated by the meaning of the word 'revolution'. In the same way we might refer to the root of the word 'identity'. Its original sense is best preserved in its derivative 'identical' which reflects the meaning of Latin *identitas*, literally 'sameness', derived from Latin *idem*, 'same'. There is a common 'identity' in all human beings residing in the primordial disposition or essential nature (*fitrah*) with which we have been divinely endowed. The word 'simple', derived from the Indo-European root meaning 'same' has the underlying sense 'same-fold' – that is, not multifarious. The semantic connection between what is simple and what is single is evident in the Latin word *simplus* ('single') derived from this root. The 'simple' person may therefore be seen in one sense as a 'single' undivided person, a person who is always 'the same', true to himself or herself. Simplicity in this sense is like a mirror which reflects the Divine Singularity at the core of every human being.

The relationship between the words 'origin' and 'orientation' can also be excavated from their common root. Both English words come from the same source, Latin *oriri* 'rise'. The verb 'orient' and its variant 'orientate' originally meant 'turn the face to the east', the direction of the rising sun. Orientation is an essential spiritual concept, whether exoterically in terms of physical direction (as in the *qibla*, the direction Muslims face in the ritual prayer, or facing east towards the altar for Christians) or esoterically as the light of God, 'neither of the East nor of the West' (24:35), the point of Unity within the Heart, the dimensionless point at the Centre beyond duality and the play of the opposites. To face to the centre in this inward direction and to perceive that 'wherever you turn there is the face of God' (2:115) entails the constant remembrance of our origin, our point of arising, and our inevitable return: 'Verily, unto God do we belong and, verily, unto Him we shall return' (2:156).

In all of these semantic excavations, we might discern a primordial language which articulates the fundamental unity and interconnection at the root of everything that exists. That 'radical unity' in its deepest sense must be at the heart of the radical educational reform needed in all societies. Rooted in living relationship between the 'self and the other', our diverse identities, orientations and values find a common origin and centre which dissolves the rigid oppositions erected by dualism. As Sardar concludes, 'Islamisation of Knowledge, like most ideas, has moved on. It was a product of its time and context. But it has left a legacy'. Its enunciation of first principles centred on Divine Unity (*tawhid*) stand as an enduring framework for educational reform. Now, we 'move forward' with 'Integration of Knowledge', to be sure, but also with that panoramic integral perspective which can only be encompassed by the totality of human faculties. This is the emerging consciousness which offers us hope for the future.

WHAT IS A UNIVERSITY?

Richard Pring

What is in a name? Does it pick out some 'essence' – an idea to which those institutions, for example, universities, claiming to be manifestations of that idea, need to conform? If so, then we need to spell out what that idea is. Much depends on it. Thus, a degree is a mark of achievement awarded by a 'university', and its value, therefore, depends on the awarding body justifying that title. Again, governments financially support institutions which go by the name of university. By what criteria are they judged to be so? We have seen recently in Britain the growth of institutions which, because they have the title of university, are entitled to receive loans for their students, mainly from abroad, but questions have been raised as to whether they should be entitled to be so called.

There are many different kinds of institutions which claim to be universities and to award degrees. But before we look at them, it may be worth trying to identify the idea or the ideal against which claims to be universities might be measured.

Perhaps we might start with John Henry Newman's account in his much quoted book *The Idea of the University*, namely, 'a place of teaching universal knowledge'. This is qualified by the claim that its objects are intellectual, not moral, and the 'diffusion and extension of knowledge rather than the advancement'. By 'universal knowledge' is meant those different logical forms of knowledge (defined by their distinctive concepts, modes of enquiry, procedures for verifying the truth) by which we have come to understand the physical, social and moral worlds we inhabit. There is an inheritance of knowing, reasoning, appreciating which needs to be preserved and passed on to future generations. Such an institution (the university), therefore, would need to be broad in terms of the different disciplines of thinking which it offers.

CRITICAL MUSLIM 15, JULY–SEPTEMBER 2015

Perhaps relatively few people are capable of this disinterested pursuit of knowledge and of gaining the wisdom arising from it. They, in Plato's *Republic*, would constitute the 'guardian class', from whom would arise the 'philosopher king'. They would, by reason of their education, form what the nineteenth century philosopher and poet, Coleridge, referred to as 'the clerisy', whose knowledge and wisdom prepared them well to lead others who were not so well endowed. And this was very much the view which shaped those early universities of which Oxford was a prime example, recruiting almost exclusively from the 'public schools' those who were reared on the civilising curriculum of the classics. Such a sense of transmitted wisdom fitted them well to positions of authority in Government and in the civil service and indeed in the continuation of civilised values through their teaching. According to Herbert Warren, President of Magdalen College Oxford, in his evidence to the *Royal Commission on Secondary Education* in 1895, the student who has read Plato's *Republic* and Aristotle's *Politics and Ethics* has whatever theory is necessary for the practice of teaching, especially if he were an Oxford man, more especially the classical student. The corollary of this ideal, to be embodied in the university, was that training for a specific role or profession was not the aim of this disinterested pursuit of knowledge. As John Stuart Mill argued in his inaugural address to St Andrew's University, 'there is a tolerably general agreement about what a university is not. It is not a place of professional education. Universities are not intended to teach the knowledge required to fit men for some special mode of gaining their livelihood. Their objective is not to make skilful lawyers, or physicians or engineers, but capable and cultivated human beings'.

None the less, this ideal is an ancient one and indeed precedes the old universities of Western Europe. In her book, *Islam and Higher Education*, Marod Muborakshoeva shows how the Islamic universities of the tenth and eleventh centuries, later influencing the development of universities in Iran and India, absorbed Greek philosophy and produced such philosophers as ibn Sina (980-1037) and ibn Rushd (1126-1198), who in turn were widely influential on the scholastic tradition of the universities of Western Europe. The intellectual currents of this period, Muborakshoeva notes, 'led to the formulation of a world-view with a pluralistic concept of knowledge and epistemology, and yet within the overall framework of revelation'.

That 'overall framework of revelation' is clearly an issue we need to return to. But it is interesting to note that Newman's classical work was written in connection with the establishment of a Catholic university in Dublin, and his belief that the religious framework, provided by the Church, was necessary for the integrity of the teaching of universal knowledge

Language, of course, changes. It reflects a form of life, and as that form of life changes so do the meanings which previously prevailed. But one must be wary of what one means by such change. The gradual shift in meaning may still owe much to the original ideal. There is continuity. The developed meaning is not an equivocal use of a word. There must be meaningful connections between the ideal (a place of teaching universal knowledge) and subsequent meanings of the word. What follows accounts for the different ways in which practices have come to shape the meanings of 'university'. But it raises the question of when the meaning of the word is being so stretched as to barely relate to the ideal. Perhaps the meaning has shifted to such an extent that the continuing use of the name 'university' would seem unacceptable, trading on a name without justification.

It is fascinating, in reflecting on Newman's account, how, for example, the role of research (the 'advancement of knowledge') seems to play little or no part. Teaching is its purpose – which, of course, does depend on the scholarship of those who are doing that teaching. But research, the systematic pursuit of new knowledge as opposed to scholarship, would not be the main or essential purpose. Such absence of research would not be characteristic of most universities today. Indeed, some are referred to as 'research universities', meaning that research is a major activity within them, supported by external grants for so doing. It is the case that most universities in the UK would see research to be an important element in the duties of academic appointments. Such an emphasis has been intensified internationally as a result of world league tables of 'top universities' based mainly on the quality of research. In the UK the Research Assessment Exercise (now the Research Excellence Framework, REF), which takes place every four years, has reshaped the idea of the university and the nature of academic life. Until the 1980s, universities were funded to teach and to devote time to research and scholarship which would support that teaching. An academic was not pressurised to produce research of 'international standard'. He or she would not be penalised for concentrating upon teaching. The Research Assessment Exercise changed all that. The third of Government funding supposedly to support research and scholarship was withdrawn and then redistributed on the basis of the quality of research – subject by subject. That sum of money is increasingly distributed to fewer and fewer universities with considerable financial consequences.

The effects of this are several, changing the idea of the university and of the role of academics within them.

First, there is clearly a hierarchy growing within the university sector, at the top of which are the 'Research Universities' – on the basis of international and national reputation and therefore of the greater income from research and from the attraction to overseas students. Further down the scale are those which are referred to as 'teaching universities' where scholarship is pursued but much within the context of their teaching responsibilities.

Second, however, within the respective universities, there is an increasing division between those who do research and those who just teach – on different contracts and different rates of pay. Only those are submitted for the REF whose published work is judged to be of national standard (howsoever that is defined). It is a brave academic who, harking back to the nature of the university only a few decades ago, feels able to focus on the quality of his teaching and not be intimidated by the need to produce four publications preferably in the few journals on the Social Science Citation Index (or the indexes relevant to other disciplines). Such is the pressure that more and more teaching is handed over to part-time teachers or to post-graduate students, raising doubts as to whether the university is seeing teaching (as with Newman) as its prime purpose. A case was recently published of a student in a 'Russell Group University' who had no personal contact with an established member of the academic staff for three years of her course.

Third, the competition between universities for league table rankings inhibits the collaboration between disciplines within a university and between universities. A good quality research paper, arising out of collaboration between researchers in more than one department or university, cannot be attributed to more than one person for the purposes of the Research Excellence Framework. Better therefore to keep the research 'within house'.

How far is there the 'tolerably general agreement', according to John Stuart Mill (quoted above), as to what universities are not, namely, 'a place of professional education'. There are quite clearly limits to how far this ever was the case. Students in the university framework of Newman prepared for medicine, the law and the Church, though no doubt in a way which was intended to produce 'the capable and cultivated human being'. Present universities, in addition, offer, amongst other professionally related courses, degrees in engineering, accountancy, social work, nursing and teaching. But in each case it would be claimed that the university course offers a wider theoretical context of the professional preparation. They would claim to be educational rather than mere training in relevant skills. Indeed, it would be argued that practical experience and skill would be the basis of the wider educational thinking which enables the students to become 'capable and cultured human beings'.

Teacher training offers a useful example. In England what were referred to as Training Colleges were re-designated Colleges of Education to reflect the wider theoretical dimension to professional preparation. A professional degree, the BEd, was developed. But then attempts had to be made to make education a respectable study for universities to adopt. At a conference of the Association of Teachers in Colleges and Departments of Education in Hull in 1964, studies for the professional development of teachers were dismissed as so much undifferentiated mush by the influential philosopher of education, Richard Peters. Hence began a purposeful attempt to inject into educational studies an academic rigour that respectability in the eyes of the universities demanded. There was an exponential growth of theory in what were called the 'foundation disciplines' – the philosophy, sociology, psychology and history of education, and finally comparative and curriculum studies.

The Aga Khan University, established in Karachi in 1970s, began with a School of community medicine, training nurses amongst other health care workers. This seemed an odd beginning for a new and ambitious university – hardly the teaching of universal knowledge. But the Aga Khan wanted to create a university which would address the needs of the wider community, and that community suffered from a lack of good health care and medical services. The School had an appreciation of its brief, namely, an understanding of the wider social context, and the ethical concerns for the needs of those in receipt of medical attention. In the course of its history the child mortality of the community it served was reduced by 50 per cent. That first faculty was followed by a second, namely, a prestigious School of Medicine which had a large hospital that trained future doctors. However, the health of the community is enhanced by understanding the range of factors which contribute to a healthy lifestyle. Hence, a third Institute was created for the better education of teachers. It is interesting to reflect on this three-fold approach to the development of knowledge and understanding, arising as it did from strong practical and ethical concerns but evolving into a wider development of understanding and knowledge. Now the university is developing a School of Humanities and Social Sciences.

On the other hand, distinctions have to be made between the preparation for a profession, which is narrowly focused on the skills and specific knowledge for practice, and the broader social, philosophical and ethical aspects of that profession. There has now been a exponential growth of degrees in business studies around the world at both undergraduate and post-graduate (MBA) levels. It is notable how few of these engage critically with the disputable orthodoxies of the business world and with the ethical questions which a university course (true to the ideal of the university as a place of critical and universal knowledge) should be engaged with. How few, I wonder, have *Capital in the Twenty-First Century*, Thomas Pickety's devastating critique of the neo-liberal principles of economic theory, on their syllabuses as a serious work of research? To what extent is there a moral critique of the practices of global banking which have brought ruin to so many? After all, most of the students pay crippling fees (£44,000 per year at Oxford University's Said Business School) to get their MBA en route to jobs within the banking industry.

The ideal of universities being places for teaching universal knowledge embodied what the philosopher Michael Oakeshott referred to as 'the conversation between the generations of mankind' in which the learners become acquainted with the voices of poetry, philosophy, science, literature, history, and so on. The metaphor of 'conversation' is an important one. We have inherited ways of seeing and understanding the physical, social and moral worlds, developed through scholarship and critical appraisal of previous attempts to make sense. Knowledge grows through criticism, as the philosopher, Karl Popper so cogently argued. That responsibility to teach universal knowledge requires the free and critical spirit – the interaction, unrestrained, between scholars, across the disciplines.

It was traditional for such an academic community to be self-governing, appointing its own Vice-Chancellor, and dominant in the governance of the community – a community of learners. Differences there were and are. The medieval university of Bologna was much governed by the learners, who could sack the staff if they were failing to provide the knowledge and understanding. But normally that community of learners was led by those who were deemed to be knowledgeable in their different fields. Autonomy and freedom from political interference were the hall-marks of the earliest universities.

In many ways, that autonomy was preserved until comparatively recently. It could never be complete in so far as universities depend in the main on Government funding. But in England certainly it was preserved through the establishment of a University Grant Committee which distributed the government money to universities independently of political influence. This autonomy was however gradually eroded – through, for example, (under UGC's successor, the Higher Education Funding Council) the influence on the research spending, one element being the 'impact' of the research; or through the intrusion of Her Majesty's Inspectorate into universities; or through the control over numbers of students that the university should take; or through the withdrawal of academic tenure . This increasing government incursion has resulted in a different language in which universities are spoken about. It is a global language affecting the understanding of universities world wide. It is exemplified in the papers coming from the UK's Treasury and the Cabinet Office: *Modern Public Services in Britain: Investing in Reform* (1988, Cm 4011); *Public Services for the Future: Modernisation, Reform, Accountability* (1998 Cm 4181); *The Government's Measures of Success: Outputs and Performance Analyses* (1999). It is a language of management with reference to targets, outcomes, performance indicators, audits. The effect on universities is a massive increase in the administrative staff. At Oxford University, the central administrative staff rose in 2013-14 by 11 per cent to 1391 – the Development Office had 98. There was a further rise of 5.5 per cent the following year, for a student body of 20,000. The central administration is double the academic staff.

This shift from academic governance of universities to that of the management class, which thinks in the business terms of measures of success: outputs and performance analyses, is going global. In the United States between 1987 and 2012, non-academic and professional employers have more than doubled at the same time as cutting back full-time tenured teaching staff. Part-time staff and teaching assistants make up over half the university teaching staff, compared to one third not long previously.

We must think therefore of the modern university in very different terms from that of Newman's idea, with it becoming less and less like an institution teaching universal knowledge as that is understood within a community of learners, and more like a corporate business teaching whatever is likely to sell in the global market – as estimated by the administrators, not by the guardians of our culture.

Universities obviously need funding in order to pay for staff and resources. Traditionally this has come mainly from governments, charitable donors, increasingly research grants and student fees. Government support was adequate at a time when only five per cent or six per cent of the relevant cohort of young people went to university, as in the UK in the 1960s. But now the aspiration is for 50 per cent to attend university. There is, therefore, an increase in fees, to be paid by the students, financed principally from loans which have to be paid back over a period of 30 years. But such an expansion has given rise to the private and for-profit organisations to offer university education. Indeed, there is in Britain the considerable growth of such institutions, some accredited by universities abroad, such as the American International University in London, or BPP University, whose parent company is the US Apollo Group. Others are single subject professional training institutions, such as Ashridge Business School and the College of Estate Management. The quality of some of the new arrivals has been severely questioned. As a result, eight institutions with award-bearing powers (including the ones just mentioned and referred to as the 'Russell Group of the alternative sector') have set up the

Independent Universities Group, to disassociate its members from other for-profit colleges.

This raises the question, which remains constant in the face of the changing idea of the university, concerning the compatibility of the pursuit of profit with the idea of a community of learners, teaching universal knowledge and exercising academic freedom. The newly appointed Vice-Chancellor of the Aston Business School, George Feiger, speaks of universities having to adapt to 'the marketisation of education with fee income following students'. They operate as businesses, though without shareholders.

Newman's 'idea of a new university' would embrace theology as one amongst many contributions to universal thought, contemplation and intellectual formation. But more than that, the religious perspective provides a distinctive background within which other areas of knowledge find a place and significance – indeed, just as a purely secular vision of knowledge so does. Thus for Newman it made sense to have a distinctively Catholic university within the different kinds of knowledge that would be taught, true to their distinctive modes of enquiry yet open to the possibility of seeing such knowledge contributing to a wider vision of human nature and well-being.

Muborakshoeva describes well the much earlier vision of teaching universal knowledge within the ancient universities of the Muslim world starting in the tenth and eleventh centuries – in Morocco at Fez and Marrakesh, and beyond the Middle East and North Africa to the universities of the Indian sub-continent. Key figures were the philosophers who interacted with the 'wandering scholars' of medieval Europe, and thereby helped to create the philosophical traditions which emerged in the nascent universities of Western Europe such as Paris and Oxford. But then, as Muborakshoeva shows, this indigenous tradition, so influential on the medieval European universities, shifted under the influence of colonialism to the more secular idea.

There are of course many so-called universities within the Muslim and Christian religious frameworks which could not claim to be teaching 'universal knowledge', but rather the knowledge which trains future clerics of the respective religions and denominations – such as the

University of Mecca. When does a university, properly speaking, become a seminary?

There is also the issue of geographical dispersion. The 'idea' of a university did once include the notion of a community, interacting through debate and questioning. 'Conversation' would have been seen as an essential element in the development of knowledge and critical enquiry. One can still see, in the medieval madrasa of Marrakesh, the student rooms surrounding and overlooking the central hall or arena where lectures took place. It was a closely knit learning community. Indeed, the medieval universities of Oxford and Cambridge were collegial, students living within the small communities of their respective colleges together with their teachers. But such tight communities became increasingly difficult to maintain as universities expanded to the sizes which prevail today.

Two developments in particular are worthy of note. First, the UK's Open University was founded in 1968, whereby part-time students, scattered far and wide, matriculated to take their degrees in a range of academic disciplines. The Open University pioneered the distance learning mode of higher education. This required a different pedagogy in order to maintain the standards of learning which are expected of an institution calling itself a university. Written material with relevant exercises and stringently assessed by panels of academic experts was distributed; weekly sessions were backed up by radio and television recordings; personal supervision was organised through correspondence. The internet has transformed all that. In 2013/14 there were over 200,000 UK based students studying for both undergraduate and postgraduate degrees in the UK of whom 150,000 were with the Open University. Students and teachers can meet in virtual theatres and laboratories. Discussions and tutorials take place on-line and in forums. MOOCS (Massive On-line Communication System), provided by world standard universities such as Stanford, Harvard and Michigan cater for many thousands of students. On the other hand, Iran's Azzad universities have well over a million students in many different centres around the world which are not necessarily linked for teaching purposes on-line. The university is physically dispersed, which necessarily diminishes the idea of a community of learners as it is managed from the centre in Tehran.

Second, there has been a further development of the Credit Accumulation and Transfer System (CATS) following the 1998 Government paper, *The Learning Age*, which had predicted (wrongly) CATS to be fully functioning by 2003. The problems were and remain less autonomy for the specific institutions taking part and a shift to a more modular system. However, 'transferable credits' may well be the way forward in a changing and more global world

So universities have changed in many ways from some ideal type of 'teaching universal knowledge' in response to changing social and economic circumstances – in particular: growth of, and importance attached to, research based scholarship; increasing relevance to economic and social needs, and to employment; restrictions on academic autonomy and freedom; growth of private and for-profit institutions; and part-time, on-line and virtual learning, together with credit accumulation and transfer of qualifications.

However, it is necessary to ask, how far these changes can develop before the title of 'university' is used purely equivocally, bearing few of the qualities and virtues normally associated with that name. For example: Is a university still a university when it loses its academic autonomy? Is a single faculty university (e.g. a business school) really a university? Should an institution be classed as a university which has no faculty of humanities or social studies? Independent quality assurance becomes a crucial issue, especially where the university is globally spread or when it is in the hands of for-profit corporations or religious bodies which see it much as a seminary. In an age of credit transfer on a global scale, universities and employers will need to be assured of the standards of those 'universities' from whom they are receiving their students.

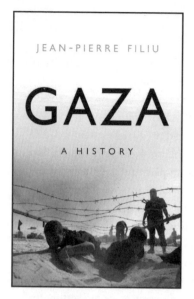

JEAN-PIERRE FILIU

GAZA

A HISTORY

ISBN: 9781849044011
£25.00 / Hardback / 424pp

GAZA
A HISTORY
JEAN-PIERRE FILIU

Through its millennium–long existence, Gaza has often been bitterly disputed while simultaneously and paradoxically enduring prolonged neglect. Jean-Pierre Filiu's book is the first comprehensive history of Gaza in any language.

Squeezed between the Negev and Sinai deserts on the one hand and the Mediterranean Sea on the other, Gaza was contested by the Pharaohs, the Persians, the Greeks, the Romans, the Byzantines, the Arabs, the Fatimids, the Mamluks, the Crusaders and the Ottomans. Napoleon had to secure it in 1799 to launch his failed campaign on Palestine. In 1917, the British Empire fought for months to conquer Gaza, before establishing its mandate on Palestine.

In 1948, 200,000 Palestinians sought refuge in Gaza, a marginal area neither Israel nor Egypt wanted. Palestinian nationalism grew there, and Gaza has since found itself at the heart of Palestinian history. It is in Gaza that the fedayeen movement arose from the ruins of Arab nationalism. It is in Gaza that the 1967 Israeli occupation was repeatedly challenged, until the outbreak of the 1987 intifada. And it is in Gaza, in 2007, that the dream of Palestinian statehood appeared to have been shattered by the split between Fatah and Hamas. The endurance of Gaza and the Palestinians make the publication of this history both timely and significant.

'A magnificent piece of historical writing: clear in its exposition, careful in its use of a treasure-trove of new sources and judicious in its analysis of competing political claims to this small and troubled strip of land. It is difficult to see how it will ever be rivalled in terms of scope, intensity and sympathetic understanding.' — **Roger Owen, Emeritus Professor of Middle East History, Harvard University**

WWW.HURSTPUBLISHERS.COM/BOOK/GAZA

41 GREAT RUSSELL ST, LONDON WC1B 3PL
WWW.HURSTPUBLISHERS.COM
WWW.FBOOK.COM/HURSTPUBLISHERS
020 7255 2201

UNIVERSITIES IN MUSLIM CONTEXTS

Marodsilton Muborakshoeva

Universities in Muslim countries are rich in heritage and conceptual diversity. But they have faced numerous challenges from the first day of their inception. These include funding, quality assurance, leadership and management, organisation of knowledge, the position of women, the integration of modernity and tradition, and the study of Muslim cultures and civilisations, in which religion is of pre-eminent importance. However, we should see these challenges not as intractable problems but as transformational opportunities.

To understand the challenges facing universities in Muslim-majority contexts, one must look into the history of these institutions. This is because higher learning in its institutional or non-institutional forms has a long-standing tradition among Muslims, and modern universities retain some cultural and civilisational ties with this heritage, even though most of them do not necessarily embrace every aspect of it. The struggle (*jihad*) to acquire knowledge, whatever the source, has been obligatory for all Muslims, both men and women, since the time of the Prophet Muhammad. The very first verse of the Qur'an, as well as several others, urged the Prophet to read, understand and reflect on the mysteries of creation, and he in turn conveyed this injunction to the believers and encouraged them to search and struggle for knowledge 'even if it be in China'. The early Muslims, therefore, actively sought to harmonise the message of Islam not only with their existing cultures but also with earlier civilisations. Since the search and struggle for knowledge was a divine command for Muslims, they endeavoured to acquire and transmit it using any appropriate means at their disposal, whether it was through memorisation, writing, reading, or a range of art forms, including calligraphy, architecture, poetry, recitation, and singing. By the middle of the eleventh century Muslims developed distinctive institutions for higher learning with their unique architecture, funding structure and organisation of knowledge and also introduced degrees (*ijaza*) and academic rankings. Some of these features were borrowed by medieval European universities, and early Muslim institutions such as Al-Azhar in Cairo, Al-Qarawiyin in Fez, and Al-Zaytuna in Tunis, have sometimes been described as the prototypes on which the Christians of Europe modelled their own universities. Nevertheless, debates about whether the Muslims or Christians were the inventors of universities do not really yield productive discussions simply because there were many cultural and intellectual exchanges in the Middle Ages. Muslims engaged in a dialogue with Christian theologians and intellectuals in the eighth and ninth centuries and learned a great deal from them, and in turn the Christians benefited from the rapid intellectual and cultural achievements of the Muslims from the ninth to eleventh centuries. Once these cultural exchanges slowed down, the universities established by Christians or Muslims developed their own distinctive features drawing on their own religious and cultural world view and their respective approaches to knowledge acquisition. Later, during the colonial period in the nineteenth and early twentieth centuries, there was a revival of cultural exchange, though this time largely a one-way phenomenon with Muslims borrowing heavily and sometimes uncritically from European models so as to establish their own modern institutions of higher education.

Universities in Christian Europe then developed into corporations where a community of masters and students gathered with the aim of seeking knowledge and truth and equipping those in professional, ecclesiastical and governmental occupations to respond to societal needs. Muslims, however, did not develop their madrasas or colleges into universities in the European sense. Associated with the development of universities into corporations in the Christian world were complex intellectual developments. By the twelfth century, separate schools for clerics and monks had been established in Europe. The former were concerned with training clerics in the liberal arts and scholastic theology, whereas the latter prepared boys for monastic life, which was more individual and had a contemplative dimension that was absent in scholastic theology. However, this did not mean that monastic learning was opposed to or unfamiliar with scholastic methods; it merely emphasised an inner, experiential and mystical dimension in addition to intellectual pursuits. From the twelfth century a new strand of philosophical and theological thinking started to emerge which dissociated itself from the experiential and mystical aspects of monastic schooling. The distinction between the knower as inquiring subject and the knowledge as object of his investigation was made. By the age of Enlightenment this culminated in the secularisation of scholasticism, whereby religious reasoning gave way to a more 'naturalistic' mode of inquiry. In addition, the scientific revolution, rapid industrialisation and economic advancement in Europe initiated many debates about the nature of universities which resulted in the cumulative reform of their curricula. By the early twentieth century several models of universities addressing the different needs of society had emerged. Various concepts of what constitutes a higher education were embedded in these evolving institutions, but in the course of their development they shared three important characteristics. First, the study of theology was marginalised or abandoned. Second, new and ever increasing numbers of disciplines were introduced, with teachers and scholars in these fields claiming autonomy for their subject and abandoning the responsibility to interconnect and make sense of all subject areas. Third, philosophy too became just one more academic discipline, with its own subject matter, methods and goals.

However, this depersonalisation and secularisation, by which there is a loss of harmony between the complementary rational and experiential faculties, should not be seen as a global trend. In Buddhism, Christianity, and certain schools within Islam the experiential aspect still plays a major role and individuals are not only pursuing knowledge but also striving to develop spiritually through inner contemplative practice.

Muslims too from early on had certain inclinations or preferences either for mystical, legal, humanistic, or purely intellectual pursuits in the search for knowledge. The *ulama* (scholars, especially those trained in Islamic jurisprudence), *udaba* (literati), philosophers and Sufis would have reflected these various inclinations. However, there has never been a sharp division between these intellectual traditions; an *adib*, for example, could have been a legal scholar, a philosopher and mystic at the same time. Places for higher learning remained diverse and methods of teaching and learning continued to be largely flexible and adapted to the needs of different groups and learners. Teaching and learning took place not only in institutional settings such as madrasas, but in places such as mosques, libraries, palaces, private houses, shrines, and market places.

Debates amongst Muslims about whether to give preference to the rational sciences sometimes led to a rigid approach to the organisation of knowledge in madrasas, with priority being given to the revealed sciences over the rational sciences especially from the eleventh century onwards. Nevertheless, the teaching of rational sciences did take place in private circles, palaces, shrines, and from the sixteenth century even in madrasas, especially in Iran and India. The secularisation of scholastic traditions did not therefore occur amongst Muslims as it had done so in the Christian world and a strict demarcation between experiential and rational approaches to knowledge acquisition remained unknown to them at least until their encounter with modern European education.

For Muslims the most obvious anomaly in the curriculum of those modern European universities established in Muslim contexts from the mid-nineteenth century was that they did not necessarily include the study of Muslim culture, civilisation or religion. During the extensive borrowing from European models in the nineteenth and early twentieth centuries, traditional universities such as Al-Qarawiyin, Al-Azhar, the madrasas in Central Asia, the seminaries in Qum and Najaf, and many others in Muslim lands were gradually marginalised and isolated from the mainstream educational enterprise and a huge part of human experience to do with religion, identity, and cultural and civilisational heritage was consequently relegated to the domain of the 'private' or 'religious' as opposed to the 'secular'. This marginalisation did not, however, reduce the influence of these institutions within society or in the political arena. In some Muslim contexts, especially amongst Muslims in India, alongside the modern universities, and sometimes in opposition to them, new types of higher educational institutions with a specific focus on the study of religion and cultural and civilisational heritage were established with the aim of mitigating the threat of marginalisation and isolation.

Muslim intellectuals and scholars in Morocco, Tunisia, Egypt, Turkey, Iran and India, sensing the shortcomings of modern universities, made some genuine attempts to bridge this gap and merge their age-old traditions of learning with the European models. This was contrary to the aims of the colonialists and some Muslim rulers who wanted a quick fix for their societies by establishing universities that prepared a skilled and appropriately educated work force for employment in the civil services. Interesting developments have taken place in these countries. Morocco and Iran pursued separate development of modern universities while leaving their traditional institutions such as Al-Qarawiyin and Qum intact and allowing them to continue with their old teaching and learning methods. Tunisia and Egypt introduced reforms into their traditional universities: al-Zaytuna developed into a modern university, whereas in the case of Al-Azhar, although several reforms were imposed and modern departments and faculties added, these reforms are regarded by critics as largely unsuccessful with no effective integration of traditional and modern approaches. These countries, like many others, have therefore developed modern universities separately. The synthesis of religious and modern education was very successful in Turkey up until the 1880s, with some features even surviving the radical modernisation by Ataturk in the 1920s.

Nevertheless, the most creative debates over the nature of modern universities have taken place amongst Muslim intellectuals in the Indian subcontinent, resulting in the establishment of a diverse range of colleges and universities. Here, in the colonial context of the nineteenth century, Muslims questioning the value of British education for their communities went on to create their own modern colleges and universities. This re-assertion of heritage saw the emergence of Deobandi and Barelwi colleges, Aligarh Muslim University, Jamia Millia Islamia, and many others by the end of the nineteenth and early twentieth centuries in the subcontinent. The first two colleges would make use of the modern structures of a school, yet their curriculum was mostly fashioned after medieval institutions so as to preserve their Islamic heritage from extinction. It was only gradually that they introduced the teaching of some non-religious subjects. Aligarh Muslim University aimed to produce intellectuals capable not only of meeting the demands of the modern age but also well-grounded in knowledge of Islamic religion and cultures, an aim which it achieved to a great extent. Overall, however, these institutions had varying degrees of success and in recent decades, their original mission and vision seems to have been largely forgotten or muddled. For instance, the Deobandi schools in modern India seem to favour an apolitical role whereas some Deobandi schools in Pakistan have been actively engaging in political affairs, especially since the 1980s. Aligarh Muslim University too is very often embroiled in the polemics of contemporary political issues rather than teaching a curriculum which creates real harmony between sciences, culture and religion.

By the mid-twentieth century, the borrowed models of a university had become dominant across Muslim contexts. Tied to the idea of the nation state, their main function was to turn out a suitably skilled and functionally educated work-force for employment in the civil services, emerging industries and economic structures. These institutions did not necessarily get involved very much in the study of what Muslim identity, culture or religion meant to individuals or communities. The consequence of this neglect and even suppression of a whole area of human experience was that the question of identity rooted culturally in the local context, history and heritage remained largely unexplored and marginalised within mainstream educational institutions.

In the past, the approach to knowledge in traditional universities was holistic in that they prepared students to undertake a wide range of occupations in society but their role has now been reduced to producing teachers of religion (and sometimes languages) and performers of rituals and ceremonies. Scholarship has become a routine regurgitation of materials handed down from generation to generation with little creativity and originality of thought. The modern universities in Muslim contexts have a similarly narrow utilitarian aim to meet the contemporary needs of society and lack creative and original approaches to knowledge acquisition and production. As a result most universities in Muslim contexts have very little to contribute either in the field of scientific and technological advancement or in cultural and religious studies.

Nevertheless, there have been attempts in some Muslim contexts to create departments within universities for the study of culture in a broader sense. In Tunisia, for instance, a department of Arabic culture was established in some modern universities which produced scholars of a high calibre. The American University in Beirut is another instance of an institution encouraging open and critical study of cultures and civilisations.

All in all, the success of state universities in most Muslim countries should not be downgraded. Despite their shortcomings, many have achieved considerable success in contributing to the establishment of their nation states, preparing human resources for civil services, emerging industries and technologies. The universities of Cairo and Kuala Lumpur, Istanbul and Tehran, Punjab and Karachi, and many others, could be listed among such universities even though their mission has revolved mostly around their nationalistic ambitions. In this enterprise, Muslims perhaps resemble the Catholics of the nineteenth century who recognised the weaknesses of modern universities yet at the same time they had to acknowledge their achievements, especially in enhancing knowledge in natural and social sciences.

Of great importance in considering the challenges for universities in the modern age is the impact of the neo-liberal model of economic development on all levels of education. Most universities globally are struggling with the pressure of responding to the economic needs of their societies, a heavy demand placed on them by governments, corporations and business enterprises. Most renowned universities are funded generously by large corporations for conducting research, mostly in sciences, thus marginalising and disadvantaging other disciplines. Such research universities have become very expensive and charge students high tuition fees. By the early twenty-first century research universities were becoming successful business corporations subsidised by tax exemptions and exhibiting all the acquisitive ambitions typical of such corporations. This is a far cry from how Muslim or Christian universities in medieval times would have defined their philosophy of education and their approach to the acquisition of knowledge.

Marketisation of knowledge has opened new avenues for Western universities to make profit by franchising their services and opening branches in developing countries. The advantage of such institutions is that they take the pressure off state universities in terms of access to university education in the Middle East, the Gulf states and Pakistan, for instance, and offer degrees that are not available at national universities. They are also attractive to students because of the prestige conferred by belonging to a renowned western university and the associated assumption that their curriculum is more advanced than what is perceived as the backward or stagnant curriculum of the state universities. However, the disadvantage of these universities, operating with an imported (and not always updated) curriculum and an English-language medium of instruction, is that they further alienate students from their cultural and civilisational roots.

Muslim intellectuals are increasingly becoming aware of these conceptual challenges as well as pressures on universities to adjust their curriculum to the economic needs of societies. In the wake of the cultural and religious resurgence associated with the movement for the 'Islamisation of knowledge' since the 1970s a new type of Islamic University began to spring up in countries such as Saudi Arabia, Pakistan, Malaysia, Indonesia and others. These universities aspired to bridge the gap between the religious and secular domains by offering a curriculum which encompasses both religion and the natural and social sciences. They also sought to apply certain principles for the inculcation of moral values and the conduct of human relations. The Kuala Lumpur based International Islamic University Malaysia (IIUM), for instance, aims to train responsible professionals aware of the consequences of scientific research and technological innovation. The budding scientist, for example, is required to take some subjects from the revealed sciences so as to be well-grounded in Islam and its ethical and moral outlook. Some notable achievements have been attributed to the 'Islamisation of knowledge' movement, especially in the conceptualisation of knowledge and also in the highlighting of the importance of the Arabic language in both secondary and university education and in the inclusion of philosophy and traditional arts in the curriculum. Nevertheless, the movement and some Islamic Universities which have followed it, are being criticised for having a political agenda and confusing religious and worldly knowledge as opposed to the Muslim thinkers of the nineteenth century who distinguished between these types of knowledge yet saw them as complementary and maintained harmony between them. Such critics maintain that as a result of this confusion there is an artificial imposition of the so called 'Islamic' worldview on natural sciences. This is in sharp contrast to the approach of medieval Muslim thinkers who sought to encompass the unity of all knowledge through a pluralistic epistemology yet within the all-embracing framework of revelation. This was so for philosophers like Al-Farabi, Ibn Sina, Ibn Rushd, theologians and travellers like Al-Ghazali, Mulla Sadra, Abu-Yaqub al-Sijistani, Nasir Khusraw, ibn Jubayr, ibn Battutah, scientists such as al-Haythan, al-Biruni and Nasiriddin Tusi, and mystics like Ibn al-Arabi and Jalaluddin Rumi. For them, the overriding purpose of knowledge acquisition was to become a humble, decent, kind and generous human being who neglects his own self for the sake of attaining perfection, knowing God and taking care of His creation.

Serious research and thought is now undertaken, before creating new universities, to determine their nature and concept in some Muslim countries. They aim to design and contextualise their mission and vision according to the needs of the time, especially with regard to leadership training, quality education, healthcare and services. Some examples of such creative universities are the Institute for Business Studies and al-Akhawain University in Morocco, the University of Tunisia, the American University in Cairo, the American University of Beirut, Ahl al-Bayt University in Jordan, Sebanci University in Turkey, the Aga Khan University, Lahore University of Management Sciences (LUMS) in Pakistan, the International Islamic University Malaysia (IIUM), and the Islamic State University in Jakarta.

In recent decades in Pakistan diverse models of universities have been emerging which also have the intention of studying the religion and cultures of Muslims at a deeper level. In creating Aga Khan University (AKU) in Karachi, for instance, a great deal of research was undertaken to explore the needs of Pakistani society as well as considering cultural and civilisational currents at a regional and global level. Questions regarding the nature of a university and the needs of the time were examined, one of which was to address the question of cultural identity and how it might be preserved and developed. The relevant architecture, the curriculum, the organisation of knowledge, the emphasis on high quality research, and the establishment of certain departments within AKU reflect this ambition of having an identity that is rooted in the local culture yet speaking and reaching out to global cultures. Others such institutions – Hamdard University, which has campuses in Karachi and Islamabad, Lahore University of Management and Sciences, and the University of Management and Technology in Lahore – have followed suit and have been producing competent graduates aware of important issues in their society. However, all these universities are private with typically high tuition fees and cater to a limited student population. Even though some of them provide scholarships for disadvantaged students, they can only provide a limited number of such bursaries, and are generally inaccessible to well-qualified applicants, including the gifted and talented who lack financial means.

It will be clear from this very brief survey that institutions of higher education in Muslim societies are diverse, ranging from traditional to modern national universities, franchises, innovative Islamic Universities, and creative, progressive universities such as AKU and LUMS. The opportunity undoubtedly exists for Muslims to build upon such richness and diversity. Giving the commonalities but also differences between the global and local institutions of higher education with regard to the concept of education, the organisation of knowledge, and methods of teaching and learning, what should be the next move for universities in Muslim countries? How can they build on the strengths of previous and existing institutions and avoid the pitfalls? How can a higher education structure with a unified philosophy of knowledge and education be created?

Although the serious thinking that has started in Muslim contexts and the resultant developments in higher education are commendable, these attempts are marginal in the larger scheme of things. The debates about what a university should ideally be are rather muted and are not generally engaged with urgently or earnestly by university academics, intellectuals, governments or Muslims at large. Muslims academics and intellectuals need to work together with governments and societies to reform and reconceptualise the idea of a university in Muslim contexts. The starting point should be the organisation of workshops, seminars and conferences to discuss the dominant conceptual issues and problems and determine where valid progress has been made and where there has been deviation from the holistic approach to knowledge of our ancestors. We should propose what type of university would best prepare responsible professionals well equipped with appropriate skills to critically examine political, economic, social, cultural, and religious issues in their societies and find solutions for them. Knowing in depth about the history of diverse medieval and modern institutions of higher education and learning, including their successes and failures, will be of a great value in this urgent process of the revitalisation and reform of higher education in Muslim societies.

An important step towards the revival of a holistic approach is for university academics to question the compartmentalisation and disconnection within university disciplines which also offer little or no philosophical insight to enrich their teaching, extend their students' minds, or explore deeper implications of scientific discoveries. This compartmentalisation and lack of coherent integration of spiritual and material aspects of human experience have potentially harsh consequences for Muslim identity, culture and civilisation. It may well be that the powerful tensions in Muslim societies between secular and religious institutions, and between different sects of Islam, as well as the extremist interpretations of religion which promote terrorism, are direct consequences of marginalising Islamic education at its best from mainstream secondary and higher education with the obvious risk of conceptual degeneration which that implies.

It is up to university academics, scholars and intellectuals to bring together the various perspectives represented by the diverse set of universities in Muslim contexts around a table and expel mistrust and mutual ignorance. It needs to be made clear that humanity cannot progress if any aspect of human life is put aside from mainstream social institutions. In Islamic studies at modern universities methodologies are not very well developed and scholars may sometimes alternate, often inadvertently, between methods of scriptural exegesis and the methods germane to the social sciences. The traditional institutions, on the other hand, follow the age-old methods of reading and writing commentaries on sacred texts which do not generally favour creative thinking and originality in research. Traditional religious universities should not be fearful of examining religion critically, any more than scientific advancement can proceed without critical inquiry. We well know that some scientific and technological inventions, which ultimately benefit only a few shareholders and corporations, have highly destructive and even catastrophic potential for human beings and the wider natural world, and yet for the sake of progress such harm is rarely questioned. In both the natural and religious sciences it is incumbent on the scholarly community to develop new paradigms and methodologies which are not fettered by dogmatism of any kind.

It is important to acknowledge that universities are not directly responsible for underachievement in society, whether economic or otherwise, but they are accountable for conducting high quality research and ensuring that the professionals they produce are capable of critically examining the principles and values that underlie economic prosperity. They also need to prepare educated professionals whose competence extends to an understanding of the human condition as a whole and an appreciation of what constitutes a civilisation.

It has also been argued that scholasticism as an intellectual tradition in contemporary universities should be recovered due to its valuable pedagogical tools and epistemology. It is worth emphasising here that in Islam the ultimate goal of this tradition, focused as it is on education through all available means, is not for its own sake nor for mere argumentation, but for the attainment of perfection in virtues and understanding of the unity of knowledge.

Muslims have a great opportunity to reconceptualise the nature and function of the university, because in Muslim contexts many institutionalised and non-institutionalised modes of traditional learning are still preserved, and these could be further built upon and improved. Although modern universities side-lined or erased the spiritual and religious dimension of Muslim cultures, the madrasas, mosques, Sufi lodges, private learning circles, shrines, and ceremonial rituals passed down the knowledge of the past to future generations and preserved it from extinction. It is time to initiate a genuine polylogue between the diverse models of universities in Muslim contexts, to transcend narrow definitions, and re-envision what a university should be and how it should serve individuals, communities and wider society.

THINKING OF RECONFIGURATION

Abdelwahab El-Affendi

In established industrialised societies, where most of the important debates about the overall general direction of society have been resolved, the debates around the purpose of higher education usually centre around the contests between utilitarianism (vocational and professional skills and employability) and some relatively more lofty ideas, such as 'self-fulfilment', 'nourishing the soul' and sustaining values, social cohesion, and even social justice. In recent years, with the value dimension of education being marginalised in the era of moral relativism, some observers have deplored the increasing tendency towards 'the rise of corporatisation and managerialisation of higher education processes, as well as the increasing political polarisation and plutocracy of public policies'.

However, in societies where the fundamentals are still being contested, the role of higher education is much more crucial and central. There is a dynamic relationship in all societies between the production of knowledge and the process of education. Institutions of higher education cannot exist without a significant body of knowledge to share, contemplate and critically engage with. During its early phase, as was the case in Athens or early Islamic history, knowledge production centred on a few gifted individuals and their circles of disciples. But as knowledge advanced, organised educational institutions arose to deal with the growing body of knowledge and manage its complexity through specialisation and long periods of intensive training.

Educational institutions have another central role to play, an ethical one this time. They seek to ensure that the production of knowledge does not become divorced from the higher values of society. As specialisations evolve, students tend to concentrate on minute details of their particular field, and may lose sight of overall objectives, guiding principles and interdisciplinary connections. Already in ancient Athens the so-called 'Sophists', the first dedicated professional teachers, were being satirised as unprincipled seekers of utility. Like modern day lawyers, they became notorious for teaching the skills of winning an argument, regardless of the intrinsic value of the position staked. At the time of Abu Hamid al-Ghazali (d. 1111), similar accusations were being levelled against professional jurists (fuqaha), reputed to seek lucrative employment and gain at the expense of lofty Islamic values. Regrettably, this remains a hazard even today.

The problem of the tensions between the higher values of seeking truth and achieving moral excellence on the one side, and the pursuit of short term advantage on the other, is thus a perennial challenge for the production of knowledge. However, the modern challenge facing Muslim education is a radically different one: Muslims may have values to uphold, but they do not have that much knowledge to share. They are also confused about their values and the context of their application, precisely because of knowledge deficit. For you cannot find the direction of qibla if you do not know where you are. Similarly, as we see with ISIS types and similar groups, a faulty moral compass is associated with combined deficit in religious and worldly knowledge.

The roots of this problem go back to the crisis which was confronted by Muslim societies from the seventeenth century onward: that almost all the knowledge Muslims possessed became worthless overnight in terms of worldly value. There were several reasons for this, starting with the long period of internal decline that, as early as the fifth/eleventh century prompted Al-Ghazali's (modestly successful) endeavour to 'revive the religious sciences'. In later centuries, persistent civil conflict, foreign invasions, economic decline and the loss of vital learning centres like Al-Andalus, accelerated this decline, and made it look irreversible. The second reason was the relative advance of alternative knowledge frameworks in the West, with new allied major political, philosophical, economic and ethical reconfigurations.

The expansion of the secular realm started from the political, where a trend had emerged since Machiavelli emphasising the primacy of power over all other considerations, including ethical and religious scruples. Unscrupulousness has more often than not been the mark of men of power. What Machiavelli did was to bring this tendency into the open and seek to legitimise it. (One can blame our own Ibn Khaldun for inaugurating this trend of insisting that power has its own irreducible logic). Political power was thus the first to rebel against religious and moral authority, and even seek to subjugate religion and ethics to its command. Economy soon followed, emulating and allying itself to power, it also wanted profit to trump all other considerations. Philosophically, the 'Enlightenment' sought to frame this rebellion by emphasising the autonomy and supremacy of human reason. Science and learning followed, trying to carve out an autonomous space, but allying themselves soon with power and economic privilege to prioritise utilitarian principles. This combination produced modern Western civilisation and its hegemonic worldwide surge.

Muslims, like many non-Western communities, began to feel the might of this new naked power in the form of military defeats and foreign invasions. Their instinct was to acquire ready-made military hardware and training to stave off this threat. They began to set up military schools to teach their soldiers the new ways of war, import weapons, hire military instructors and even send men to train in the West. They believed, as some 'wealthy' Muslim states still do, that you could buy your way out of this problem. But they soon realised that your wealth cannot be protected in this way, since those with might could – and often did – take it without bothering to sell you the knowledge or ability to defend yourself against them. Even when they did sell you a little, countries like Egypt and Tunisia became so heavily indebted that they were easily taken over under the pretext of 'debt collection.'

By the end of the nineteenth century, perceptive minds like Sayyid Jamal al-Din al-Afghani and Khayr al-Din al-Tunisi began to notice the barren nature of the new school system set up in Istanbul and Cairo, and the paradoxical status of depending on your enemies to sell you the means to defend yourself. Afghani noted the failure of the new schools – sixty years after the first were established – to produce any self-sustaining system of autonomous knowledge production. His diagnosis at the time was that it was because those schools did not teach philosophy. There was a sense in which he was right, since teaching fragments of knowledge and technical expertise without an over-arching framework or worldview is not likely to produce knowledge in any meaningful sense of the word. Afghani gave an example of the fundamental 'philosophical' transformation the Qur'an had brought about in the Arab frame of mind, thus providing the galvanising and decisive factor which brought the Islamic civilisation into existence. Although he did not say this, the implication was that the radical philosophical transformation in Europe, in this case the Enlightenment, was the decisive factor in creating the new framework of knowledge production and acquisition.

Since then, great minds like Muhammad Iqbal, Malik Bennabi, Muhammad Asad, Ali Shariati and Ismail Raji al-Faruqi, among others, have continued to grapple with this core challenge of locating the decisive factor(s) needed to galvanise Muslim intellectual and spiritual life back from its current status of living death. Each of these intellectuals has tried to offer a formula for a civilisational revival, based on the emergence of a new type of intellectual combining spiritual depth, ethical commitment and contemporary erudition. However, while these intellectuals have appeared indirectly to indicate that their own careers were an embodiment of this new charismatic figure (and that was partly true), they have provided no formula to ensure his reproduction. Thus while the questions posed by these figures, and some of the answers they offered, are still relevant, they are neither completely satisfactory nor coherent. They have all emphasised the centrality of education. But the question remains: which type of education? And what content should it have? Above all, where is the viable paradigm that could and should guide our knowledge production, our own new 'Enlightenment'.

The challenge faced by the earlier generations of Muslims confronting modernity has now radically changed. A century ago, the focus was on basic education: literacy in home languages, mastery of at least one foreign language, basic maths, science education, technical training, etc. At a later stage, higher education became a necessity, and it was often delivered in a foreign language, that of the colonial overlords. At present, most Muslim countries have widely available primary education, and higher education is accessible to many. The basic needs of society in technical skills are largely being met, if often through imported technology, expertise and labour.

However, the quality of higher education is still not up to international standards, regardless of the question of authenticity and originality. As a consequence, most of our students who can afford it seek post-graduate studies in the West almost as a routine. However, the question posed by

Afghani over a century and a half ago is still relevant: Why aren't our institutions generating original knowledge? Even more fundamentally, our contributions to international knowledge are so meagre as to remain virtually non-existent. The only two Muslims to win Nobel prizes in science did so in British and US universities.

This is puzzling, given that well-established reasonably accessible and objective procedures for the operation of institutions of higher learning now exist. It is true that a self-reinforcing dynamic of established reputation that in turn attracts talent and funds continues to sustain the better known prestigious institutions. However, there is nothing preventing others from reproducing that experience elsewhere. Talent is fairly mobile, and some Muslim countries have no shortage of funds. Nothing need have prevented them from setting up centres which could benefit from the best talent. (After all, many governments, businesses and benefactors have taken to endowing chairs and centres in prestigious Western universities). But we have yet to see a significant breakthrough in this area.

What is more worrying than the absence of originality and innovation in modern science is the falling behind even in our own indigenous sciences: Islamic sciences, Arabic and other local languages, etc. Our students who want to excel in Islamic learning or research Arabic, do not go to Al-Azhar or the University of Madina. If they did, they would usually emerge with less capacity for knowledge than when they went in. It is thus not just the lack of capacity to absorb and develop knowledge generated elsewhere, but also incapacity to absorb or develop our own indigenous resources!

This points to a fundamental crisis of knowledge-processing capacity, and cannot be just ascribed to an inability to grapple with the products of 'alien cultures'. We do not lack bright and gifted students, but we have rarely been able to turn these into gifted and inspiring researchers and teachers. One result is that the initiative on *ijtihad* has been taken over by semi-literate groups, such as ISIS and its clones. We do have a crisis, indeed. We have yet to have respected learning institutions that do more than produce 'technical knowledge' in the most limited sense, let alone exude moral authority and an aura of excellence. Even Al-Azhar and similar institutions seem barely able to do so.

We seem to have a circular problem here: in order to generate new knowledge, we need viable institutions. But in order to have viable institutions, we need new forms of knowledge and knowledge-producing and knowledge-absorbing capacities. So where and how do we start?

More to the point, what is the source of this problem of perennial barrenness in the area of knowledge absorption and production? We do have talented students and teachers, we have ample funds, and we have great traditions of learning. Even in the poorer countries, children are happy to walk miles to go to school, and teachers provide dedicated service at meagre salaries, which are often not paid for months on end. So what is the problem? One argument is that governments do not prioritise education. The 2002 *Arab Human Development Report* complained that the GDP percentage expenditure on research and development in the 1990s averaged about 0.4 per cent, less than a third of that of Cuba and one seventh of Israel's expenditure relative to its GDP. This was reflected in research output, which was two per cent of the rate of output in industrialised countries according to available statistics at that time. However, expenditure on higher education as a whole was higher, reaching about five per cent of GDP by 2008, as the number of Arab universities rose to 385 (from 233 in 2003), of which 115 were private. However, this did not seem to improve the quality of education or the equality of access, while the complaints about the limitations of research output both in terms of quality and quantity persisted. This was ascribed again to low expenditure on research, in addition to lack of freedoms and poor training.

Statistics alone cannot explain the problem, though. For if the problem is one of funding, one would expect to find oases of excellent here and there, in particular within the proliferating private schools and the clones of foreign universities that are mushrooming in some Gulf regions. One senses here a deeper problem, an inability to provide a hospitable environment for learning and to build up viable higher learning research institutions that could compete internationally. Since, as mentioned, Muslim students and scholars do flourish in foreign schools when the right enabling atmosphere is created, the challenge is to provide this atmosphere at home.

In the modern experience, as well as in Islamic history, schools (in both senses of the word) have tended to emerge from new paradigms of thought initiated by exceptional individuals. Thus we had Malik and Buhkari and then the science of Hadith, Shafi'i and fiqh, Kindi and philosophy, etc.

Similarly, we had Galileo, Machiavelli, Bacon, Comte, Kant, Marx, Weber, Freud, and then modern schools of thought and disciplines emerging from their investigations and ideas. In the second stage, the need for exceptional individuals has almost been eliminated. Today, in spite of the Nobel prizes, it is usually research groups, companies or departments which produce and reproduce inventions and innovations. Individuals still matter, but their achievements are necessarily those of their institutions. Without the enabling environment universities and research institutions create, and without the overall competitive set up provided by academic associations, journals, conferences, prizes, etc., it is not possible to have a thriving scientific life.

In sum, the generation of self-sustaining institutional set-up of knowledge production makes the function of the exceptional individual largely redundant, or at least subsidiary to the knowledge-generation 'machine'. An atmosphere is created where the production and dissemination of knowledge becomes self-sustaining and has the space to flourish.

Our problem is that we have probably moved to the second stage without passing through the first. So we have set up schools and companies without first establishing the paradigms according to which they should operate. An enabling atmosphere that allows knowledge to blossom and flourish is also absent. The default paradigm remains too restrictive, favouring *taqlid*, if not rigidity; it is far from favourable to innovation and *ijtihad*. We need really to develop a new learning paradigm that encourages students to develop wings, rather than attaching deadweight to their feet. We should thus seek to determine which specific aspects of the paradigm are holding us back, and cut them loose.

We have to note here that this is not specifically a problem for Muslim societies. Many Third World countries have been struggling with higher education from the perspective of quality and utility (not to mention cost). As we have seen above, some Western circles in higher education have been expressing anguish about crass utilitarian approaches to education. However, the question is posed in Muslim discussions about 'authenticity' and the quest for civilisational regeneration. It is not only about achieving technical excellence and catching up; it is —more importantly- about catching up without losing one's soul.

There is no point here into getting into a sterile debate about the possibility of specifically 'Muslim' knowledge (let alone the now stalled 'Islamisation of Knowledge' project), for this will be just a distraction. The Muslim's world's premier contribution to world civilisation has not been through the production of esoteric 'Islamic knowledge', but through the furnishing of knowledge which everybody else could –and did- use to build the basis of modern civilisation. By the same token, Muslims do not need to sacrifice their soul in a Faustian bargain to gain knowledge. By its very nature, true knowledge is one that is accessible to all.

Still, the chief concern for many Muslims was to achieve a holistic revitalisation of society, where material gains would not be achieved at the expense of spiritual vitality. However, the essence of the crisis has been that even when some were prepared to sacrifice everything for modernisation, as Kemalist Turkey and a few other Muslim countries have done, the results were not that impressive. Ironically, Turkey only managed to achieve palpable progress when it significantly relaxed its obsession with wholesale Westernisation. More recently, some Arab countries have adopted a combination of policies that amounted to wholesale Westernisation. This included imposing English as a language of tuition, and importing branches of established Western (mainly American) universities and transplanting them on their territories. They also took to sending full cohorts of students to the West to study there. These policies are too recent to enable us to assess their impact. But their very adoption is a sign of despair about the ability to build home-grown viable higher education systems.

Still more remarkable is the tendency to set up elite private schools from the primary level up, where the tuition language is English (or French), and where foreign curricula are adopted. Such schools are frightfully expensive, with the only the upper elite able to access. But it is more interesting to note that even ultra-conservative countries, like Saudi Arabia, or fanatically 'Islamist' countries, like Sudan, have permitted the proliferation of such schools. Ironically in Sudan, where the regime has precipitately and controversially Arabised higher education and imposed wholesale 'Islamisation', children of the state and business elite are sent to these new elite schools, rather than to the underfunded state schools. Although it is too soon to say how this anomalous situation is going to transform the educational scene, the early signs are not encouraging.

Earlier this year, about thirteen university students, all studying medicine or pharmacology at a private university owned by a Sudanese 'Islamist' minister, left unnoticed by their families to join ISIS in Syria. What is remarkable is that almost all were either British or American citizens, whose families had sent them to 'Islamist' Sudan for 'safe-keeping'. With the useful incentive of affordable education available from a younger age, the hope is also that exposure to one's own culture creates a bond with extended family. This clearly did not work in this instance. This is further proof that this wholesale failure has nothing to do with the 'Muslim mind' or 'Arab culture', for the simple reason that students who have graduated from the least prestigious institutions in Muslim countries have consistently proved able to integrate and excel in advanced universities. Institutions like the British NHS would collapse without the third world-educated professionals (many of whom come from Muslim societies) manning the front line. This tells us that the problem is primarily institutional, rather cultural.

We can conclude from this that the challenge is to provide the institutional set up that would enable the emergence of a healthy higher education sector. This would by necessity entail significant social and economic reforms, if not political as well. At the minimum, basic freedoms and institutional autonomy should be guaranteed for educational institutions. Adequate funding is also essential for an overall enabling atmosphere. No less important is the creation of a vibrant learning community through networks, associations, publishing and debating forums, research funding, access to international research, etc.

However, it might be enough at this stage to entertain a modest goal of securing 'enclaves' where a viable cycle of knowledge acquisition, sharing and production could flourish. The objective is to set up Centres of Excellence at several locations, where sufficient conditions of economic viability and guaranteed freedoms could be secured. These centres should also be networked, both among themselves and internationally, to enable fruitful exchange of knowledge and benefit from experience.

One is reminded here that in many areas of Africa and the Middle East, such centres did exist in the past, such as the universities of Makerere, Ibadan, Khartoum, Cairo and Kuwait. Having said this, these centres have fallen victim to political vandalism and economic decline. But some, such as the American University of Beirut, still thrive, while new ones, such as the University of Singapore, are emerging. So this task is not an impossible one.

But lessons need to be learned from these and other experiences. This in turn might require in-depth studies and careful planning, including a careful examination of successful – and failed – cases in order to benefit from good practice and know what to avoid.

The task is urgent, however, and it is important not to waste more time than necessary. Quite a few centuries have been lost already, and we are a bit behind schedule. So the need for more study should not be used as another excuse for further delay.

REFORMING SELF AND OTHER

Abdulkader Tayob

The Other occupies a dominant place in modern Islamic educational reform. Khayr al-Din al-Tunisi in the nineteenth-century urged Muslim educators to look at European developments, and questioned if the current approach followed in Muslim societies was beneficial. Muhammad 'Abduh, in the twentieth century, identified one of the chief causes of decline in the influences exerted by 'the beliefs and opinions introduced into Islam by different groups like the Sufis and others'. Deobandi *madrasa* in the Indian subcontinent pictured themselves as the forts of Islam *(islam ke qile)* protecting Muslims from the corrupting influence of Westernisation. In the last quarter of the twentieth century, Isma'i' al-Faruqi framed the theory and plan of Islamisation in relation to Western social sciences, aiming to replace them with authentic, indigenous ones. It is clear that modern educational reformers have thought about reform in relation to a significant other. The West has often occupied a dominant place, but it is not the only partner through which reforms are conceptualised, planned and executed.

Reformers have justified their attention to the Other as a quest to break free from dependency and alienation. They have been distressed about a deep and persistent tendency among modern Muslims to value and emulate the West. They have criticised Muslims for believing that the best solutions, the most creative applications, and the best products come from the West. Reformists have identified a crisis of dependency that debilitates the self to produce, to create and to make history. There are often other objectives in educational reform, but Muslim educational projects in the modern world are first and foremost a desire for freedom, and a pursuit of authenticity.

In their search for authenticity, indeterminate Muslim educational reformist projects rely on a particular conception of identity; and construct self and other as deeply divided. They are conceptualised as utterly separated and alienated from each other. They cannot share goals, aspirations and futures. In this view, the self and other can only relate to each other on the basis of difference – at best respect when they meet and engage, at worse conflict and war. Such ideas of self and other presuppose a natural state of difference, incommunicability and alienation between peoples, individuals and societies.

However, Muslim educational projects could pursue a vision of self and other that is not founded on difference and incommensurability, but on unity and non-identity. There is an alternative framework of self and other in the work of the great mystic Jalal al-Din Rumi (1207–1273) whose vision is rooted in unity and sameness. It is a vision that sees the other as a mirror of the self, and as a path to self-discovery. It is a vision that would enrich Muslim educational reforms in the modern world – characterised by globalisation, multicultural societies and communities, and intense interaction.

Mapping Islamic Educational Reform

There are three distinct dispositions in educational reform in Muslim societies that promote identity and authenticity. These dispositions may be represented by the terms rejection, bifurcation and integration. They capture assessments of what education is and what it ought to be within contemporary Muslim societies. They include views and ideas about what has happened to Muslim education under the impact of imperialism, colonialism and modernisation; and how Muslims should respond to these challenges. They have inspired curriculum reforms, textbook writing, and new institutions. Recently, they have also inspired rejectionist movements. The three dispositions are deeply implicated in the struggle over identity and authenticity in modern Islamic educational reforms.

Rejection is the first of the dispositions, and is graphically and tragically illustrated in the Boko Haram of contemporary Nigeria. *Boko* represents the books of the West or derived from the West; and is associated with colonial and post-colonial Nigerian schools and universities. Boko Haram is not the official name of the movement, but given by its opponents to a movement that has vehemently rejected all modern forms of schooling.

Boko Haram and other similar groups consider modern education to be covert Western education. They see it as part of a consistent attack on the institutions, territories and values of Muslims. They argue that modern education is an intellectual attack or raid (*al-ghazw al-fikri*) that cannot be dissociated from colonial and post-colonial plans to subjugate Muslims. This intellectual attack, they believe, is more insidious than a military attack, hardly noticeable before it tears down the fabric of Muslim society. The Taliban in Afghanistan and northern Pakistan have also embraced this disposition with deadly effect. Like the Boko Haram, they have not shirked from attacking individuals and schools that they believe support the intellectual war against Muslims.

This disposition is not only the preserve of radical movements. It reflects a widespread sentiment among Muslims that modern education may be dangerous to one's faith and way of life. In many countries, for example, Muslims refused to attend the first modern schools established by the colonial British, French and their local supporters. Saudi Arabia in the early twentieth century had to go to extraordinary lengths to open modern schools. Elsewhere, in India, West and East Africa, schools were regarded as nefarious projects to turn Muslims away from their religion and culture. The total rejection of modern education is no longer present, but the suspicion towards its social and political effects persists.

Many who share this sentiment do not completely reject modern schools. They accept, sometimes grudgingly, that such schooling was a necessity that should be tolerated for the pursuit of worldly objectives. Based on this line of reasoning, a second disposition towards modern education may be identified as bifurcation. It is a conviction that education may be divided between religious and worldly methods and objectives. This disposition was first justified by Muslim statesmen who believed that a major technological gap had developed between Muslims and the West. Ottoman rulers, followed by others, sent delegation after delegation to Europe to acquire knowledge of the new sciences and technologies developed there. Sometimes, an Imam or religious scholar would accompany such delegations for spiritual and cultural guidance. Such projects construed the world of knowledge as bifurcated between techniques that would be obtained from the West, and values and mores that originated at home. The West would be the source of updated and modernised armies, better bureaucracies and other technological and professional goods. But the source of values, and ultimately salvation, lay in the history and origins of Islam.

This disposition towards education and knowledge was further developed in schools and institutions founded in Muslim communities from the nineteenth century. One of the great religious leaders of India in the twentieth century, Ashraf 'Ali Thanvi illustrates and justifies this bifurcation in a short treatise on the centres of learning (Dar al-'ulums) founded in British India from 1867. He makes a number of proposals to promote and strengthen such centres. One of these proposals is that such institutions should pursue entirely 'religious' objectives: 'It should be a purely religious school. It should neither be influenced by, nor mixed with, worldly concerns'. Mixing 'worldly concerns' with religious objectives in such a school, he continued, would threaten the deeper objectives of the religious school: 'If this institution pursues a mixture of worldly and religious aims, then experience shows that worldly gains, being immediate, attract people sooner. Therefore, to make a mixture of worldly and religious aims would ultimately lead to a worldly orientation'. Mawlana Thanvi recognised the attraction of worldly objectives in such schools, and their threat to religious objectives. His statement illustrates a determination to maintain a clear separation between religious and worldly orientations within education.

This bifurcated model of education is probably most widespread in Muslim societies. It has guided the development of two streams of education. Religious schools are separated from so-called 'secular' or government schools. In Muslim-minority contexts, children attend the latter in the mornings, and go to religious schools in the afternoons or weekends. In many Muslim-majority countries, schools offer religious and secular subjects in one school, often in great tension with each other. In this bifurcated model, children are exposed to two curricula, two orientations and two philosophies. Both are considered necessary, one for success in this world, and one for salvation in the hereafter.

There is a third disposition that has been developed in response to these two earlier models. Muslim intellectuals have been disturbed by the problems and inconsistencies in the rejectionist and bifurcated models of modern Islamic education. In their place, they have argued in various ways for an integrated model of Islamic education. One can find signs of such thinking among the earlier modernisers like Sayyid Ahmad Khan and Muhammad 'Abduh. Khan in particular called on Muslims to adopt modern sciences, but also said that a new theology ('ilm al-kalam) would have to be developed for such modern societies. More recently, most of such integrationist models for education have been proposed by those exposed to Western social and human sciences, who felt that new theologies or reconstructed theologies, hermeneutics and epistemologies are needed to face the challenge of the modern world. In their view, technologies are not sufficient for the revival of Muslim societies – they must be supported by a revised and rejuvenated intellectual tradition.

Islamisation of Knowledge has been the most prominent project for an integrated model of knowledge promoted by leading intellectuals like Seyyed Hossein Nasr, Syed Muhammad Naquib al-Attas and Ismail al-Faruqi. Al-Attas, Nasr and al-Faruqi differ on key terms such as modernity, Islam and the secular, but they argue that Muslims need a reconstruction, or at least a restatement, of the human sciences as much as they need new technologies. Al-Faruqi established a major proposal and plan for the Islamisation of the Sciences. He founded the International Institute of Islamic Thought in Virginia, USA, which became a major catalyst for Islamisation worldwide. Some universities were established on the basis of this vision, and many Muslim schools, particularly outside Muslim majority countries, became the supporters of the programme.

According to al-Faruqi, Muslims should develop a new paradigm of knowledge on the basis of tawhid. Beginning with the unity of God, the new knowledge project would be founded on the unity of humankind, of creation, and of life. Al-Faruqi lamented the dependency of Muslim intellectuals on the West, but also warned them of the dangers that lay inside. Sufis and Sufism, in particular, were the main culprits whose 'egoism' directed them only to 'the state of consciousness of the practitioner'. It was a grand and ambitious plan captured in the following quote:

Muslim ought to master all the modern disciplines, understand them completely, and achieve an absolute command of all that they have to offer. Then, they ought to integrate their certain achievements into the corpus of Islamic knowledge by eliminating, amending, reinterpreting and adapting its components as the world view of Islam and its values dictate. They should determine the exact relevance of Islam to the philosophy – the method and objectives – of the discipline and blaze for a new way in which the reformed discipline can serve the ideals of Islam. Finally, by their example as pioneers, they ought to teach the new generation of Muslims and non-Muslims how to follow in their footsteps, push the frontiers of human knowledge even farther, discover new layers of the patterns of Allah ta'ala in creation, and establish new paths for making His will and commandments realised in history.

The plan promoted an integrationist disposition towards knowledge and education in a consistent and fundamental way. It asked that Muslims grapple with modern sciences, not turn away from them in fear and trepidation. It also asked Muslims to approach the legacy critically, and produce a new integrated vision of knowledge and education.

Identity making is an important, if not the most important, objective of these three dispositions. Rejectionists want to preserve the self at all cost, even at great cost to the other. The interests of the self come first in all instances. Those who support bifurcation accommodate the other, and even benefit from a symbiotic relationship. Dividing education between Western and Islamic sciences, they divide the self neatly between the technological and non-technological spheres – one deriving its strength from superior Western technologies and the other from the secure sources of revelation, belief and practice. But the self and other remain separate and distinct, and the borders between them are maintained at great cost and effort. Intellectuals within the third group have grappled and struggled to put the divided self together. They want to overcome the bifurcation of the self, decrying the impact that such an approach has had on Muslim communities. They lament the loss of integrity that such an approach entails. But they too focus their energies entirely on the reconstruction of the self, ignoring the other in the process. From Khayr al-Din al-Tunisi to al-Faruqi, integrationists pine for unity rooted in the creation of a new self. The other fades away, as all the energies are directed at reconstruction. They take one step in the direction of universality and unity, and retreat as quickly with another step to distinction and difference. And generally, it is the second step to distinction and difference that has been appreciated by Muslims in the modern world. Unity, universality and commonality are repeatedly ignored and forgotten as the self distinguished from the other.

In spite of their differences, the three dispositions that dominate Muslim education reform agree with each other on identity at a deeper level. These radically different educational projects see the self as distinct from the other. The other is identified as utterly different, either a source of threat or value. Generally, a politics of identity supported these projects. And that politics was founded and rooted on the self and other that were basically different from and incommensurable with each other. There was very little common ground between self and other: no common history, common values or common destiny.

This conception of identity within Islamic educational projects was compatible with general concepts of identity in the modern world. The latter turned around the individual ideally located within a nation and state, neatly defined even as it struggled to break free. The works of Charles Taylor, Sygmunt Bauman and Stuart Hall reveal this deep framework. In his exploration of the fundamental makeup of the self since the Enlightenment, Taylor's book presupposes the nation within which the self explores and constructs itself – sometimes against the other and sometimes with the other. The sociologist Bauman is more explicit on the project of identity of modernity within a nation, now deconstructed in postmodernism. Similarly, Hall's critical work on the construction of the self does not contradict its rootedness within the nation. He only argued that it was not permanent and primordial. They all work with identities based on difference, distinction and opposition.

Rumi's Way

Jalal al-Din Rumi offers a very different approach to identity for Islamic educational reform. Rumi's poems and poetry have become a source of great inspiration in the last few years. His discourses on human experiences, God and society have been widely recognised for their flashes of brilliance, insight and wit. In one of his *Discourses*, Rumi addresses a breakdown in relations, first between God and an individual, and then between two individuals. Rumi's advice provides food for thought for thinking about identity and authenticity for modern educational reform. Instead of a self that is antagonistic or set apart from the other, Rumi directs the self to unity and union with the other.

Rumi's discourse turns around 'pain' and estrangement that a person experiences in her relation with the other. He deals first with this pain in relation to God, and then in relation to human others. It would be natural, Rumi says, for a person to feel reprimanded in her relation with God. He uses the word 'hurt' to identify and acknowledge the reprimand. But Rumi directs her to the underlying 'truth' of being 'stung' by pain. According to Rumi, the pain is a sign of love. It is a sign that 'God loves [her] and cares for [her].' Rumi does not deny the pain; a reality that cannot be put aside. But he wants her to recognise the deeper truth of friendship and estrangement between the self and the Great Other. Pain is part of a relationship; threatened only by indifference and complete forgetfulness.

Rumi then turns to relations with a human other and finds pain there as well. But he presents a different set of scenarios of how this pain manifests itself between self and other. He begins with the pain, faults and errors that are often so clearly evident in the other:

> If you find fault in your brother or sister, the fault you see in them is within yourself. The true Sufi is like a mirror where you see your own image, for 'The believer is a mirror of their fellow believers.' Get rid of those faults in yourself, because what bothers you in them bothers you in yourself.

Rumi's discourse is a commentary of the Prophetic statement narrated in the hadith collection of Abu Dawud: 'The believer is the believer's mirror, and the believer is the believer's brother who guards him against loss and protects him when he is absent'. Rumi picks up a subtle point in this Prophetic statement that refers to a relationship of mutual support and protection. He directs our gaze at the self that wants to correct the other, and turns its attention to what it feels for the other at that moment. Rather than succumbing to a desire to reprimand, Rumi shows an opportunity to know the self through the fault that it sees so clearly in the other.

In his characteristic style, Rumi begins with an image of an elephant turning away from itself: 'an elephant was led to a well to drink. Seeing itself in the water, it shied away. It thought it was shying away from another elephant. It did not realise it was shying away from its own self'. Turning away from another in a personal encounter was a deep turning away from the self. The elephant was convinced that it was turning away from another that threatened her. It was only turning away from itself.

Rumi brings us back to the pain of this encounter, emanating essentially from a natural human feeling towards negative qualities: 'all evil qualities – oppression, hatred, envy, greed, mercilessness, pride – when they are within yourself, they bring no pain. When you see them in another, then you shy away and feel the pain'.

These negative qualities and values are rejected when they are recognised in the other. They are painful because they are negative qualities shunned by all human beings. It is interesting that Rumi thinks of the rejection as painful, to be kept at a distance from the self. But the rejection of the other and the pain that was identified in the other is part of the self's pain. The self only recognises the pain because such qualities can be seen in the other. The other was thus important in recognising the pain (negative qualities).

From the other, Rumi then turns our gaze once more to the self:

> We feel no disgust at our own scab and abscess. We will dip our infected hand into our food and lick our fingers without turning in the least bit squeamish. But if we see a tiny abscess or half a scratch on another's hand, we shy away from that person's food and have no stomach for it whatsoever. Evil qualities are just like scabs and abscesses; when they are within us they cause no pain, but when we see them even to a small degree in another, then we feel pain and disgust.

The self is easily blinded by its own faults and pain. Unlike the elephant which turns away from this illusionary other, the pain in the self is ignored or easily accommodated. Rumi reminds us that if the same pain ('scab and abscess') was seen on the other, it would be repulsive. Rumi asks us to recognise the mirror effect of pain between self and other.

Just as you shy away from your brother or sister, so you should excuse them for shying away from you. The pain you feel comes from those faults, and they see the same faults. The seeker of truth is a mirror for their neighbours. But those who cannot feel the sting of truth are not mirrors to anyone but themselves.

Rumi develops a universal significance from the hadith about the self and the other. The reprimand that emanates from the hadith is a command to do Good. Rumi plays on the pain that such a command generates within the self and other. The pain is real, and represents a deep aspiration to do good and a desire to shun evil. But following the pain in the self and other, Rumi brings out the challenge of transformation. The self and other are mirrors to each other, sharing pain in the encounter. Sharing in the recognition, they know the command and their relation to it. Rumi concludes with a telling reminder that without the pain shared between self and other, we only have self-reflections ('But those who cannot feel the sting of truth are not mirrors to anyone but themselves'). Inward gazes cannot reveal the truth; they cannot know the truth that is so clear in the other. Moving from the self and other, Rumi shows how pain and recognition appear and disappear in the self and other with great power and subtlety.

There are signs of reformist projects breaking the hold of a conception of identity founded on separation, difference and incommensurability, but Rumi takes us one step further. The discourses of Rumi help us to radically locate ourselves outside this maelstrom of identity-making. By thinking about identity as self and other looking at each other, we can imagine a different way of thinking about Self. Such a perception has profound and radical implications for educational reform.

Rumi's discourses are replete with the challenge of unity and plurality. He wants readers and listeners to fully appreciate both unity and multiplicity in the world. He reflects on the multiplicity of objects, events and histories. He does not want to reject such phenomena, but urges his readers and listeners to pay attention to the unity underlying all multiplicities. His comment on the self and the other reflects this deeper truth. The self is endlessly replicated in variety, but the self that recognises itself in the other begins the discovery of unity. When the self sees the other as self, then it begins to see the self in all others. Rumi does not want to reject multiplicity, but says the self cannot ignore unity with others.

Moreover, this is not an idiosyncratic insight of Rumi. It should not be rejected or set aside as the inspiration of a great poet and mystic. The balance between unity and multiplicity, sameness and difference lies at the heart of Islam as a religion. We might think of the very origins of Islam as first preached by the Prophet Muhammad when he reminded his listeners that his message was no different from the truth brought by all the prophets and righteous people that came before. He did not claim Islam to be a new religion, only a confirmation of that which had come before. This was a deeply universal appeal. At the same time, Islam in Medina and beyond laid the foundation for a unique community, identified around the Prophet as leader of a community. Henceforth, the truth took on unique shape and structure. The universal truth was not forgotten or ignored, now in a unique shape and form. This balance between sameness and difference lies at the heart of Islam as religion, represented in its teachings, its practices and its values. Rumi's reflection on the self might be seen as a deep resonance of this reality. The self was only truly a self in its deep appreciation of the other. The ultimate self was also the other, while it maintained its uniqueness.

Rumi's commentary provides much food for thought and reflection on what we call identity construction today. Moreover, it is a perceptive comment on modern educational reform that is fixated on the self and heedless of the other as a source of truth. Rumi's idea of self is deeply connected with the Other. The self was not founded on separation and difference. In fact, his concluding statement that 'those who cannot feel the sting of truth are not mirrors to anyone but themselves' is a deeply powerful comment on identity projects that do not appreciate the other as self. Those who only see themselves, absorbed as they are in their ultimate fulfilment without recognition of the other, do not 'feel the sting of truth!' For Rumi, the road to the self passes through the other. It is a conception of self that is rooted in the other as self. And this is the 'sting' of truth that must inevitably be felt in an identity encounter.

Furthermore, Rumi turns his attention again and again to pain and hurt in the encounter. This is very interesting and appropriate for modern educational reform projects. He would not deny the feeling of alienation and dependency that has struck a deep chord in modern educational reformers. It is a pain that cannot be denied. It certainly should not be replaced with an uncomplicated feeling of unity and universality. The pain of colonialism, the destruction of communities and livelihoods through rampant capitalism, and other dysfunctional systems in the modern world, cannot be denied. This pain, though, is not easily located in the other or the self. Rumi's metaphors suggest that we follow this pain from the self to the other, and back again. The recovery of dignity and selfhood cannot be completed on the self or the other alone.

If one begins with Rumi's insight that the other and the self are windows to each other, then a more radical and bolder approach to identity in educational reform might be pursued. Following Rumi, the radical critique of the West should not be the beginning of radical difference. It should be the beginning of radical unity. The pain that one recognises in the destruction caused by the West does not only lie in the West. It is also a pain and an ethical challenge that lies in the self. The West's faults would not be so clear if they were not present in the self as well. The reprimand should not stop at the fault lying in the other, but be the beginning of self-discovery and self-healing.

In even more practical terms, the vision of unity and universality as suggested by Rumi would mean the major political, social and ethical challenges facing the world would be included in a reformed programme of education. For example, Muslims are often proud to say that they do not have the same challenges of secularism, individualism, and ethical malaise that is afflicting the West. And they proceed to develop research programmes and institutions that are uniquely suited for Muslims, as if they hardly face such problems and challenges. If one were to take Rumi seriously, these problems of politics and ethics that are clearly evident in the West, in the Other, call for serious examination of the self. As a mirror of the self, the Other provides a perfect reflection of the self. The only way of understanding the scab in the other is to recognise it in oneself. And the only way to reform has to begin with what one identifies as the problem so prominently in the Other. The West provides an excellent point of departure for reform, not a point of repulsion and rejection. The self and other are mirrors to each other. Let one's perception of the other be an invitation to a serious exploration of the self.

Taking Rumi seriously means values, not identity, would be the starting project of reformed education. What values should be promoted in our contemporary world marked by science, capitalism, diversity, mediatisation and globalisation? What values should be promoted in educational institutions in relation to the other as the enemy, the neighbour, the stranger and the environment? I think that the answer to these questions should be the beginning of educational reform. They will prepare the ground for the self rooted in unity and commensurability with the other.

Rumi offers a fundamental resource in the intellectual history of Islam for thinking about identity, self and other. It is well known that identity and authenticity are critical issues in modern societies, endlessly debated in philosophy, the humanities and the social sciences. Rumi's perspective on self and other goes beyond modernist and postmodernist readings of identity. The intellectual history of Islam offers similar opportunities for thinking about values, religion, politics and the world. As a deep well of human experience, it shows current challenges in a completely different light; it has grappled with some fundamental issues on knowledge, ethics, self and society. I see these historical debates as resources for critical reflection in our times. There are no neat and complete solutions to be found in this intellectual history. It consists of contradictions and radical alternatives, but in general presents extensive material that deserves to be appreciated. I hope that my example of thinking about identity through Rumi is a good indication of the potential that exists out there.

Taking the insight of Rumi even further, it is also time that Islamic education reform locates itself more clearly in comparative perspective. What we find in Muslim educational reform is also evident in discussions going on in India, Brazil, China, Japan and even in the West. Educational reform is not a challenge shared by Muslims in different places in the world. It is the concern of those who are worried about the future of humanity and about life on earth, providing excellent partners and Others. The colonial and post-colonial condition of our world provides a rich tapestry of self and other in which pain and reprimand should be seen as opportunities for critical self-reflection. Partnerships and cross-cultural reflections might be the beginning of this comparison.

THE SHEEPSKIN EFFECT

Martin Rose

The kingdom of Libya became independent of Italy under King Idris in 1951. Just over a decade later, Algeria finally followed after its long war of independence with France in 1962. During this period, the five countries of the southern Mediterranean coast each in different ways took control of their own futures. Amongst a sobering battery of challenges, one of the more pressing for all of them was education. A large proportion of colonial civil servants, businessmen, skilled workers and teachers left at Independence, especially from the francophone countries where settler colonialism was particularly dense. In Egypt the 1952 Revolution, followed by the Suez War and the expulsion of the *mutamassirun*, resident foreigners (Jews, Armenians, Greeks, Italians), had a similar effect, though Egyptian capacity was already far more developed than that of the Maghreb. In late Protectorate Morocco, for instance, there were three times as many French *fonctionnaires* as there were British civil servants in India, with its population forty times the size of Morocco's – quite apart from large European commercial and artisan classes. Each country faced an urgent need for skilled manpower to fill the vacuum. Each country's educated local elite was both much too small, and mostly unsuited, to fill that need itself, and at the same time largely unequipped to train the next generation. Each government faced a pent-up demand for the social escalator that education represented, and from which the vast majority of the Muslim population had been excluded under French rule. Constructing a new education system was for each an urgent and absolutely crucial area of national development.

Libya and the francophone countries of the Maghreb started from a very low base. Egypt was better placed, with a proud legacy of elite education and the highest level of school enrolment in the region, at around 50 per cent. In Morocco in 1956 only 13 per cent of Muslim children of school age attended school, and the country boasted a total of 640 native graduates. Tunisia, where 33 per cent of Muslim children were in school, counted 1,300. In Algeria the enrolment figure was 21 per cent (this reflected a recent growth from around 8 per cent during the Second World War). In the brand new United Kingdom of Libya more than 90 per cent of the population was illiterate and there were just over 800 students in secondary school. Girls were of course vastly underrepresented in, though not entirely absent from, schools across the region as a whole.

Education during the colonial period had resolved, in slightly different ways in the three countries of francophone North Africa, into a differentiated system of European and native instruction. Where it was available to Muslims, education was limited in scale and had an effective ceiling: with a small number of exceptions from the local elites, it was very hard for Muslims to become educated beyond what was necessary for the subaltern positions to which their institutions were carefully geared. In Algeria there was for many years 'no public conception of education of and for the locals,' and settler pressure led to virtual exclusion of Muslims from state schools. In Morocco, French schooling was closed to all but a few of the Moroccan elite; and only in Tunisia, where the system was the most open, with a *collège* or high school in Tunis open to native students, had some real progress at opening up the system been made. And as for employment, 'the public service,' in the words of Pierre Vermeren, 'was out of bounds for native people, in Algeria because only French citizens could be employed in it, and in the Protectorates because these were foreign countries.' With few exceptions, the best that most native Muslims could hope for was vocational schooling and artisanal employment. Of Libya, UNESCO reported in 1951 that 'few countries in the world are less advanced economically, have a higher proportion of illiteracy or have been longer under foreign domination than Libya,' which was made up of three disparate and very poor provinces brought together for the first time at Independence. Its largest exports were scrap metal and esparto grass.

The new governments urgently needed skilled administrators and industrial and agricultural workers in order to develop their economies, and producing this skilled workforce was the task of their education systems. Getting many more children into school and retaining them for as long as possible formed the central challenge. Many of the urban population certainly saw education as a way to open up chances for the future from which they had hitherto been excluded; but in the countryside there was often more resistance, with attitudes conditioned, if at all, by the traditional experience of the Qur'anic *maktab*, *kuttaab* or *msid*. Extending educational opportunities into the poorer rural areas was a constant theme, though growing urban migration was shifting the balance in favour of the cities. Schools were built, scholarships were established, and the growing needs of the public sector as an employer made sure that there was a clear reward, in terms of secure jobs, for pupils and students who persevered. Vocational education systems were established to train skilled workers; secondary schools and universities were expanded to supply graduates to the public administration and particularly, in numerical terms, to its largest branch, the education system itself.

The result was a generation during which opportunity expanded dramatically, and the education systems grew to accommodate them. Graduates of secondary schools and universities found immediate employment, largely in the government service. School enrolment grew, reaching about 50 per cent by 1970 in all three countries. The first wave of expansion took the colonial education systems as its model, and continued to educate its young largely in French, though with a nationalist political urge to Arabise as that became possible. Egypt, the cultural giant in terms of Arab identity, played a special role in this process, setting the example followed across North Africa of offering free education as a constitutional right to all citizens, and at the same time supplying many of the teachers needed to fill the yawning gaps in Algeria and Morocco as Arabic became the medium of instruction. But French culture remained dominant in this first generation, with many more French than Egyptian teachers in those two countries.

In the 1970s, a corner was turned, and a tide of Arabisation swept through education in North Africa. It was a development with clear political and cultural motivation in a post-colonial world of pan-Arab sentiments, dominated by Nasser's Egypt. Seldom well enough planned or well enough resourced, the change proceeded in fits and starts, conquering primary schools first, pausing, and then sweeping through secondary schools and finally universities. Arabisation has never been entirely completed, STEM (science, technology, engineering and mathematics) subjects at university being largely taught in French to this day and showing little sign of lowering their barriers. Pushed forward for reasons of doctrinaire Arab nationalism, it also reflected a growing governmental unease at the political unrest seen as rooted in access to foreign-language teaching and teachers, Western ideas and subjects like philosophy. In this sense the rise of Arabic-medium teaching, often accompanied by Islamic Studies, has been a fumbling method of social and political control in several countries, of which Morocco in the 'leaden years' of Hassan II is an obvious case.

This development in North African education clearly needs to be judged on a number of different criteria. It may have reinforced national and Islamic sentiment (though the form of the latter, and the Islamist ballast that many of the Egyptian teachers brought with them do not perhaps seem quite as welcome today as they once did); but it has not been kind to educational achievement, and many would argue that the unruly speed of change, the linguistic confusion caused by generally poorly-taught Arabic and the requirement to change language in mid-education if pursuing the sciences, have all contributed to something approaching an educational disaster. Educational outcomes, as we shall see below, are generally very disappointing, and while Arabisation is not the only reason, it is clearly a major contributor.

This is the grand contradiction of North African education and its development since independence: how can a process so earnestly and expensively entered into have yielded quite such slender dividends? It has certainly not come cheap. The five countries have been amongst the biggest spenders in the world, fairly consistently putting some 5 per cent of GDP and about 20 per cent of government spending into education over the last half-century. This money has been spent on expanding provision in a highly centralised way. Ministries of Education have employed, contracted, posted and rewarded teachers and teacher-trainers. They have set targets, allocated funds and run national exams. They have built schools in inaccessible places, commissioned text-books and run school transport. The objective has been, very laudably, a consistent delivery of good quality education to students across each country. In a region that half a century ago was largely illiterate, this has meant some pretty basic things: universal primary education, education for girls and the massive extension of literacy.

These three things are of course also the components of the second Millennium Development Goal (MDG2), which is headlined as the achievement of universal primary education by 2015. The UNDP's 2014 MDG progress report shows North Africa as leading the developing regions of the world, with a net primary enrolment ratio of 99 per cent. This is certainly a big achievement, and quantitative measures are very positive. Apart from the net enrolment ratio, retention from first to last year of primary is a respectable 90 per cent plus, and youth literacy ranges from a low of 81.5 per cent in Morocco to a high of 99.9 per cent in Libya. Gender disparity is under 5 per cent in Libya, Algeria and Tunisia, 8.3 per cent in Egypt and 14.8 per cent in Morocco. Much has been achieved, certainly. And yet there are serious reservations.

Writing in the preface to *The Road Not Travelled*, the seminal World Bank report on education in North Africa published in 2008, Daniela Gressani, Vice-President for Middle East and North African (MENA) region, says: 'The modern history of education reform in MENA is a tale of brazen ambition, struggle against internal and external odds, unintended consequences, tactical error and success, accomplishment and unfinished business. It is also the story of the interaction of competing visions of the purpose and ends of education, pitching global trends in education strategy and content against age-old education traditions. Along this tumultuous path the region should be proud of its accomplishments. However ...' And that 'however' is the substance of the World Bank's report, as of any thoughtful critique of North African educational achievement. Summing up, Gressani writes, 'in particular, the relationship between education and economic growth has remained weak, the divide between education and employment has not been bridged, and the quality of education continues to be disappointing.'

King Mohamed VI of Morocco said in 2013, soon after the completion of a three-year, €2.7 billion Emergency Plan of investment in his country's education, 'I am indeed sad to note that the state of education now is worse than it was twenty years ago ... we still have a long, arduous journey ahead of us …' Honest commentators in all five countries would probably say something very similar, and it is important to understand the nature of the crisis. It is rooted in the history, coupled with the sheer scale of the problem, and the failure to address satisfactorily a number of fundamental, structural problems. These could be summarised brutally as demography, quality, the employability of those that it educates and – different but utterly central – the question of language.

Of demography it is important simply to note that the youth population of the region has been growing very fast during the whole period of educational reform, a growth whose impact on the educational systems of the region has been magnified by the steadily growing proportion of this steadily growing youth cohort that has needed educating. The proportion of the population under the age of 14 ranges from 23 per cent in Tunisia to 31 per cent in Egypt; and the next segment – aged between 15 and 24 – ranges from 27 per cent in Tunisia and Libya to 31 per cent in Egypt. Nowhere, in other words, is the proportion of the population under the age of 24 smaller than 50 per cent, and at the high end in Egypt, it reaches 62 per cent of all Egyptians.

The end of the crude demographic bulge is in sight: by the mid-century only Libya and Egypt will still have growing youth populations, the other three countries anticipating drops of between 13 and 20 per cent. But demand for education will continue to rise for some time to come, peaking earlier in Tunisia and Algeria than in Morocco and Libya where demand at the primary stage will peak only in 2020–30. Successful universalisation of primary education has devastating consequences as the pupils work their way up through the system. Each stage of education has significantly higher per capita costs than the ones before it, and the effect today on overflowing universities is clear across the region in ever-increasing numbers, vastly increased costs and inevitably imperilled standards. One simple vignette of scale is the reflection that the Egyptian school system has a population double that of the state of Tunisia: adding tertiary students to the number makes it 90 per cent of the size of Morocco. And estimates of Egypt's population growth suggest that from 86.8 million today it may reach as high as 140 million by 2050.

Quality has much to do with fitness for purpose, and a large part of the World Bank's argument is that the region has essentially failed to progress from an extensive, quantitative reform engineered from the centre, to a delegated, decentralised, incentive-driven, quality-orientated, child-centred education focussing on skills development, employability and international competitiveness. It has thus failed too in producing the kind of skilled, versatile young people who are needed for the growth and prosperity of the region's economies in today's world. The problem – the static, even regressing, nature of education in the Arab world as whole – was recognised clearly by the Arab Human Development Report of 2003, which noted that 'the most serious problem facing Arab education today is its deteriorating quality,' and that 'curricula taught in Arab countries seem to encourage submission, obedience, subordination and compliance, rather than free critical thought.' This had much to do of course with the 'decolonisation' of education, the impulse to renationalise it, which gathered steam after the mid-1970s and of which Arabisation was only one aspect. It resulted in what Vermeren calls baldly 'the failure of nationalism to build a new, democratic high school system.'

The deterioration of quality is clear from international comparisons, but the truth is that there are relatively few of these that can be easily made. State-run systems are by nature generally non-competitive (in terms of inter-institutional competition), and across North Africa measurements have become largely self-referential. Tunisia offers the most extreme example of this, with school examinations that have no external component, all exams being set, marked and moderated within the individual school, until the Baccalaureate (and even this has an input of 25 per cent from the examinee's own school). Any notion of competition between public and private provision is blurred by the fact that teachers from the public system routinely moonlight in private institutions, not infrequently commercialising key elements of their public courses that have then to be bought by their own state-school students as private goods. This inwardness is reinforced by a rigid exam-based system relying heavily on rote-memorisation, in which each certificate is a cashable end in itself. An 'Integrity Audit' commissioned by the OECD in 2013 noted that 70 per cent of all Tunisian secondary school completers had taken private lessons at one time or another, and that 54 per cent of secondary students were taking private lessons from their current classroom teacher. In Egypt, CAPMAS, the national statistics agency, states that over 60 per cent of all educational investment in the country goes into private tutoring.

The standard international comparison tools are PISA (Programme for International Student Assessment), PIRLS (Progress in International Reading Literacy Study) and TIMSS (Trends in International Mathematics and Science Studies), regular assessments of basic skills that allow a good measure of international comparison. Only Tunisia, Morocco and Egypt have taken part in these, and the most complete participation is from Morocco. It takes a good deal of courage to submit to such comparisons. The results are not altogether positive – but as educational policy-makers understand, change can only begin with clear measurement of the problem. What these exercises show is very clear. In TIMSS (Science and Maths) 2011 Morocco and Tunisia ranked in the bottom three of the 45 participating countries, with only 26 per cent and 35 per cent respectively of Grade 4 pupils passing the lowest international benchmark (international median 90 per cent). On top of that, another 15-20 per cent and 25 per cent respectively scored so low as to be unassessable. There was no statistically significant score at the Advanced Benchmark (international median 75 per cent) by either country.

At PIRLS (reading and writing), where only Morocco took part in 2011, 21 per cent of Grade 4 students reached the lowest benchmark (international median 95 per cent) and again another 25 per cent of students scored so low as to be unassessable. Pausing for a moment to reflect on what these figures mean, we realise that in Morocco 79 per cent of Grade 4 pupils failed to reach the lowest international benchmark, of whom more than 25 per cent scored worse than the mark which a random choice of answers would have given them. It is hard in this case to understand how, in the same year, 2011, *Education for All*, records Morocco's youth literacy as 82 per cent. It seems unkind to single Morocco out, because it is the only country in North Africa to have put itself forward regularly for PIRLS. Tunisia took part in PISA 2012, and ranked 58th in reading out of 66 countries, its score unchanged since 2009. Yet *Education for All* lists Tunisia's youth literacy rate as 97 per cent. It is quite clear that the headline figures for literacy, and by implication all figures relating to educational achievement, need to be taken with a generous pinch of salt right across the region.

An alternative view is offered by the WEF, which in its *Africa Competitiveness Report* of 2013 places Morocco 105th, Algeria 131st, Egypt 139th, Libya 142nd and Tunisia 68th out of 144 countries in the world for 'Quality of Education System.' And it is worth noting that even Tunisia, apparently ahead of the pack, had been demoted to 68th from 12th in 2007, suggesting either a catastrophic decline in national education standards or – more likely – an access of serious doubt at the WEF about the reliability of the information and statistics being offered.

It is necessary therefore to look for other measures, and the next question posed by the World Bank – employability – provides one. One recent writer on Tunisia refers to 'the Tunisian Paradox,' whereby the more educated a young Tunisian is, the more likely she or he is to be out of work. But in truth it is not a Tunisian Paradox at all – it is a North African Paradox. In each country youth unemployment is a major problem, and in each country graduate unemployment is a greater one. It is all too clear that the labour markets of the five countries are unable to absorb the flood of school and university graduates that the systems produce each year; and equally that the systems themselves are unable sufficiently to adapt their curricula and ethos to the needs of a modern economy. Catch-22, in other words.

'It seems,' as one UNDP report drily puts it, of Egypt, 'true that an educated person is at no advantage when it comes to finding his/her way in the job market. In fact the opposite seems to be true.' The figures corroborate this. In Egypt those with secondary education make up 42 per cent of the population and 80 per cent of the unemployed. In Algeria those figures are 20 per cent and 40 per cent. In Morocco, 16 per cent and 30 per cent. Graduate unemployment – *le chômage diplomé* as it is known in the francophone Maghreb – is significantly worse. Only in Tunisia is the graduate employment rate a little below that of general unemployment (at 33.2 per cent to 37.6 per cent) but is still progressive in a very negative sense: Master's degree holders, a mere 15 per cent of the Tunisian student population, make up 55 per cent of the graduate unemployed. In Algeria 20.3 per cent of graduates are unemployed against a global 9.8 per cent (though 24.3 per cent of Algerians aged 15-24 are unemployed); in Morocco 22.7 per cent of graduates are unemployed against 8.9 per cent globally (and 17.6 per cent of youth); in Egypt has 19 per cent graduate unemployment, as against a global 12 per cent and 17 per cent for youth. Libya is more difficult to call, though 'World Bank estimates show that youth unemployment has remained at about 50 per cent, *with the majority of unemployed holding university degrees*' (my italics). It needs noting, though, that grim as it is graduate unemployment is in many (but far from all) cases a luxury available to those who can afford to be unemployed, often through family support, while they wait for public sector employment, so that 'those who can afford to spend time queuing for public sector jobs, with the expectation of relatively high pay for low productivity,' do so.

An even greater tragedy is hidden away beyond the statistics: the young who are not in education or employment – but are not registered as unemployed – and who make up 30-40 per cent of the youth cohort in all countries. Egypt has about 35.9 per cent of 15-24s (and 40.5 per cent of 15-29s) in this condition; Tunisia, 25.4 per cent (and 32.2 per cent). Young women are hugely over-represented: Egypt's 40.5 per cent breaks down into 9.3 per cent of young men and 49.5 per cent of young women. Tunisia's 32.2 per cent into 22.4 per cent of young men and 42.2 per cent of young women.

There is clearly therefore a mismatch between educational provision across North Africa, and the needs of the labour market. The fundamental challenge is of course the changing global economy. A globalised, knowledge-based economy demands 'a well-educated, technically skilled workforce producing high value-added, knowledge-intensive goods and services ... in enterprises that have the managerial capacity to find, adapt and adopt modern up-to-date technology and services in local and global markets.' A low-educated and inflexible workforce is no longer the answer to any country's developmental needs, and the education systems of North Africa are not yet producing anything like enough graduates at each level equipped with the transverse skills, the 'expert thinking,' and the 'complex communication' capacity that the world demands and their countries need. Low-skilled economies have not, and will not, produced the growth necessary to absorb the region's young productively.

A lot of this is the result of low literacy levels and educational outcomes which are discouraging of critical thought in favour of obedience, subordination and compliance. But there are also systemic problems which are worth noting, in the relative failure of the region's technical and vocational education systems, the destructive obsession with public sector employment and the failure of all countries to adapt educational provision and choices to the demands of the market. These three problems are closely interrelated. The public sector has traditionally offered jobs to graduates in the humanities and social sciences, and a shrinking public sector has left many of these graduates stranded with skills that are not useful elsewhere. The academic route through education has been so overwhelmingly more prestigious than the technical vocational education and training (TVET) route, in all countries, that the latter has much more often been seen as a sign of failure than as a route to specialised employment. And none of the countries has created the conditions for a lightly regulated private sector, confident in its security and financing and the openness of its markets, able easily to hire and invest in staff and create wealth.

The Public Sector and its dominance both of employment and aspiration is universal, though it is beginning to be seriously addressed in most countries. Beside a private sector that is still largely informal and without security, the attractions of the public service are clear, with relatively high salaries, pensions and other benefits, a high level of job-security and – very often – low demands that allow secondary employment. By the first decade of this century, the 22 per cent of Tunisians in the government service were absorbing 63 per cent of the government's budget; the 10 per cent of Moroccans, 51 per cent of their government budget; the 29 per cent of Algerians, 31 per cent, and the 29 per cent of Egyptians, 29 per cent. In Libya, where comparable figures are not available, 66 per cent of the workforce was on the public payroll in 2000. These figures are beginning to change for the better, but the inevitable result is growing graduate unemployment and anger at the apparent breaking of the implicit bargain that the state would employ graduates – an anger clearly visible in the regular demonstrations outside the Moroccan parliament by unemployed graduates demanding 'unconditional and non-competitive absorption into the public administration.'

In a 2010 poll, 60 per cent of young Egyptians, 55 per cent of young Tunisians, 44 per cent of Algerians and 38 per cent of Moroccans expressed a preference for public sector employment, for which a simple degree is the pre-requisite. This, and the inflexibility of the region's higher education systems, helps foster a phenomenon which has been called 'the sheepskin effect,' whereby the degree certificate itself is more important than what it represents. 'The public sector,' as one commentator puts it, 'not only regulates the education and training system – with very little involvement of employers – but also is its main client,' and 'as a result, the education system has created signals for public sector hiring rather than equipping graduates with the employability capital needed to succeed in the wider labour market.' Since the public sector is only interested in the sheepskin, this tends to cluster students in the low-cost open-access faculties which provide a degree that is fine for the shrinking pool of public sector jobs, but of little relevance to the private sector.

It's not easy to attribute unemployment to discipline studied, figures being hard to come by, though Algeria shows 27 per cent of humanities graduates unemployed, as against 29 per cent of social scientists, 18 per cent of science graduates and 15 per cent of engineers. Morocco's leading authority on graduate unemployment writes that 'unemployment affects principally those educated in Arabic Literature, Islamic Studies, biology, chemistry and physics, who in 2010 made up more than 80 per cent of the graduate unemployed recorded in the Prime Minister's database.' (The sciences feature here because they are studied for teaching in school, and for the majority who do not succeed in the competition for public sector teaching posts, are not effectively re-deployable in industry.) Governments are tackling this by reducing the size of the public sector, and – particularly in the case of Tunisia – by encouraging students into 'applied' courses with better employment prospects.

Vocational training, at school and post-school levels, should be producing skilled workers for the changing employment market. Unfortunately it isn't really succeeding, anywhere in the region. All five countries have found it very difficult to maintain 'parity of esteem' in a context where the academic route is overwhelmingly prestigious, and where good public sector employment requires a degree. The World Bank in 2013 noted that education must be made 'more inclusive, more directed towards learning, and less directed towards selecting and exclusively rewarding the academically able while leaving the rest behind.' TVET is not only less prestigious, but is also (and partly as a result) the victim of serious under-investment. And it has become progressively less popular. Between 1999 and 2009 there was a 35 per cent drop (the highest in the world) in TVET enrolment in the Arab World. In North Africa, Egypt's was the most dramatic drop, from 30 to 20 per cent; and Tunisia actually bucked the global trend by increasing TVET enrolment, albeit on a very low base, from 10 to 14 per cent. Employers cite lack of skilled workers as a constraint on business creation. It is grimly interesting to note a comment by the World Bank on the Don Bosco Institute, a private TVET college in Egypt, which 'offers three and five year diplomas that provide a path to employment, decent pay and career progression – the very elements lacking in most public TVET institutions.' That is quite a comprehensive lack.

So the picture is alarmingly clear: a series of relatively inflexible education systems geared still, for the most part, to a phase of national development that is past, and finding great difficulty in adapting to the needs of a modern world economy. All this is a reasonably conventional analysis, and one which the World Bank, among other national and international institutions, has offered repeatedly. Some in the region feel that it seems unduly utilitarian, seeming to deny the humanising mission of a liberal education and the role that it plays in producing intelligent, critical citizens. The obvious answer to this is that however humanising it may be, the first priority of a government must be to see food put in its citizens' mouths, and this means that they need employment.

There is however, a nexus of important cultural issues which to a surprising extent escapes utilitarian discussions. By far the most important is that of language, and the intractable political, religious and cultural baggage that 'the language question' trails in its wake. It has at least two main dimensions. The first is the tension between *fusHa* – Classical Arabic – and its colloquial cousins, *'aamiya* or *darija* and the various Tamazight dialects of the Maghreb. And the second is the tension between all of these and the colonial languages – English, French and Spanish – which have been overlaid upon them and have in many cases assumed dangerously divisive roles as class, educational and employment markers. Language has become a matter of politics, and the political disagreements and vested interests involved have a severe impact on education. I shall focus here as an example, Morocco because it exemplifies at their most extreme all these tensions, which have different resonances in each of the countries we are considering.

In Morocco today there rages a peculiar argument (which is important for the whole region) over the language in which early school education should be conducted. A country where 79 per cent of young people are (if we accept the PIRLS figures) at best inadequately literate, clearly has a major educational problem. The same is true of Algeria and Tunisia (though much of the corroboration is anecdotal, given the stellar literacy figures asserted) – and may well be the case of Libya too where a literacy figure of over 99 per cent seem too good to be true. There is a strong link between literacy-acquisition and language, and it seems very clear that the doctrinaire determination to educate very young *darija* and Tamazight-speaking children in Classical Arabic is a significant contributor to this problem. It is not limited to Morocco, but current debates there exemplify its intractable nature: an Islamist government regards any attempt to dilute the stranglehold of Classical Arabic on literacy education as beyond discussion for religious reasons. A governing elite which uses Arabic as the language of administration and justice is equally defensive of its own linguistic achievement and monopoly. And where pan-Islamism and elite interest do not suffice, there is a sentimental pan-Arabism, reforged in the independence struggle, which fills the remaining gaps. The losers are Morocco's children, who remain, in effect, substantially illiterate.

The second question is also one of entrenched interests. French, in francophone North Africa, has a number of functions. It is the language of high culture, and of business (though English is making significant inroads into the latter). It is the language of higher education at least in the STEM subjects. And it is the ineradicable marker of the social and political elite. Morocco retains, outside its state education system, an archipelago of more than 20 'Lycées de Mission' owned and run by the French government. A recent analysis of graduations since independence shows that 45 per cent of Moroccan *lycée* graduates come from 500 families, 34 per cent from 200, 27 per cent from 100, 21 per cent from 50 and 15 per cent from 20 families. So as the system was Arabised in the 1980s the elite remained firmly outside the process. Even the then Minister of Education, who rushed Arabisation through the state schools, had his children at French *lycée* where they were educated in French. The francophone elites remain closely wedded to France in educational terms. Large numbers of North Africans study in France, at university and Grande Ecole, and recruitment fairs for managerial jobs in large corporations take place in Paris as much as in Casablanca or Tunis.

So North Africa faces a very difficult challenge on education reform. The demographic pressures remain intense, the costs crippling, the sheer size of the task alarming. There are vested interests in the semi-reformed state in which the regions education systems find themselves; but there is also great goodwill, considerable expertise and a sense of urgency. There is good work going on in all the countries of North Africa, but it is not yet clear that the political will, the educational wisdom and the administrative excellence co-exist in the necessary constellation.

The stakes are high. The apparently fruitless process of education undertaken by the large numbers of young people from Suez to Agadir who remain unemployed, or underemployed, is dangerously destabilising. Quite apart from the tragic waste of human potential, the blighted lives and the stuttering development process, there is a cost in terms of political stability.

Mohamed Bouazizi, whose self-immolation triggered the 'Arab Spring,' saw education as the only way out of his dead-end existence in Sidi Bouzid. Not for himself – he had dropped out without completing secondary school – but for his sisters. His sister Samya told a journalist that 'my sister was the one at university and he would pay for her, and I am still a student and he would spend money on me.' Another sister, Basma, said 'his dream was to see his sisters go to university.' This dream is the head of steam behind the demand for betterment through education. It continues to build up.

THE INEVITABLE CALIPHATE?

A History of the Struggle for Global Islamic Union, 1924 to the Present

REZA PANKHURST

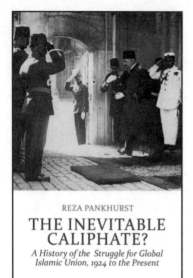

REZA PANKHURST
THE INEVITABLE CALIPHATE?
A History of the Struggle for Global Islamic Union, 1924 to the Present

ISBN: 9781849042512
£18.99 / Paperback / 256pp

While in the West 'the Caliphate' evokes overwhelmingly negative images, throughout Islamic history it has been regarded as the ideal Islamic polity. In the wake of the 'Arab Spring' and the removal of long-standing dictators in the Middle East, in which the dominant discourse appears to be one of the compatibility of Islam and democracy, reviving the Caliphate has continued to exercise the minds of its opponents and advocates. Reza Pankhurst's book contributes to our understanding of Islam in politics, the path of Islamic revival across the last century and how the popularity of the Caliphate in Muslim discourse waned and later re-emerged. Beginning with the abolition of the Caliphate, the ideas and discourse of the Muslim Brotherhood, Hizb ut-Tahrir, al-Qaeda and other smaller groups are then examined. A comparative analysis highlights the core commonalities as well as differences between the various movements and individuals, and suggests that as movements struggle to re-establish a polity which expresses the unity of the ummah (or global Islamic community), the Caliphate has alternatively been ignored, had its significance minimised or denied, reclaimed and promoted as a theory and symbol in different ways, yet still serves as a political ideal for many.

'Reza Pankhurst provides a unique and probing examination of modern thinking on the caliphate. ... This detailed analysis of the ways in which the Muslim Brotherhood, Hizb ut-Tahrir, and al-Qaeda as well as smaller groups reformulate and use the concept today is both judicious and informed. It provides the most reliable guide available to an idea and political symbol that holds attraction for many Sunni Muslims while inciting anxiety, even fear, among others, including many non-Muslims and Shi'a.' — Professor James Piscatori, Durham University

WWW.HURSTPUBLISHERS.COM/BOOK/THE-INEVITABLE-CALIPHATE

41 GREAT RUSSELL ST, LONDON WC1B 3▮
WWW.HURSTPUBLISHERS.COM
WWW.FBOOK.COM/HURSTPUBLISHERS
020 7255 2201

MEASURING QUALITY

Paul Ashwin

Higher education is in a state of flux. The shift of the funding from the government to students is changing many aspects of higher education. One stated aim of this move was to improve quality, attract students and offer students a richer experience. But this aim raises all kinds of questions about what counts as a good undergraduate education and about the appropriate nature of the higher education that is offered by universities. It also has important implications for how quality and student experiences of higher education are improved.

Debates around quality and student experiences of higher education have highlighted three different ways in which quality might be thought about, which have different implications for the improvement of quality. Any position we take on quality is based on our personal values and so I first outline my own engagement with teaching and learning in higher education and consider how it has shaped my position in relation to these issues.

My position on quality has been informed by my experiences as a student and member of staff in both further and higher education. My undergraduate degree was in Applied Social Science at Kingston Polytechnic (although it became a university in the year that I graduated). I basically studied the politics, sociology, economics and philosophy of welfare. The teaching we had was brilliant and the students were from a diverse range of backgrounds. From here, I managed to get British Academy funding to do a Masters in Philosophy of the Social Sciences from the London School of Economics. I hadn't realised that whilst I had studied philosophy from the perspective of social sciences at Kingston, at the LSE I would be studying the social sciences from the perspective of philosophy. I spent the first term and a half being told I wasn't making philosophical arguments and whilst I found the challenge of learning how to do this rewarding, I was shocked by the lack of care for us as a group of students.

One incident summed this up for me when I began work on my dissertation. I turned up to see my supervisor and we had a useful initial chat about the topic. I then asked when we could meet again to discuss my progress and was told 'no, you now go away and write it. We will not be meeting again'. The contrast with my polytechnic experience was stark.

Whilst at Kingston, I had begun to get involved in peer learning schemes. First as a peer supporter of other students on my course and later as someone who supported peer supporters. Whilst at the LSE, I worked the six hours I was allowed by the British Academy at Newham College of Further Education in east London organising peer learning schemes there. Following the completion of my master's programme, I applied for a full-time job at Newham organising peer learning schemes across the college. I worked with teachers and students on a range of programmes to design and implement schemes in which students could support each other. This included schemes on programmes such as A levels in the sciences, social sciences and humanities, and vocational qualifications in electronic engineering, accountancy, and art and design. This work led to a PhD in which I examined the ways in which these schemes developed, were shaped by the courses that they were supporting, and the manner in which those who acted as peer supporters developed a more social view of effective learning. In all, I spent seven years working at Newham and was struck by the dynamism and intelligence of the students and staff that I worked with.

After completing my PhD, I got a post-doctoral research job examining students' experiences of learning at the University of Oxford. As part of this I studied students' and tutors' ways of understanding tutorials at Oxford as well as the factors that affected the quality of students' learning. A few of the people I met at Oxford were truly remarkable but most were not that much different from those I had worked with in Newham. The main difference was in their sense of entitlement and certainty that they were the brightest and the best. When I suggested that the students I worked with at Newham would not understand the culture at Oxford, even those who were keen to widen participation looked at me as if I were mad. I eventually realised that Oxford was its culture. What was unfair was its claim to take the brightest and the best whereas it actually took a particular kind of student to thrive there.

These experiences have made me sceptical about accepting established hierarchies of what were considered the 'best' universities and to question the ways in which notions of quality are informed by ideas of prestige that can have little to do with the programmes that students study and their experiences whilst studying. They have also informed my subsequent research into the quality of teaching and learning in universities.

How do you know the quality of a degree course? This apparently simple question raises fundamental questions about what is valuable and valued about higher education. Is it the prestige of the institution in which the course is located that tells you about its quality? Is it information about what is done on the course or what students who have studied the course say about it? Is it what students go on to do after they have graduated? Or is it something about the ways in which those students have been transformed by studying on the course that really tells us about its quality?

Within all these ways of thinking about the quality of courses are uncertainties about how much it is the process of studying a particular course at a particular institution that leads to high quality outcomes or whether it is the prestige of simply being associated with courses and institutions that we all 'know' are high quality. This reflects the tensions that are engendered by these questions in relation to the competing roles that the notion of quality needs to play. On one side measures of quality need to be portable and durable across contexts and time. We need ideas of quality that are not ever changing so that we can make meaningful comparisons. On the other side, notions of quality need to tell us something valid about how particular courses change the particular students who study them, which is by its nature an individual and unpredictable process. It is also dependent on the relations between the course and the students – students need to take full advantage of the opportunities that are offered and this is not something that can be guaranteed at the outset.

Towards the portable and stable end of the pole, we have national university league tables that are generated by newspapers and websites. These travel across a number of contexts and audiences; having resonance for prospective students and their families, employers, policy makers, academics and universities, and international bodies. They tend to be fairly stable largely because they are based on measures which reflect historical reputation and financial advantage such as staff: student ratios, expenditure and entry standards. These different measures are brought together into a single score by algorithms and weightings that change year on year and lack any statistical credibility because they combine the scores on unrelated and incomparable measures.

The stability of league tables is also driven by the need to ensure that they appear credible to those who are reading them. People will only accept higher education league tables that match with their pre-conceived ideas of which are the top universities. In research into league tables, those who construct national university league tables cheerfully admitted this, arguing that this provided a safety check on the make-up and relative weightings of the measures used to construct particular league tables. It is easy to understand their thinking on this, if Oxbridge and London do not feature heavily near the top of your league table then readers are likely to suspect that there is something wrong with your league table because, after all, we all know which are the really top universities in the UK. We may be uncertain whether this is because of their history, their research, their teaching or the social mix of their students but we simply do know that they are the best, don't we? However, there is an obvious and dangerous circularity to this thinking. It is dangerous because it reinforces privilege: higher status institutions tend to take in a much greater proportion of privileged students and the measures that are used in league tables strongly and wrongly suggest that students who have been to these institutions have received a higher quality education and are likely to have developed greater knowledge and skills than students who have been to less high status universities.

In a project with Monica McLean and Andrea Abbas, examining the quality of sociology and related undergraduate degrees, we found that the key elements of quality were the quality of the teaching and the quality of engagement with academic knowledge that the programmes supported. We examined four institutions whose programmes were very differently ranked in national league tables: Prestige and Selective were consistently in the top third of league tables for Sociology, whilst Community and Diversity were consistently in the bottom third. Based on an in-depth study of the quality of these courses which followed students through the three years of their degrees we found that league table position said nothing useful about the quality of the courses. We found strong evidence that the quality of the courses at Selective and Diversity seemed to be higher in terms of the quality of the teaching and the quality of students' engagement with academic knowledge than the courses at Prestige and Community. However, National League Table position did appear to have real impact on students' perceptions on their own achievements. Whilst students at Prestige talked about their pride of attending a good university, some students at Diversity who were performing very well were dismissive of their achievements because they felt they were not at a good university. That the students had internalised these hierarchies as well as the way they are used by employers to measure 'good graduates' show how notions of quality based on league tables serve to reinforce inequalities.

This means that overall national league tables as measures of quality have high portability and stability but weak validity meaning that they are both convincing and thoroughly misleading. For all of these reasons, league tables are very unlikely to support increases in the quality of undergraduate education. Our pre-conceived ideas of prestige and reputation serve to keep league tables too stable and most of the measures used will be unaffected by any efforts that institutions make to improve the quality of students' experiences. So from university's perspective, the best strategy in relation to such league tables is to find the one that they perform best in and seek to promote this as the most valid league table.

Another source of evidence about the quality of undergraduate courses is students' ratings of the quality of their educational experience. In the UK, this is currently provided by the National Student Survey (NSS) which is completed each year by final year undergraduate students. This is a measure that is a single factor in many UK higher education league tables. Despite criticisms of the survey for reducing education to the meaningless grunt of student satisfaction, research shows that student satisfaction with their courses tends to be related to their perceptions of the quality of their teaching which in turn is a reasonable predictor of the quality of their learning outcomes. This makes the outcomes of such surveys a more valid measure of the quality of an undergraduate education. Considering the outcomes of such surveys can also support improvements in the quality of undergraduate degree programmes. This involves using the survey as a starting point to explore students' experiences on these programmes more deeply, through conversations between programme teams and students, which are aimed at improving the educational experience offered.

The criticisms of the NSS show that it is slightly less portable than league tables. It is also less stable as institutions' positions tend to fluctuate more than they do in relation to national league tables. There are also problems with the ways that the outcomes of the NSS are used. The first is a problem that is shared more generally by national league tables. This is that institutions with very small differences in their national student survey scores can be separated by many places in rankings. This means that meaningless differences are presented as if they are large, significant and meaningful. Whilst one obvious solution would be to rank institutions in bands between which the differences actually mean something, this would involve sacrificing simplicity for the sake of validity and this is a sacrifice that no one has been willing to make.

The second problem is that, despite its potential for supporting improvements in quality, the NSS suffers from a version of Goodhart's Law that when a measure becomes a target, it ceases to be a good measure. What happens in this case is that institutions spend vast amounts of time and energy trying to fix students' responses rather than trying to improve the quality of students' educational experience. The classic example of this is the response to students consistently giving lower scores to the quality of feedback they receive compared to the quality of teaching. This response has involved attempting to make students more aware of when they are having a 'feedback moment'. It is routinely suggested at meetings to discuss NSS outcomes that when a tutor talks to a student about their work they should highlight that the student is actually getting feedback. This kind of nonsense will have no positive impact on the quality of students' educational experiences but is a predictable outcome of the logic of trying to fix the measures that are used to indicate quality.

There is another problem. While focusing on a single dimension of quality improves its validity, it also means that there are plenty of elements of quality that the NSS does not tell us about. So overall, the National Student Survey has greater validity in examining quality than league tables but this involves sacrificing some of the portability and stability of league tables as well of focusing on a narrower definition of what counts as high quality student experiences of higher education.

In our research on pedagogic quality, we argued that the ways in which students engage with academic knowledge should be at the centre of the way we think about the quality of an undergraduate education. Our argument was that in defining quality we need to focus on what is the central purpose of an undergraduate education. Our sense was that it is the critical relations that students develop to knowledge that is the defining feature of higher education. It is the ways that students' engagement with knowledge changes their sense of who they are and what the world is that marks the transformational elements of higher education.

This way of thinking about quality involves examining students' trajectories through their undergraduate education and exploring how they change through their engagement with knowledge as part of this process. As part of the project, we developed survey items that attempted to capture students' engagement with knowledge that appeared to be reasonable predictors of their learning outcomes. Whilst we would argue that this way of thinking about quality has strong validity because it focuses on the central purpose of an undergraduate education, it is much less portable and stable than league table notions of quality. This is because these relations to knowledge will be discipline-specific. The items that we used to capture students' relations to sociological knowledge would not be appropriate for students studying Chemistry. There also may be disciplinary differences in the extent to which these relations to knowledge have resonance internationally. Some disciplines, such as the natural sciences, engineering and economics, tend to have similar curricular internationally whereas other social science and humanities disciplines tend to be more nationally defined. For example, it is difficult to conceptualise what would be an international curriculum in Sociology or Literature studies.

Whilst this may be a heavy price to pay in terms of portability and stability, this way of thinking about quality also supports more thoughtful approaches to improving the quality of undergraduate education. This is because it focuses attention on developing environments and teaching that are focused on helping students to develop transformational relationships to knowledge. This is in marked contrast to the focus in recent government policy documents on improving quality through the creation of a competitive market for students-as-informed-consumers. The emphasis in these documents on assuring quality through competition for students is likely to encourage universities to focus on how their undergraduate courses and reputation are perceived externally rather than focusing on improving the quality of the teaching and learning experiences that they offer students.

It is also problematic because this notion of improving quality is silent about what quality should be. Rather quality is defined in terms of ensuring high demand for courses rather than in terms of how those degree courses should transform students and their identities. A similar thing happens when quality is defined in terms of the employability of students. Rather than the quality of an education being valued for what students become, it is defined in terms of students having the correct dispositions for an ever-changing employment market. The problems with both of these approaches is that they are silent about the forms of knowledge that students should have access to and it is this knowledge that is central in the transformative power of higher education. It is also this knowledge that makes higher education, a higher form of learning.

The three ways of thinking about quality reveal a central tension in the very notions of quality. It is important to be clear that both sides of this tension (portability and stability on the one side and validity on the other) are important. It would be wrong to be dismissive of the need for portability and stability because this is crucial in providing people with ways of understanding what quality is and making meaningful comparisons of the qualities of different programmes. There is no point in having rich and valid accounts of particular examples of quality if these do not allow a sense of the relative nature of this quality. However, there is equally no point in having highly comparable measures of qualities that are meaningless and tell us about prestige and history rather than about the quality of the education that students actually experience.

In conclusion, there are two important things to bear in mind when thinking about the quality of a university education. The first is that all measures of quality will simplify and give us a partial picture of what is going on. What is crucial is to seek to be clear what elements are being used to create this picture and to question what they actually say about the educational experience of students. Second, a central element of thinking about quality is the extent to which particular degree programmes give students access to knowledge that changes their understanding of the world and themselves. This may seem obvious but it is remarkable how little discussions of knowledge feature in policy documents relating to higher education. For example, in the 2011 White Paper 'Students at the Heart of the System', there was very little discussion of knowledge. Where it was discussed, it was either a junior partner in the couplet of 'skills and knowledge' or was not discussed in particularly positive terms, for example 'A good student is not simply a consumer of other people's knowledge, but will actively draw on all the resources that a good university or college can offer to learn as much as they can' (paragraph 3.1, p.33). This matters because prestige and reputation are such distorting factors in our ways of thinking about educational quality. Focusing on how knowledge changes students is essential if higher education is not simply going to reinforce existing social hierarchies.

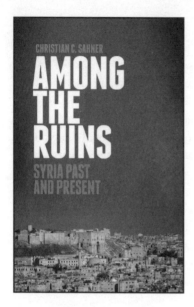

ISBN: 9781849044004
£20.00 / Hardback / 240pp

AMONG THE RUINS

SYRIA PAST AND PRESENT

CHRISTIAN C. SAHNER

As a civil war shatters a country and consumes its people, historian Christian Sahner offers a poignant account of Syria, where the past profoundly shapes its dreadful present.

Among the Ruins blends history, memoir and reportage, drawing on the author's extensive knowledge of Syria in ancient, medieval, and modern times, as well as his experiences living in the Levant on the eve of the war and in the midst of the 'Arab Spring'. These plotlines converge in a rich narrative of a country in constant flux — a place renewed by the very shifts that, in the near term, are proving so destructive.

Sahner focuses on five themes of interest to anyone intrigued and dismayed by Syria's fragmentation since 2011: the role of Christianity in society; the arrival of Islam; the rise of sectarianism and competing minorities; the emergence of the Ba'ath Party; and the current pitiless civil war.

Among the Ruins is a brisk and illuminating read, an accessible introduction to a country with an enormously rich past and a tragic present. For anyone seeking to understand Syria, this book should be their starting point.

'*Among the Ruins* is a uniquely vivid evocation of the past of Syria and a prescient record of its present state. Deeply humane and drawing on subjects from all walks of life, Sahner has a gift for presenting them against a past that is as varied and as ancient as the country itself. We are brought to the edge of the precipice over which, alas, a magnificently diverse society appears to have stumbled. We will be both better informed and wiser for reading it.' — Peter Brown, Rollins Professor Emeritus of History at Princeton University

WWW.HURSTPUBLISHERS.COM/BOOK/AMONG-THE-RUINS

41 GREAT RUSSELL ST, LONDON WC1B 3PI
WWW.HURSTPUBLISHERS.COM
WWW.FBOOK.COM/HURSTPUBLISHERS
020 7255 2201

RESEARCHING ISLAMOPHOBIA

Sindre Bangstad

I have probably dedicated more time and energy to researching and teaching the topic of Islamophobia than any other academic in Norway, yet I cannot quite recall where and when I first encountered the term. It would be a fair assumption that the first time I came across it was back in 2009 when I hosted a visit from an American academic. I was launching a series of public lectures in anthropology at the then recently established House of Literature in Oslo.

From 2009 to 2014, I invited a number of accomplished international scholars in my own field of anthropology to Oslo to provide them with a platform to discuss their own work and engage with a largely non-specialist audience. The core funding for the series was provided by Norway's Fritt Ord Foundation, established in 1974 to protect and promote freedom of expression in Norway and internationally. At a time when my own field of study seemed to be retreating in the face of Norway's neo-liberal marketisation of universities, and engaging with the public on issues of contemporary concern (a process brilliantly described in the case of the UK by Stefan Collini in his book *What are Universities for?*) was shunned, the series was intended to promote the continued relevance of public anthropology. My main criteria for the scholars I invited, in co-operation with other education institutions and research centres in Norway, were that they had an exceptional academic record, wrote about issues of broad concern and interest in international affairs, and they were willing, able and enthusiastic about engaging with non-specialist audiences. The first guest in my series was Matti Bunzl, at that time a professor at Illinois University at Urbana-Champaign in the USA. Bunzl had published an article, in 2005, in the anthropological journal *American Ethnologist* on anti-Semitism and Islamophobia, that has subsequently become one of the scholarly reference points in the literature on

Islamophobia. This article, which had generated a lively, yet respectful debate in the pages of the *American Ethnologist*, was picked up two years later by Marshall Sahlins, one of the real grand old men of US anthropology, and published as a pamphlet by Prickly Paradigm Press. I had ambitiously booked the largest hall at the House of Literature for Bunzl, but did not quite know what to expect either of him or the audience. Bunzl, whose profound interest in art and literature would a few years later see him become artistic director of the Chicago Humanities Festival, proved to be a perfect start to the series. A lively, witty, bald and bespectacled gay Jewish man with a large frame in his thirties, who might have come straight out of the sitcom *Seinfeld*, Matti seemed to relish the opportunity. It was extra touching that he had invited his ageing father, the Austrian scholar and historian John Bunzl, who, I did not know at the time, had also published extensively on Islamophobia in his native German.

The event with Bunzl at the House of Literature, which took place in September 2009, subsequently providing the basis of an article for the anthropological journal *Ethnos* in 2010, consisted of a one-hour conversation between myself and Matti, followed by a one-hour question and answer session between him and the audience. I have little record or recollection of the Q&A itself, although I do remember that there was hardly any reservation from the audience to Bunzl's extensive usage of the term Islamophobia. After all, the term was then relatively new to a Norwegian general public, and Norwegian far-right activists were not paying much attention to discrediting it or dissuading its use. As for myself, I was at that point still undecided about using the term in my work.

A foretaste of the future came, however, in the form of an academic seminar at the Center for the Studies of The Holocaust and Religious Minorities (The HL-Center) in Oslo held the day before Bunzl's appearance at the House of Literature. The centre was established in 2001, partly funded out of the 450 million Norwegian kroner (around £38 million) awarded by the Norwegian Parliament to the small Jewish community in 1997 as compensation for the economic liquidation Norway's Jews suffered during the Nazi Occupation and the forced deportation of 772 jews by Norwegian Nazified state police officers to

Auschwitz between 1942-43. The HL-Center is located in the villa the Norwegian Nazi and collaborationist Prime Minister Vidkun Quisling (1889–1945) had built at Bygdøy in Oslo West. Together with the HL-Center's senior researcher Cora Alexa Døving I had invited a number of distinguished Norwegian academics to the seminar. Present at the proceedings was also the cultural and op-ed editor at the liberal-conservative *Aftenposten*, for many years Norway's most influential mainstream newspaper, sitting at the back silently taking notes. In the break, he came up to me and asked whether it was correct that Bunzl was Jewish. To which I responded that I believed so. I could not quite understand what that had to do with anything, but from the comment column he penned, which appeared in the pages of *Aftenposten* on the following day, it became much clearer. In this, the editor took Bunzl to task for even mentioning Islamophobia and anti-Semitism in the same breath. To do so, the column implied, was to betray the memories of the darkest chapter of modern European history: the Nazi extermination of some six million European Jews in the Holocaust during World War II. And for a scholar of Jewish background such as Bunzl to do so, was even worse.

Now, as it happens, some of the scholars who have written most insightfully about Islamophobia in recent years, like Bunzl, happen to have a Jewish background. To imply that it should matter to us whether an academic happens to be of Muslim, Jewish, Hindu, Sikh, atheist or other background in the evaluation of their work seems to me to open up a kind of scholarly identity politics which I personally find both reductionist and abhorrent. Now, at the very same seminar, there was also a young and aspiring left-leaning journalist. She had, I was later told, taken the opportunity to interview Bunzl while they were both travelling back to central Oslo on the same bus. This led to an item in the Norwegian weekly for which she worked, *Dag &Tid*, bearing a title which suggested that Bunzl had implied that 'Muslims were the new Jews' of modern Europe. In light of the fact that Bunzl had, in his various publications, explicitly argued that the analogy had serious limitations, this was most unfortunate.

So the first question I posed to Bunzl at the House of Literature the following day was 'is the analogy valid?'. 'I have a feeling that sometimes newspaper editors', Bunzl replied, 'are quite attracted to lines like that because they sound good and they do have some punch, as we would say in the US. But on a general level, two groups are never identical. This is a philosophical point: Jews and Muslims will never be the same, and Muslims of today could not possibly be the Jews of the early twentieth century. On a purely formal philosophical basis, such a statement does not make sense'.

Perhaps the most insightful guide to the limits of the analogy between Islamophobia and anti-Semitism is the Oxford philosopher Brian Klug. In an article in *Patterns of Prejudice*, Klug notes that in Islamophobic representations there are no equivalents to classical anti-Semitism's ideas about the 'hidden hand of Jews' controlling and orchestrating international finance. Nor are the Muslims of Islamophobia, unlike the Jews of classical anti-Semitic tropes, represented as agents of materialistic modernity or as 'Christ-killers'. Yet even if Klug, much like me, is averse to direct analogies between the two terms, he is a clear proponent of the view that comparisons between Islamophobia and anti-Semitism may have their uses.

The Norwegian Context

At this point, I need to say something about the context for, and of, Islamophobia in Norway. Norway is in no way a unique case. As elsewhere in Western Europe, what the American political scientist Erik Bleich referred to as 'indiscriminate negative attitudes towards Islam and Muslims', articulated in the public sphere, have become part of Norwegian mainstream politics, particularly after 9/11. These sentiments have become a mobilising factor for the far-right in Norway. In our time, more than ever, ideas travel, and they travel very fast. In tracing the origins of specific ideas which form part of the Islamophobic repertoire in Norway, I have often been struck by the extent to which these ideas have originated elsewhere, but have been adapted to the local context and put rapidly into circulation. I have often, in jest, remarked to Muslim friends that the only idea I have yet to encounter in the European Islamophobic repertoire is that Muslims represent a mortal threat to Norway's favourite pet – dogs. Such is the case with 'Eurabia', which is certainly of transnational provenance. 'Eurabia' is the idea that the European Union and various Middle Eastern and North African countries have, since the petroleum crisis in 1973, secretly plotted to turn the continent of Europe into an Islamic territory (state or caliphate) by means of high fertility rates, mass immigration and terror. As British writer Matt Carr and others have pointed out, the 'Eurabia' genre is a contemporary far-right conspiracy theory that shares significant structural resemblances to the anti-Semitic Tsarist forgery *The Protocols of The Elders of Zion*. As a conspiracy theory, it is non-refutable on factual and empirical grounds to those who happen to believe in it, for those who do argue against it are often cast as part of the conspiracy itself. The term 'Eurabia' originated with the late Italian feminist Oriana Fallaci in 2004, but the idea was first systematised by the octogenarian far-right Cairo born, Swiss-Israeli, author Bat Ye'or (pseudonym of Gisèle Littmann) in his 2005 book, *Eurabia: The Euro-Arab Axis*. By the following year the term was adopted by Norwegian far-right bloggers such as the biological racist 'Fjordman', (Peder Are Nøstvold Jensen), an MA student at the University of Oslo whose writings, calling for Europeans to arm themselves against Muslims and for the ethnic cleansing of Europe, would later provide the main inspiration for the right-wing extremist and mass murderer Anders Behring Breivik.

Another early and eager convert to the 'Eurabia' conspiracy was the Norwegian lesbian secular-feminist civil society activist Hege Storhaug of the Progress Party, which is supported by the think-thank Human Rights Service (HRS). By 2007, a former Member of Parliament and Member of the European Parliament, Hallgrim Berg of the Conservative Party, had made the first Norwegian contribution to the 'Eurabia' genre in the form of the self-published pamphlet *Letter to Lady Liberty: Europe in Danger*. Yet the central ideas of the 'Eurabia' literature are hardly novel, and what Ye'or and her followers did during the US-led 'war on terror' (2001–08) was simply to systematise ideas that had been in wide circulation in far-right circles in Western Europe and the USA for quite some time. An early precursor of the genre in Norway is in fact a speech made by the Progress Party's legendary chairman from 1978 to 2006, Carl Ivar Hagen at a Progress Party election rally ahead of the Norwegian county and municipal elections of September 1987. Reading out what later became known in the media as the 'Mustafa letter', Hagen claimed to have received a letter from a Muslim from Oslo called Muhammad Mustafa. Hagen pointed to the letter as manifest evidence of a Muslim plot to turn Norway into an Islamic state. For in the letter, Mustafa asserted that Hagen was 'fighting in vain' against Muslims, since 'Islam will conquer Norway too' and 'one day, mosques will be as common in Norway as churches are today'. Ominously, the letter warned that 'one day, the heathen cross in the flag would be gone'. And the cause of this future state of affairs was, according to the letter, that 'we' Muslims 'give birth to more children than you' and that 'many right-believing Muslim men of fertile age' were arriving in Norway every year.

The real Muhammad Mustafa, a hard-working pizza baker and married man with children from the inner-city suburb of Tøyen in the capital of Oslo, had never written such a letter. After being awoken by racist phone-calls for days and nights on end, he decided to sue Hagen for forging the letter. The matter was settled out of court, and Hagen is reported to have been forced to pay hundreds of thousands in financial compensation to Mustafa. Yet Hagen knew very well what he was doing: he never apologised, but claimed to have acted in good faith, and asserted that it could have been true. In the elections that followed Hagen's speech the Progress Party polled higher than it had ever done before, winning 12.1 per cent of the total vote. The Progress Party, originally established by rather crank libertarian right-wingers as a party opposed to taxation and bureaucracy, had discovered its winning formula.

Ever since then, opposition to immigration and anti-Muslim rhetoric has been a regular feature of the Progress Party's electoral campaigns, helping bring its best result to date in the parliamentary elections of September 2009, when the party obtained 22.9 per cent of the total votes cast, and became Norway's second largest party in parliament. The years 2001–11, which I have covered extensively in my own monograph *Anders Breivik and The Rise of Islamophobia*, saw a gradual but steady turning up of the volume and intensity of the Progress Party's Islamophobic discourse, to the extent that the party chairperson (and from 2013, Norway's Finance Minister) Siv Jensen in a speech to the party's congress in February 2009, ahead of that year's parliamentary elections, referred to an alleged ongoing 'islamisation by stealth' of Norwegian society. What she meant by the term was rather unclear, for the only actual instances of 'islamisation' Jensen was able to refer to in her speech were the provision of halal foods for Muslim prison inmates, failed demands to gain state acceptance for female Muslim police officers to wear the hijab as part of their uniform, and alleged gender segregation at Norwegian schools with Muslim pupils. To the extent that such demands had been made by Norwegian Muslims, they had gone through democratic channels and procedures, openly, and not stealthily. The very notion of an ongoing 'islamisation by stealth' of Norwegian society had originated in Norwegian far-right circles. The US Islamophobic kingpin and ideologue Robert Spencer (also to become a significant inspiration for Anders Behring Breivik) had even dedicated a whole book to the topic, published in 2008.

What is crucially important to note about the Norwegian context, however, is that Norway has weathered the recurrent and ongoing financial crises in Europe extremely well. Although Norway has increasing levels of social and economic inequality, it has comparatively extremely low levels of unemployment, especially youth unemployment, and comparatively high rates of minority labour market participation. The reasons for the existential fears generated by the presence of Islam and Muslims in the Norwegian context must therefore be sought in other places than material factors. A key, I have long argued, is to be found in the resentment and feelings of marginalisation from deliberative democratic processes experienced by certain sections of the white Norwegian working class turned service class in the course of the de-industrialisation that Norway experienced between 1970 and 1990. This, coupled with the rise of a technocratic politics, neo-liberal economics and state feminism, has left many voters open to the appeal of a party – which though it was in government since 2013 demonstrated that it is as dominated by technocratic elites as any other party, and as ready, if not more, to abandon the interests of ordinary Norwegian workers for the sake of political expediency as the rest – claims to represent the interests and the voices of the average Joe and Mary. And perhaps more Joe than Mary, for in line with research findings about the supporters of other far-right political formations in Europe, it is now a well-established fact that the overwhelming majority (91 per cent in the parliamentary elections of 2009) of Progress Party voters are male, white and relatively poorly educated. So why the focus on Muslims, who after all on current estimates represent no more than 3.8 per cent of the Norwegian population? To understand this, we have to link the Norwegian context to the international situation which has pertained since 2001 in which Muslims have been often cast as threats not only to national and international security, but also to various liberal freedoms, a development examined by Joseph Massad in his recent book, *Islam in Liberalism*.

Choosing 'Islamophobia'

'Men make history, but not under conditions of their own choosing' is a statement often attributed to Karl Marx. In my own case, it was not until the Norwegian winter of 2010-11 that I actively chose to use the term Islamophobia in my writings. Like many others, I had reservations. Firstly, the term has both descriptive and denunciatory properties. To declare something or someone to be Islamophobic is not a neutral act: it is to declare that such a person or a movement which engages in Islamophobia as ranking low on one's moral spectrum. Secondly, the term has the risk of conflating (often warranted, and perfectly legitimate) criticisms of Islam or interpretations of Islam – which in our time should by no means be exempt from criticism, whether by Muslims or non-Muslims – with unreservedly negative attitudes and sentiments towards Muslims in general. If one, for the sake of the argument, finds criticism of Saudi Arabia and Iran's appalling record on human rights and women's rights 'Islamophobic', or finds the fears for the global influence and reach of the moronic and barbaric creed of salafi-jihadism, as represented by ISIS, Boko Haram, Al-Qaeda and the Tehrik-e-Taliban 'Islamophobic', then one has certainly entered into the realm of the absurd. And thirdly, the term often seems to imply that people who express negative ideas and sentiments about Islam and Muslims are somehow 'phobic'.

So what, then, were the circumstances that let me to choose and use the term Islamophobia? In late November 2010, the private but national Norwegian TV channel TV2 screened a speculative documentary on the 'Eurabia' genre featuring a number of secular-orientated Egyptian intellectuals along with representatives of the Egyptian Muslim Brotherhood. Entitled *Freedom, Equality and The Muslim Brothers*, and funded by TV2 itself in conjunction with the Fritt Ord Foundation, it was directed by the Norwegian documentary filmmaker Per Anders Magnus. The script was written by a Norwegian-Iraqi atheist political activist, poet and popular author by the name of Walid al-Kubaisi, who also played the lead as the documentary's investigator and interviewer. In the documentary, which was set to an ominous musical score, these Egyptian intellectuals, more or less all aligned with the interests of the corrupt and authoritarian regime of Hosni Mubarak and his National Democratic Party, told the filmmakers about their fears for a future Egypt run by the Muslim Brothers. These fears were of course genuine, but the documentary had nothing at all to say about the increasingly repressive rule of Mubarak and his neo-liberal cronies: the plot line basically being that everything would have been hunky-dory in Egypt if it was not for the Muslim Brotherhood plotting to take power. Through investigative reporting by the leftist daily newspaper *Klassekampen's* Cairo-based Middle East correspondent Amal Wahhab, it later turn out that neither the Iraqi-Norwegian filmmaker nor the director had informed the Egyptian intellectuals appearing in the documentary that in the final product their statements would be used to imply that the Muslim Brotherhood in Egypt were secretly plotting to 'establish an Islamic caliphate in Norway' through the means of 'baby trolleys, the hijab, democracy and freedom of expression'. The Norwegian-Iraqi filmmaker appeared in numerous media interviews, in which he declared, virtually uncontested by any journalists or editors, that he had made a film 'against the fascism of our time'; and charged any number of moderate mainstream Muslims in Norway with being either Islamists or 'errand boys for the Islamists'. In the ensuing media storm which inevitably followed, the Progress Party launched another parliamentary motion proposing the banning of the hijab in Norwegian public schools, citing previous op-eds from the filmmaker to the effect that the 'hijab was the Islamists' uniform'. The filmmaker of course wanted everyone to believe that his target was Islamism, and not Islam, but in fact he had for a number of years actively contributed to blurring the line between the two in Norway's mediated public spheres, by accusing all and sundry among mainstream Norwegian Muslim representatives of being 'Islamists'. This was the 'hermeneutics of suspicion' writ large in order to cast aspersions on Norwegian citizens of Muslim background in general, and clearly a contribution to the 'Eurabia' genre.

In an opinion poll taken shortly after the screening of the documentary, a full 61 per cent of those surveyed in a national representative sample of Norwegians declared that they feared 'conflicts with Muslims' more than anything else in the future. By February 2011, central Progress Party members in Oslo were referring to Islam as 'Nazism' and thereby implying that Muslims in general were akin to Nazis. It was in this context that I, as the first Norwegian academic to do so, started to sound the alarm about the state of public discourse on Islam and Muslims in Norway, and decided to use the term Islamophobia. My first recorded use of the term in a scholarly essay was in a piece for the Social Sciences Research Council (SSRC) blog 'The Immament Frame' published on 16 June 2011. The worst terror attacks in Norwegian history, perpetrated by a white right-wing extremist from Oslo West, who had unknown to all but his closest family, shut the windows on the real world and immersed himself in the darknet's netherworld of far-right Islamophobia and 'Eurabia' ideas, were to occur a few months later.

Though I have opted to use the term Islamophobia myself, as does various UN and EU organs, *The Economist*, *The Guardian*, *The New York Times* and others, I have long favoured an agnostic and pragmatic attitude to its usage. I can understand why other people would opt for terms such as 'anti-Muslim attitudes' or 'anti-Muslim hatred' instead of Islamophobia, if only to underline the point that it is unreservedly negative attitudes and sentiments about Muslims, rather than Islam itself, that we should be worried about if we are concerned about equal rights and the ability for all citizens regardless of background to live their lives in dignity and peace in liberal and secular societies. In the context of my teaching, I have heard from Norwegian Muslim civil society activists who refrain from using the term because they consider it to be too much of a 'conversation stopper'. And they have a point: for if the debate about this becomes one of the appropriateness of specific analytical terms rather than what to do about the regrettable situation which these terms seek to capture, it is too easy for all parties to get side-tracked. The attempts to dissuade scholars and the wider public from active use of the term have been relentless, have come from various quarters, and have involved senior media editors in the

Norwegian mainstream press. One of the early strategies was to launch genealogies of the term which had no basis in any historical research. The Spanish historian Fernando Bravo López established, in a 2011 article published in *Ethnic and Racial Studies*, that the first known scholarly usage of the term dates back to 1910, in the work of two French West Africanists (one of whom was a French colonial administrator in West Africa to boot, and not likely to have been overly sympathetic to Muslims) namely Maurice Delafosse and Alain Quillien. However, in far-right online media in Norway the idea that the term emerged variously from the Muslim Brotherhood, the Islamist regime in Iraq, or even with Tariq Ramadan, continues to be put forward as a serious proposition. In my monograph *Anders Breivik and The Rise of Islamophobia*, written as my personal way of dealing with the darkest days many Norwegians had ever experienced in July and August 2011, following Breivik's massacre, I catalogued some of these fabricated genealogies. I soon discovered that these genealogies were never ever accompanied by any substantiating references or data: it was as if their mere enunciation in various places online meant that they were to be taken seriously. That also tells us something about the time in which we live, in which distortions and fabrications have become ubiquitous and so commonplace that trying to insist on facts and substantiation involves one in a series of futile exercises leading to exhaustion. Another strategy has been to trivialise the actual experiences which the term Islamophobia is meant to capture. A female literary reviewer in Norway's *Aftenposten* writing in April 2011, compared Norwegian Muslims complaining about the prevalence of Islamophobia in Norway to small children exaggerating in order to obtain favours from their parents. Perhaps the most amusing attempt at discrediting the term came from another literary reviewer, this time in Norway's *Dagbladet*, who simply informed his readers that since he was not able to find the term in his dictionary, the phenomena to which it referred could not possibly exist.

The term Islamophobia has now been used so regularly and frequently as to warrant Brian Klug's conclusion that it has 'come of age' in scholarly literature and in the media, if not yet in the general public. Regardless of this, attempts to discredit the term and dissuade scholars from using it are likely to continue for the foreseeable future. So scholars and intellectuals need to do much more. We need to move from a phase in which we deliberate over intellectually responsible definitions of the term to operationalising it, for it to be used as a tool through which to explore and measure European Muslims' experiences of stigmatisation, discrimination and racism. In contemporary Europe, we find ourselves in troubled times.

THE CASE FOR FICTIONAL ISLAM

Ruqayyah A. Kareem

'Those people don't read!' I heard an administrator at Texas A&M University blurt out. He was speaking about people in Qatar. He was wrong of course; Qatar has a literacy rate of over 96 per cent, above Australia, but below the Gaza Strip.

The administrator may not have known this. So what was the reasoning behind this opinion? Where did the idea that 'those people don't read' come from? What the administrator was actually referring to is the reading of fictional literature or reading for pleasure. This is where you most often find a discrepancy between what is viewed as literacy and what is read. For the administrator the acquisition of knowledge was embedded in the act of reading fictional literature and from that perspective he concluded that the Qatari population just does not read.

In the traditional Islamic perspective the universal concepts of knowledge are viewed in terms of the sacred versus the profane. The weight of any acquisition of knowledge is measured against these two values. For some Muslims, sacred knowledge – Qur'an, hadith, and religious text – allows one to maintain a connection with the Creator. By contrast, profane knowledge in the form of fiction, in particular speculative literature, such as science fiction, fantasy and comic book literature, moves one away from the Creator and towards worldly pursuits. Of course, there is no religious basis for such a separation, unless you conflate fiction with the act of lying. Fiction, particularly science fiction, fantasy and comic books, represents a concrete way to encourage reading, writing, and imagination that can spur creativity and innovation in all areas of learning for Muslims. Through fiction, the reader and the writer can also bridge and strengthen both branches of knowledge. As an educator whose research and teaching is grounded in American Islam, I use what I refer to as fictional Islam in much of my pedagogical work.

So how do we encourage Muslims to acquire not just sacred knowledge but all knowledge? The Prophetic tradition is the ideal starting point. The injunction to seek knowledge from the cradle to the grave is a common saying you hear from Muslims all over the world. The Prophet Muhammad enjoined his followers to 'seek knowledge even if it is in China', thus encouraging the seeking of knowledge beyond the spiritual realm. Muslims are told to contemplate, think, learn, comprehend, and examine everything around them. As the social scientist Anas Al-Shaikh argues, knowledge, education, and the acquisition of learning for Muslims, reinforce 'the values of humanitarianism, morality, citizenship, peaceful coexistence, revulsion of racism and discrimination, acceptance of the "other", and is married to actively taught skills of critical thinking and awareness'. So how does that square with the reluctance to read fiction we have seen in Muslim countries?

As with most problems in the world, one can view this particular issue as one of power. Unsurprisingly, the imagination is seen as a challenge to those whose authority lies in religious dogma, the power of interpretation, and understanding. The notion of sacred versus profane knowledge can and is being used to stifle any attempts to read 'for pleasure.' In many Muslim societies, reading science fiction and fantasy are seen as profane and therefore not only useless but harmful to those trying to elevate their understanding of the Creator. In some Muslim countries, such as Saudi Arabia and Iran, this literature is regularly banned; in others it is heavily censored.

Yet the scientific invention and innovation of Muslim civilisation serve as literary tropes in much of contemporary science fiction and fantasy literature. Many of the instruments created by Muslims such as the astrolabe, the quadrant, and the detailed navigational maps have helped in the expansion of the literary heritage of science fiction, fantasy, and speculative writing as a whole. The astrolabe and the quadrant have been staples within popular science fiction television shows and movies such as *Star Wars*, *Star Trek*, and *Dune*. The use of the astrolabe and the Alpha, Beta, Delta, and Gamma Quadrants as spaceship monikers demonstrate the longevity of these early inventions and their importance as tools of discovery.

Another science fiction trope, time travel, also has roots in Islam. One of the greatest examples of such paranormal travel is the account of the Prophet's ascension from Jerusalem to Paradise while sitting in the Great Mosque in Jerusalem. For Muslims, these ideas were neither strange nor foreign. Yusuf Nuruddin, who teaches African Studies at the University of Massachusetts Boston, suggests that the Prophet's ascension is an example of what he calls the science fiction motif – a belief system that stimulates the imagination. Nuruddin also argues that some of the stories in *Arabian Nights*, for example, 'The City of Brass' and 'The Ebony Horse,' are early examples of science fiction mixed with fantasy elements.

Contemporary Muslim writers often draw on these early prophetic parables and religious stories in developing their science fiction and fantasy narratives. Donald Moffitt's *Crescent in the Sky* (1990) and *A Gathering of Stars* (1990) are early examples of science fiction about Muslims where a longing for the glory of Islam undergirds the plot. Moffitt's novels portray an Islam that has spread throughout the known universe, but lacks a single leader, a Caliph. In order to claim leadership of this interplanetary empire, the person must travel to Mecca, a venture fraught with danger and intrigue. The journey from the planet Mars to Mecca represents the obligation that all able-bodied Muslims must accomplish at least once in their lifetime. Another interesting, and earlier, example is *The Book of Strangers* (1972) by Ian Dallas, who later transformed into the Sheikh Abdul Qadir as-Sufi. Dallas's story is set in a technologically advanced world where the distribution of information is controlled by a computer. The main character is a university librarian who has control of the information and discovers a series of Sufi/religious writings that sets him off on a journey to find what is missing in his life. His travels eventually take him to North Africa where he meets the former university librarian who provided the impetus for his inner transformation. Dallas incorporates his personal journey to Islam in this story, while noting that technology and spiritual enlightenment are not conflicting but offer mutual benefit.

How can educators use science fiction, fantasy, and comics as a pedagogical method? What can this method offer in terms of new approaches to the study of Islam? The answers are multiple. Science fiction (SF) provides a means for the telling of stories from perspectives that confront our assumptions and stereotypes, and push for a new dialogue about race, privilege, and power. SF, like its sister literature of fantasy, can engage readers with its foundational use of imagination, nightmares, dreams, the unexplainable and the impossible. Fictional Islam offers opportunities for educators to expand pedagogies and skills that encourage critical thinking, communication, and innovation; and for exploring themes within the human condition that allow others to 'walk a mile in my shoes' without judgment. As a device for thought-experiments, it offers fertile opportunities for cultural study and understanding. Literature, films, music, and games inspired by Islam can challenge students to revise old assumptions, discuss controversial topics, voice their opinions, and to write fearlessly. Students can develop critical thinking by exploring the variety of perspectives and the complexities of Islam, an act possible only if students understand that no complex issue can be understood thoroughly in a binary framework. Knowing how to research the diverse Islamic practices in Muslim societies requires, among other things, that students identify authentic resources, understand search strategies that go beyond Google, develop analytical and interpretive skills that can also provide valuable and enduring proficiencies. A unique and creative way for students to develop cross-cultural understanding within the framework of science fiction would be to create their own characters and dialogue in the genre.

Indeed, educators have begun to take advantage of science fiction, fantasy, and comics as pedagogical tools in the Muslim world. A number of workshops and conferences have been held both in the West and the Muslim world to promote the idea. The Middle East Film & Comic Con in Dubai and the Sindbad SciFi conference at the British Museum in London are good examples of the acknowledgement that this genre has transnational opportunities for education, collaboration and conversations.

Another example is *Yatakhayaloon* – or the League of Arabic SciFiers – set up by the Saudi Arabian computer engineer, writer, and entrepreneur, Yasser Bahjatt. *Yatakhayaloon* ('They are imagining') is based on the belief that science fiction and science are intrinsically linked. As the renowned science fiction writer Isaac Asimov once said, 'true science fiction could not really exist until people understood the rationalism of science and began to use it with respect in their stories'. In collaboration with another

Saudi writer, Ibraheem Abbas, Bahjatt has written a wonderful science fiction romance novel called *HWJN (Hawjan)*. It tells the story of the relationship between a jinn and a human being and the numerous obstacles they face. The human society of *HWJN* has abandoned the teachings of Islam and is mired in magic and sorcery while the Jinns follow the Qur'an and are much more rational. All this has been too much for the Saudi authorities. In 2013 the Saudi Commission for the Promotion of Virtue and Prevention of Vice halted sales of *HWJN*, while they decided whether or not to ban it for blasphemy and promoting devil worship. The investigation may have been spurred by rumours that the book was 'leading teenage girls to experiment with Ouija boards'. Although the Saudi authorities stopped short of banning *HWJN*, the Kuwaitis and Qataris announced they would do so. The success of *HWJN* shows that despite the presumption of our Texan administrator, there is a thirst for fiction in the Muslim world. Before the book came to the attention of the Saudi religious authorities, it had sold 25,000 copies and shot to the top of the Saudi bestsellers' list. As Bahjatt said of the official reaction to *HWJN*, 'I expected the noise, as we realized from monitoring Saudi social media that schools started complaining from the fact that students are reading *HWJN* all the time at school. So I did expect that schools would start banning the book as it was disturbing the class day. But we never expected that teachers and schools would start rumours about the content of the book without even reading it. And, unfortunately, it is still banned in Kuwait and Qatar, and most bookstores are still afraid to put it back on shelf in Saudi".

But to ban such works of science fiction is appallingly short sighted. It is also being totally blind to their utility as a pedagogical tool that can further discussions about real world issues and assist in finding concrete solutions to problems of racism and xenophobia that plague our societies. Consider, for example, Steven Barnes's two novels *Lions Blood* and *Zulu Heart* from his Insha'Allah series. These novels confront the issues of racism head on – but by inverting the convention. Set on an alternative world where the Africans and Asians are the enslavers and the slaves are from Europe, these novels are uncanny in their reflections on current events throughout the Muslim world. The stories main characters are two children, one a Muslim and the son of the most powerful leader of Bilalistan, Kai ibn Rashid, and the other an Irish slave boy, Aidan O'Dere who has lost his village and most of his family to the slave trade. Barnes's stories are particularly concerned with what was once called Ancient Africa, an Africa that encompassed the regions that in our postcolonial world are now considered part of the Middle East. The overarching desire to find relief from constant strife, patronage, and dependence on an inhumane enterprise forces readers to confront and challenge assumptions about the systems of slavery. Barnes uses Islam to mitigate some of the harsh realities of race and racism, power and privilege that underpin our twenty-first century knowledge of slavery. He pushes this 'so called' humane characteristic throughout the storylines and emphasises that Islam's view of slavery was not race-based nor was it an impediment to advancement within society. The slaves on Dar Kush are treated well, families remain intact, and not only are they allowed to practice their religion, the plantation maintains a grove that the slaves use as their sacred ground. The whites are given their freedom in Bilalistan when they fight for their masters, as did many blacks who fought on the Union side of the American Civil War. The struggle for the freed fictional slaves is how to find their place, recover their culture, and establish communities that prosper in a black dominated world. As Kai and Aidan mature they discuss the need to abolish slavery, the humanity of whites, and the religion of Islam and Christianity; they speak as equals. Aidan forces Kai to understand what slavery does to people who are enslaved and to the slave owners, speeches that could have come from the mouth of Frederick Douglass or any anti-slavery advocate. His views on Islam mirror Douglass's statements on the Christianity of slave traders. Aidan, Kai, and Babatunde's characters recreate many of the discussions and debates regarding the legitimacy, ethical and moral aspects of slavery and the slave trade that were ongoing within the Muslim and non-Muslim communities in this alternative world, and mirror the debates that occurred in the Americas. Their discussions echo the words spoken by abolitionists, pro-slavery figures, and former slaves. The novels straddle both the world of fantasy and science fiction literature, employing both genres in ways that push us to rethink commonly held beliefs, makes us uncomfortable, to think critically about slavery and question the long term impact of slavery and the systemic effects of the peculiar institution.

These issues are central to countries throughout the Middle East and Africa, but are not discussed, not least in Egypt, with its dual identity - African and Arab. What Barnes's novels and the current state of affairs throughout the world impress upon us is the time-honoured truism that it is often the actions of individuals rather than groups that provide the spark for change, impacting and altering the lives of thousands. Instructors can use these two works to confront notions of identity and oppression, issues that are connected to current world events. What is the impact of colonialism and imperialism on the conquerors and conquered in this alternate universe? The novels offer multiple conversations about gender roles, polygamy, colonial and postcolonial impacts on societies, religious tolerance, and even maritime laws!

G. Willow Wilson's graphic novel *Cairo*, which speaks to and advocates tolerance, and recent work on the new Pakistani American superhero *Ms Marvel* which seeks to 'normalise' the Muslim experience in a pluralistic view of America, can also serve as excellent educational tools. Both stories introduce the public to the diversity of characters, plots, and storylines within Islamic traditions. Studying *Cairo* can provide an excellent opportunity to discuss current events and controversial subjects such as Muslim/Jewish relations as well as the Israeli/Palestinian conflict from a historical and contemporary point of view. Interestingly, the novel offers insights that speak to the Europeans, Americans, and Arabs currently travelling to Syria and Iraq to become fighters with ISIS, in the character of Shaheed, a Lebanese-American who travels to Egypt to become a suicide bomber. *Cairo* attempts to present these ideas wrapped up in a story that includes fantasy elements including a Jinn who is key to the storyline. This lively book can provoke difficult but necessary conversations that require someone who can lead these discussions with an understanding of history, economics, and the ideas of 'nation building' within Islam.

Gender roles in Islam can be unpacked with the help of Wilson's comic book superhero *Ms Marvel* and other works by Muslim and non-Muslim writers. For example, how many people know of Roquia Sakhawat Hussain (1880–1932)? Hussain was a prolific writer and social worker in undivided Bengal in the early twentieth century. Most famous for her efforts on behalf of gender equality and other social issues, she established the first school aimed primarily at Muslim girls, which still exists today. Her book, *Sultana's Dream* is an early work of feminist science fiction, involving a utopian male/female role-reversal. *Sultana's Dream* was first published in 1905 in a Madras-based, English language periodical the *Indian Ladies Magazine*, then as a book in 1908. Too often male and female writings that feature Muslim women characters tend to, unfortunately, perpetuate the stereotypes of submissive, oppressed, and 'veiled/silenced' persons, but many of the newer stories challenge that narrative, offering more nuanced and opposing views. Saladin Ahmad's *Throne of the Crescent Moon* (2012) includes a female warrior/ shape shifter as one of its main characters, Larissa Sansour's experimental films and art installations such as Nation Estate feature female leads, and *The 99*, a comic book series created by Kuwaiti Naif Al-Mutawa, includes a number of heroic Muslim females. The work of writer, poet, and storyteller Pamela Taylor is also a valuable source for discussion of Muslim women, poetry writing, and activism. Taylor has written books for children and presents storytelling performances using stories from various Muslim communities including Palestinians, Americans, and Turkish cultures. Her *50 Fatwas for the Virtuous Vampire* has been celebrated for its humour and imagination.

Fictional Islam can also give rise to interesting assignments to spur the writing of poetry. Using the effects of global warming as a backdrop, students can examine the African American poet and musician, Jalaluddin Nuriddin's epic poem *Beyonder*. Nuriddin is one of the founding members of The Last Poets, an iconic group of poets and musicians that evolved out of the Harlem Writers' Workshop in New York in the late 1960s. His poem is considered a masterpiece of art and spoken word poetry; ahead of its time in detailing an apocalypse brought on by man's destruction of the environment. The notion that technology is the panacea for all our ills is proposed through the creation of an android called Sir Mankin (kin to man), but to no avail, the world is lost. Another poem worth tackling in the classroom is the Persian epic *The Shahnameh*, currently available as a series of comic books and graphic novels. Written by the poet Ferdowsi between c. 977 and 1010, and consisting of some 60,000 verses, it details the mythical and historical past of the Persian empire from the creation of the world until the Islamic conquest of Persia. Students can compare the stories throughout this poem with other works of fiction and poetry. For example the well-known children's story Rapunzel (Rapunzel, Rapunzel let down your long hair) is actually from a story in *The Shahnameh*, the romance between Zal and Rudaba.

Numerous other subjects, such as politics and politicians, Sunni and Shia distinctions and similarities, can be studied with the help of fictional Islam. The choice of content must be determined in light of the desired outcomes of course, but there are countless ways in which supplemental works portraying Muslim peoples through film, comic books and graphic novels, literature, games, and other discourses can be integrated into many syllabi. Indeed, there is no shortage of resources and opportunities available to assist in teaching about Islam. There are websites, film festivals, book fairs, conventions, and conferences that now feature prominent Muslim science fiction/fantasy writers and critics. A recent celebrated work is *Frankenstein in Baghdad* by Iraqi novelist Ahmad Saadawi, which won the International Prize for Arab Fiction. The novel, a mixture of science fiction and horror, offers a fresh take on the Frankenstein story as well as a critique of the American invasion of Iraq. It tells the story of Hadi al-Attag, a man who stitches together body parts of those killed in explosions in the Iraqi capital. The monster thus created come to life and begins a revenge campaign against those responsible for the deaths. This is an excellent example of how fictional Islam can illuminate a subject from a very different but also deeply historical and multicultural perspective.

To truly appreciate the educational value of science fiction, fantasy, and comic book literature will take time and commitment. We must continue to emphasise the connection between science fiction and scientific inquiry in the Muslim world: an interest in science fiction will spark an interest in science, and vice versa. An education that exposes Muslim societies to fictional Islam can shape a positive and viable future for Muslim societies.

Sectarian Politics in the Persian Gulf

Edited by Lawrence G. Potter

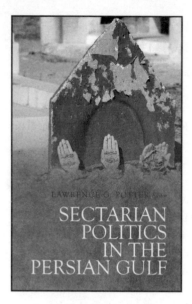

ISBN: 9781849043380
£20.00 / Paperback / 320pp

Long a taboo topic, as well as one that has alarmed outside powers, sectarian conflict in the Middle East is on the rise. The contributors to this book examine sectarian politics in the Persian Gulf, including the GCC states, Yemen, Iran and Iraq, and consider the origins and consequences of sectarianism broadly construed, as it affects ethnic, tribal and religious groups. They also present a theoretical and comparative framework for understanding sectarianism, as well as country-specific chapters based on recent research in the area. Key issues that are scrutinised include the nature of sectarianism, how identity moves from a passive to an active state, and the mechanisms that trigger conflict. The strategies of governments such as rentier economies and the 'invention' of partisan national histories that encourage or manage sectarian differences are also highlighted, as is the role of outside powers in fostering sectarian strife. The volume also seeks to clarify whether movements such as the Islamic revival or the Arab Spring obscure the continued salience of religious and ethnic cleavages.

'A timely contribution to understanding sectarianism on both sides of the Persian Gulf. The contributors are well-established historians and social scientists who offer nuanced interpretations of a malaise, at once contemporary and ancient, which threatens to redraw the region's political map. The result is an erudite exploration of the meaning of sectarianism in the context of old nations, and in newly forged ones — weaving local political contexts with transnational connections and outside interventions — which all seem to have escalated sectarian divides against a background of negotiated and fluid identities. The book paints a compelling picture of past and present coexistence and conflict.' — Madawi Al-Rasheed, Visiting Professor at the Middle East Centre, London School of Economics and Political Science

WWW.HURSTPUBLISHERS.COM/BOOK/SECTARIAN-POLITICS-IN-THE-PERSIAN-GULF

41 GREAT RUSSELL ST, LONDON WC1B 3F
WWW.HURSTPUBLISHERS.COM
WWW.FBOOK.COM/HURSTPUBLISHERS
020 7255 2201

FACING MUSLIM HISTORY

Farid Panjwani

Education is both the most lamentable reflection of the conditions across Muslim contexts and the most important element requiring attention if the situation is to be improved. While teaching about Islam is only an aspect of educational landscape in Muslim contexts, it has much wider ramifications given the continued centrality of religion in Muslim societies. Not surprisingly, Muslim reformers from the Egyptian thinker Rifaa al-Tahtawi (1801–1873) to American Pakistani scholar Fazlur Rahman (1919–1988) have engaged with Islamic educational thought and practice, seeking rapprochements between the received Muslim traditions and modernities of their time. During this period much has been changed, much has been achieved and been lost. Still, some fundamental questions about education remain. A recent conference at St. Anthony's College, University of Oxford, held on 22–24 April 2014, for example, was organised around the question: 'What are the aims of education in Islam?' From *Arab Human Development* reports to the so-called Trojan horse row in Birmingham, there are both internal and external concerns about teaching Islam. Clearly, a new pedagogical approach to the 'teaching about Islam' is needed that would seek to reconcile the seemingly contesting aims of identity formation and the development of personal autonomy in students. We can witness the problem in Muslim faith schools in Britain, but the issues have wider relevance wherever Islam is taught.

In Britain, certain schools, about a third, officially have a religious character. In informal parlance these are known as faith schools, rooted as they are in many different religious traditions, including Islam. In some traditions, these schools are along denominational lines, such as Roman Catholic Schools, Church of England Schools and Evangelical Schools. In others, such as Islam, they are called Islamic or Muslim schools, when in fact these too are often divided along denominational lines such as Deobandis, Barelwi, Shi'a and Salafi.

Notwithstanding this long tradition of faith schools, their desirability and role in British society remains controversial. One significant flashpoint in this ongoing debate is the weight attached to the rights of parents and children. Defenders of faith schools claim that these schools allow parents to exercise their constitutional rights to raise their children within their own religious traditions and nurture particular religious identities. Against this, those opposed to faith schools point to the rights of the children to be educated in a way that promotes their autonomy in a variety of matters, including religion. At a deeper level, this debate is about the different ways in which human beings are conceptualised. Whether as a primordial member of a religious community for whom education is seen to be a process of 'remembering' that given identity and enculturating into it; or, as a unique individual who must choose his/her identity afresh and for whom education is seen to be a process of developing a child's capacity to make this choice. In recent years, the issue of autonomy and identity has been the point of contention between two major philosophical traditions, liberal and communitarian. Proponents of faith schools and parental rights often make arguments which resonate with the communitarian position while opponents of faith schools support children's rights and often lean towards the liberal tradition.

It could be argued that the liberal and communitarian debate has led to the emergence of new positions which seek to recognise the importance of both individuality and community – seeking to promote autonomy but recognising that genuine autonomy is always rooted in culture and community, just as innovation is always rooted in tradition. Less successful has been the developments of pedagogies for religious education that can help achieve a calibration of identity and autonomy.

The idea of autonomy in contemporary educational thought can be traced back to Rousseau and Kant. In the character or dispositional sense of the term, it has been important in modern conceptions of liberal education, and as an aim of schooling. By dispositional autonomy we mean the inclination to determine one's own actions. To possess this trait is to have a preference for relying on one's own judgment, to be independent-minded, free-spirited and disposed to do things in one's own way. Despite its widespread recognition as an educational ideal in the liberal tradition, there is no detailed consensus on what autonomy means and how it can be nurtured. However, recent thinking about autonomy has helped bring the liberal and communitarian approaches closer.

It is useful to note that to be free is not necessarily to be autonomous. We are free when we are not constrained in our actions. While a person in prison is relatively less free than a person outside, the former could be more autonomous than the latter. Autonomy requires acting with a degree of self-direction; acting not just out of desires and motives but out of desires and motives that are a person's own.

One of the reasons that writers on Islamic education in last quarter of the twentieth century saw the liberal stress on autonomy as inimical to their understanding of Islamic education was their belief that an education seeking autonomy means developing a person outside all social influences – the notion of unencumbered self, as characterised by the American political philosopher Michael Sandel. In fact, their discomfort – since it is never lucidly articulated – was very suitably captured by the communitarian critique of the classical liberal understanding of autonomy. This critique can be summarised as follows: we neither come to the world as autonomous individuals nor do we have a reasoning process that stands outside of all traditions of thought. Nor does the world exhibit a range of options to choose from as part of the natural order. Both the subjects and the objects of freedom evolve through a process whereby the individual and the social are in dynamic interaction. To think of isolated individuals as able to make detached choices between disconnected options, through a universal process of reasoning is deeply unsound. Conventional accounts of autonomy falter because they posit an opposition between autonomy and socialisation that seems difficult to sustain in light of our understanding of human development.

In response to these strong criticisms, there arose a move towards dialogical and relational models of autonomy which acknowledges that 'the acquisition and exercise of personal autonomy is much more socially rooted' than earlier conceptions have usually accepted. The key point here is that socialisation does not equal indoctrination. The person who grows up in a religious tradition and comes to discover his/her identity-defining commitment to that tradition may still be able to subject that commitment to critical reflection.

Culture, socialisation and listening to expertise are an essential part of being autonomous. The claim, more accurately, is that an individual is then able to process the information and fashion their own path – and therefore become the author of their life. John Stuart Mill, one of the architects of liberal thought, makes this point lucidly. It would, he writes,

> be absurd to pretend that people ought to live as if nothing whatever had been known in the world before they came into it; as if experience has as yet done nothing towards showing that one mode of existence, or of conduct, is preferable to another. Nobody denies that people should be so taught and trained in youth as to know and benefit by the ascertained results of human experience. But it is the privilege and proper condition of a human being, arrived at the maturity of his faculties, to use and interpret experience in his own way. It is for him to find out what part of recorded experience is properly applicable to his own circumstances and character.

More recently, Canadian philosopher Will Kymlicka has responded to communitarian critique along similar lines:

> What is central to the liberal view is not that we can perceive a self prior to its ends, but that we understand our selves to be prior to our ends, in the sense that no end or goal is exempt from possible re-examination. …My self is, in this sense, perceived prior to its ends, i.e. I can always envisage my self without its present ends. But this does not require that I can ever perceive a self totally unencumbered by any ends…

Similarly in an educational context, Hanan Alexander claims that it is 'entirely unclear how we could go about determining what is best for a person other than within the context of a tradition concerning what ought to count as better or worse'. He thus argues that education should help children 'to discern how prevailing traditions can serve as a source of, rather than a hindrance to, moral independence'.

Nurturing identity by introducing children to religious and cultural traditions is not antithetical to developing their capacity for autonomous thinking, provided it is done with the appropriate pedagogy. The social nature of the self thus does not preclude autonomy. In fact, given that we are embedded in multiple ways, discovering points of intersection can propel a deeper search for self-knowledge and thus help in gaining an important trait of autonomy. The difference between an autonomous and non-autonomous person is not whether they are socialised or not, but in the manner in which their socialisation is carried out. Autonomy and identity formation are thus not necessarily inimical to each other.

Writing in the 1970s and 1980s on Islamic education, writers such as Naquib al-Attas, Ali Ashraf and Hossein Nasr often postulated a clear demarcation between Islamic and liberal conceptions of education. For instance, al-Attas builds his notion of Islamic education by claiming that with respect to the idea of knowledge, 'there exist such profound and absolute differences between Islam and Western culture such that they cannot be reconciled'. In contrast, more recent writers postulate a significantly different vision of Islamic education, one which can lead to a positive engagement with the liberal tradition. Abdullah Sahin, for example, argues that hitherto Islamic education has been interpreted as a religious endeavour. As a result, 'Islamic education and education in general, within Muslim societies across the globe, has been reduced to a process of mere training, instruction, and, often if not always, indoctrination'. He then proposes a new interpretation of Islamic education that is 'critical, dialogical and transformative'. Increasingly, writings on Islamic education appear to recognise the importance of nurturing children's autonomy even when the education is framed within a religious orientation. Abdolkarim Soroush captures this broader spirit well when he notes 'even those who adopt the path of religion and submission are valued because they have chosen this path freely. True submission is predicated upon the principles of freedom; indeed they are one and the same'.

This emerging openness – in the philosophy of education and in Muslim educational thought – indicate that after all, the dichotomy between identity and autonomy may not be as unbridgeable as previously thought. The self is situated and encumbered, and can only be developed in the context of identity, community and culture. Hence, to nurture autonomy does not mean to shun identity and traditions. Rather, genuine autonomy, like genuine creativity, can arise only through engagement with traditions, received ideas, culture and community. It is in these developments that we can find support for an education that can reconcile the demands of identity and autonomy.

What are pedagogical issues of developing children's autonomy and how do we relate it to the teaching of Islam? Clearly this is a complex issue and varies according to students' profiles, levels and subjects. Yet, it seems that one pedagogical tool widely believed to enhance autonomy is the exposure to alternatives; be they competing historical explanations of events, diverse interpretations of texts, various positions on existential and religious questions or vying hypotheses in science. As Charles Bailey argues in his book *Beyond the Present and the Particular*, introducing students to points of views, traditions, literature, explanations and interpretations other than those that they are likely to imbibe while growing up at home and from within their communities, is to help them transcend the present and the particular.

> The possibility of autonomy increases as the opportunity for observing and imagining alternatives increases, since to be autonomous in decision-making, a person must be able to imagine alternative courses of action and choose between them. This is an extremely important consideration for those who educate and train teachers.

Developing children's imagination is an important element if their autonomy is to be nurtured. In the case of teaching about Islam, is expansion of imagination would mean exposing students to as wide a range of Muslim traditions as possible, helping then see the variety of ways in which it has been possible to be a Muslim. Students would thus be inducted into traditions through a pedagogy that would seek to build their capacity to engage with them as active meaning makers.

However, Muslim faith schools rarely expose their students to interpretations that differ from the denomination followed by the students' families or school as well as other pedagogical sites where Islam is taught. With some exceptions, there is rather, a quest for collective identity. In a 2008 interview with the head teacher of a publicly funded Muslim school, I had the following conversation:

> Q: Is there a conscious attempt to introduce students to various positions in Muslim history? For example, the Shi'a and the Sunni positions?

A: Well, we try to avoid such controversy and give a unified account.

Q: What is that account given that we have two distinct positions, let's say about the continuation of authority after the death of the Prophet?

A: But, we can only give one account because parents already know which school they are choosing. And they send their children accordingly. For example, why would you or I not send [our children] to Al-Burhan and send [them] to al-Hijra? Al-Burhan is Barelvy while al-Hijra is Sunni oriented. So then there is no problem in teaching in accordance with what the families teach their children.

Recent research has confirmed that this emphasis on a singular narrative remains the focus of advocates of and practitioners in many Muslim faith schools.

There are both sociological and epistemological reasons for this emphasis on a singular narrative. The sociological reason is well summarised by Claire Tinker and Andrew Smart in their 2012 article when they note that 'the overarching theme that emerged from the data analysis was a perception that Muslim identity was under threat and/or attack, and that separate Muslim schools were an appropriate means of protection or defence'. They point out that 'the conditions for such expressions include: the minority status of the religion and its adherents (in terms of religious affiliation and often in terms of ethnicity); Britain's dominant secular (but historically Christian) culture; prominent global and national political contexts; perceptions and experiences of prejudice and discrimination'. However, it is to be noted that an emphasis on collective Muslim identity and discomfort with diversity exists even within Muslim majority countries where many of these conditions would not exist. For instance, Matthew J Nelson in his 2009 paper on Pakistan noted that 'most of our respondents drew attention to a general pattern in which religious and sectarian differences were consistently, and repeatedly, denied.' He goes on to observe that 'everyone could see these internal "sectarian" differences. Everyone could feel the mounting pressure associated with their expanding influence and importance... But even so... the differences themselves had become surprisingly difficult for the public at large to discuss'. In fact, the discomfort with diversity can be traced back to the first decades of Muslim history when the unity of the community was seen to be broken through a series of social and political events termed as *fitna*, a word with many meanings but whose primary reference has been 'revolt', 'disturbances', 'civil war'. There are thus both particular contextual reasons as well as long established historical reasons for the prominence of a singular narrative about Islam.

There is also an epistemological reason for the avoidance of diversity and this has to do with the way the very idea of religion (in this case, Islam), is understood by faith schools as well as across religious education, more broadly. Muslim faith schools and religious education generally, operate with the idea of religion as a finished product, a reified object or an abstract idea made into something concrete – which provides guidance, and about which students must acquire an inert body of knowledge. This reductive tendency becomes easier to recognise if we think of the widespread tendency to ask questions such as: what is the Islamic approach to economics? What does Islam say about human rights? What is Islam's relationship with democracy or science or other religions? In each case the underlying assumption is that there is something called Islam, a Platonic form, an object which has a particular relationship or attitude towards equally reified objects such as science or democracy or other religions. It is assumed that there is an Islamic answer to these and other questions which can be read straightforwardly from sacred texts. This reifying tendency underpins education about Islam.

However, even a cursory look at Muslim history shows that such assumptions are untenable. That there is a difference of opinions and interpretations between Muslim, on almost all major issues, is true both historically and in contemporary times. On the question of knowledge, for instance, there were internally diverse philosophical, theological and mystical perspectives, often at complete variance with each other. Similarly, today the Shari'a, often translated as divine law, represents a finished legal system ordained through revelation to many Muslims and non-Muslims. In fact, the Shari'a is an on-going project in Muslim history to bring various aspects of life closer to the requirements of religion. However, these aspects and requirements are constantly debated and discussed, resulting in not one but a number of schools of law that have developed over time. Abou El-Fadl noted that,

A student commencing the study of the Islamic legal heritage is immediately struck by the complexity of doctrines, diversity of opinions and enormous amounts of disputations over a wide range of issues. Early on, the student learns that other than the main jurisprudential schools…there are many extinct schools…(and) even in one school…there can be several strands. Furthermore, the student is taught that a major contributing factor to the diversity of Islamic legal schools is the acceptance and reverence given to the idea of *ikhtilaf* (disagreement and diversity).

Abou El-Fadl's observations about law are also applicable to other areas such as theology with its multiple schools and sub-schools of Maturidi Mu'tazila, Ash'ariya, Murji'ah and others. This diversity makes suspect the belief that we can find the will of God without any human interpretation and the assumption that texts have meanings contained in them and that all a reader has to do is to find them. The history of Muslims shows that the Qur'anic text has always been interpreted, and different theological, legal, ethical, political and doctrinal positions have emerged rooted in these interpretations. It is for these reasons that the teaching about Islam should start with this interpretive approach to understand the tradition.

What are the educational implications of taking the fact of interpretation seriously? What kind of education emerges if we seek to reconcile the demands of identity and autonomy?

The first pedagogical implication is that there is a need to shift the questions asked when teaching about Islam. Instead of asking what Islam's view of X is, we should be asking how Muslims have viewed X? Questions that focus on the social actors, the Muslims, allows for the recognition of historical, cultural and social forces that shape societies. Ideas can then be understood within their social contexts.

Let me illustrate this further with the question about Islam's position on other religions. It is common to ask what Islam's view of other religions is. How do we answer this question? If we turn to the Qur'an to find the Islamic position on other religions, we will not find it. Instead, we will find a variety of attitudes towards Christians and Jews ranging from that in verse 2:62, which creates a bond among people from different religions that rests on faith in God and good deeds, transcending particular theological and doctrinal positions and identities, to that in verse 5:51 which admonishes Muslims against taking Jews and Christians as *waly* (allies and, in some translations, as friends). In verse 29:46, the Qur'anic recognition that 'our God and your God are one' is made the basis of discussions among people of different religions. These different attitudes reflect the changing nature of the relationship between the neophyte Muslims, and Jews and Christians of the time. Without going into the details of the complex ways in which Muslims, Jews and Christians interacted during the period of Qur'anic revelation, it can be stated that the modes of interactions varied widely, ranging from civic arrangements for peaceful co-existence to warfare and from mutual support to hostility.

In the subsequent history of Muslims, the interpretations of founding texts and events mingled with the dynamics of theological, social and political developments, led to a wide range of Muslim positions towards other religions, in particular those of Jews and Christians. Jacques Waardenburg has found seven different ways or degrees of openness in Muslim views of other religions in the pre-modern period. These include: (1) indifference to other religions as they were seen as having been superseded by Islam; (2) suspicion of people of other religions as subverts who wanted to undermine Muslims and Islam; (3) a degree of curiosity to learn about other religions but primarily as sources of falsehood to be refuted and safeguarded against; (4) a degree of positive interest in learning about other religions and even integrating some doctrines and ideas into one's conception of Islam; (5) the view that 'all things true and good in other religions and cultures were evidently already present in Islam itself' (p. 21); (6) a tolerant attitude which saw 'one universal world in which adherents of different religions lived side by side, accepting the reality of religious plurality'; and (7) the stance which saw essential spiritual unity among all religions underlying and superseding apparent differences of rituals and doctrines.

When students are introduced to this variety of historically situated responses to the question of Islam's relationship with other religions, they are likely to observe that there is no ready-made answer to the question. And, having noted that it is appropriate for Muslims to give different responses, they may feel empowered to do so for themselves. Such an approach can propel a deeper search for self-knowledge and thus help in gaining an important trait of autonomy.

This diversity of Muslim positions is also true for many other issues such as Islam and science, Islam and human rights, Islam and gender and others. In each of these cases, we do not have an Islamic view but instead, a range of Muslim views. In fact, we could go further and propose that we simply cannot teach about Islam. Rather, we can only teach about how Islam is understood, invoked, believed in and appropriated in Muslim thought and practice. Islam, itself, is an idea in the minds of those who invoke it; it is not an external reality that can be studied.

This then leads to the second pedagogical implication. One of the legal responses to modernity in Muslim contexts has been the emergence of an eclectic approach in the Sunni context called *talfiq* which enables jurists to choose the most suitable legal ruling from different schools of law instead of unbendingly adhering to the interpretations of a single law school. In this approach, the students would have access to a much wider repertoire of tradition to draw from, as they grapple with the questions and challenges of their time. Whether these are questions of science, governance, ecology, gender or rituals, students who seek to ground their lives in their religious tradition will have many more resources to dip into than would be available to them if they are taught only within a single denominational setting.

A third pedagogical implication is greater understanding – if not appreciation – of the internal diversity among Muslims. In our increasingly inter-connected world, the internal religious 'other' is no longer at a distance. By bringing out the inescapable role of interpretations and human agency in the making of religious traditions, students will have the possibility of recognising how the same texts held sacred by all Muslims can lead to meanings, doctrine and worldviews that can be dramatically different from each other. In some, this may nurture epistemological humility. As Rumi says, 'The truth was a mirror in the hands of God. It fell, and broke into pieces. Everybody took a piece of it, and they looked at it and thought they had the truth.'

Finally, the proposed approach may also serve as a bulwark against the appeal of the Islamist narratives, including those of violent extremism. It often surprises people to note that Islamist movements are attractive to many well-educated young men and women. It is common to meet educated Muslims who carry strikingly un-historical views about their religious traditions. While their professional knowledge is state-of-the-art, their knowledge of their religious tradition comes from approaches that are emotionally powerful but intellectually deficient. They carry an emotional attachment to Islam and a rudimentary knowledge of terms such as Shari'a, *Jahaliya* and so on. Having not had a chance to learn about their tradition in a sound manner, if and when they search for 'Islam' they often find it in the pamphlets, booklets, websites and gatherings of Islamists. By successfully re-interpreting traditional concepts, Islamism's discourse is able to give people both the assurance of tradition and hope for the resolution of modern problems such as unemployment, a lack of social services, police state, corruption, and cultural imperialism. Many young men and women who are attracted to Islamism's discourse do so in the belief that they are following the essential teachings of their faith. Instead of being aware of the plurality and contested nature of norms and institutions, many believe these to be eternal and monolithic from the beginning of Islam. The emotional identification to Islam is thus often conjugated with a superficial and ideological knowledge about it. There is thus a destructive vacuum in critical engagement with religious tradition, which the extremist discourse is able to fulfil.

By reconciling the demands of autonomy and identity we will enable young people to learn not only about the morally and intellectually inspiring aspects of Muslim history but also those aspects which may challenge modern moral sensibilities but which nevertheless happen to be a part of the tradition. These include some challenging verses in the Qur'an (for example, about women, non-Muslims and war and peace), the problems with the *fiqh*, the doctrine of jihad, and the inimical attitude towards philosophers, the absolutist approach to truth and many other examples. Currently, none of these difficult issues are raised in education about Islam. But these are among the very issues that extremists draw upon to create their narratives. In the absence of an intellectual framework to deal with extremists' claims of authenticity, many young people easily fall prey to such narratives. The approach suggested here would help young people understand the Janus-faced nature of religions whereby sacred texts can be invoked for a variety of causes.

A key challenge in implementing the approach I am advocating will be to avoid the spectre of interpretive relativism. Theoretically, there is no limit to what can be interpreted but practically acknowledging the role of human agency in the making of religious knowledge does not mean that any understanding of the Qur'an will be accepted as valid, or at least, equally valid. It may not mean that anything goes. Two constraints limit what can be considered as legitimate interpretation. The first is the text of the Qur'an (and other texts considered sacred) itself. Open ended and immensely rich it may be, the Qur'an also places limits on what it could mean. The second constraint is the Muslim communities. These two – the text and the communities – put hermeneutical limits on what can be interpreted from the Qur'an. Interpretations violating these limits will find it very hard to gain wider acceptance among Muslims. Still, the diversity in Muslim intellectual thought – even among major and widely accepted figures – shows that these limits are very broad and capable of sustaining immense differences. The way ahead is not in suppressing them but coming to terms with them.

Tradition cannot be inherited passively. Each generation must acquire it afresh and with labour. There were thinkers in the Muslim past who had this sense. Abu Hamid al-Ghazali (1058–1111) was among them. A brilliant scholar by any account, al-Ghazali's life was dramatic, with each new turn hardly predictable from his earlier phase in life. He summarised his spiritual/intellectual journey, his doubts and phases of scepticism, his exploration of wide range of truth claims and his labour to inherit the tradition in his book called, *Deliverance from Error*. In the process al-Ghazali followed, there is much to offer for Muslim educationists who seek to bring together the quest for identity and demands of autonomy.

WHAT ABOUT SCIENCE?

Moneef R. Zou'bi

Some years ago, a young Muslim cleric walked into my office at the Islamic World Academy of Sciences (IAS) in Amman, Jordan. He objected to what he had read in some of our books about the status of science and technology in the Muslim world. He insisted that Muslims had made great discoveries in science, and the Muslim world had enormous wealth, agricultural and minerals resources, land mass and human capital, and that it was doing much better than the West in all domains. The IAS and similar scientific organisations were doing disservice to the ummah by suggesting that the Muslim world was seriously lagging behind in science and technology. I asked the cleric to look at some of the indicators we, and others in the international community of scientists, had adopted to measure science development: expenditure on science, research institutions, patents and publications produced. I went on to highlight that the Gross National Product (GNP) of the whole of the Muslim world was less, at the time, than that of Germany. Somewhat befuddled at the assortment of indicators I presented, he asked me to give a lecture on the subject to his colleagues and fellow students of *fiqh* at his college.

A few weeks later, I did. I talked about science and development in the Muslim world to an initially passive audience of around 500 young scholars of Islam. The would-be imams were subdued as I discussed the dire state of science and technology in the Muslim world. I argued how science could help in improving the economic situation of a country, providing water and energy security, better agriculture, and the provision of health and education services. The facts and figures I offered sadly fell on deaf ears. The only time the clerics reacted was when I pointed out that the Qur'an included numerous verses urging Muslims to contemplate and investigate life and the world around us.

There is a basic contradiction in what we read in the Qur'an, and hence believe, and what we actually do about science. In intellectual debates and discussion in Muslim circles, science seldom emerges as a subject of deliberation. When we talk about educational reform, we talk almost always about social sciences and hardly ever about science. The 'Islamisation of Knowledge' project, for example, had nothing really to say about natural sciences. When we do talk about science, it is always in terms of nostalgia, the 'Golden Age' of Islam when we made great strides in science and learning.

Both, the serious neglect of science in Muslim societies and the constant harking back to the past, have had serious consequences. Instead of considerate discussion about the role of science in the advancement of knowledge, thought and development in Muslim societies, we have allowed spurious ideas about 'scientific miracles' – the so-called *ijaz* literature – to spread far and wide. Indeed, it now seems to be the de facto position amongst Muslim theologians: when they talk about science at all it is all about how everything from electricity to relativity can be 'discovered' in the Qur'an.

In fact, the situation is getting worse. Recently I watched a video on YouTube showing a young Saudi theologian declaring before a full house in Sharjah that planet Earth is stationary and does not revolve; rather it is the sun and the moon that revolve around the Earth. My initial reaction was 'is this for real?' In less than ten minutes, the young man managed to overwrite eight centuries of accumulated trans-civilisational evidence-based science. Towering figures of the 'Golden Age', such as al-Tusi (1201–1274) and ibn al-Shatir (1304–1375), would be turning in their graves.

Unfortunately the ridiculous views of the YouTube 'theologian' indicate a wider malaise: many Muslim societies today exhibit grass roots signs that are the antithesis to science. This is manifested in the lack of appreciation of time, the prevalence of a culture of fatalism, absence of a sense of precision or accuracy (perhaps excluding countries with a long tradition of craftsmanship and skilled professionals). Against such a backdrop, vital science education and innovation cannot flourish in Muslim societies, there can be no progress, however it is defined, no matter what 'educational reforms' we may introduce.

The difficulties Muslim societies face in nurturing a culture of science are formidable. The ability of societies to solve problems and initiate and sustain economic growth depends partly on their capabilities in science, technology and innovation. Scientific and technical capabilities determine the ability of a society to meet basic needs, to provide clean water to their inhabitants, good health care, adequate infrastructure, and decent food. There is ample evidence that science, engineering, technology and innovation have a direct effect on economic growth and development. The conversion of research findings into innovation-based products, processes and services is essential to ensure that economic benefit from scientific research is realised.

At the international level, and within the circles of international academe, the last two decades have witnessed an increasing drive for science education at all levels. At the Budapest World Conference on Science in 2000 the French academician, Pierre Léna, emphasised the importance of science education as a fundamental need of modern societies to achieve peace, justice and sustainable development. It was Léna who, with others, under the auspices of the Academy of Sciences of France, launched the famous science education-in-schools programme called *La main à la pâté* (the hands-on, or the hand in the paste), which eventually became a template of science education of children at a global level. In Africa, the Ugandan National Academy of Sciences (UNAS) views education as the single most important activity in which the scientific community can be involved. Some Asian academies are also pushing the domain of science education, including the Academy of Science Malaysia (ASM).

However, the lack of interest shown by Organisation of Islamic Cooperation (OIC) countries in promoting science education does not match that of the world's leading countries. When it comes to 'learning from history', Muslims tend to be mediocre students. There are many things that can be learned by studying the storyline of science in the past, particularly in the context of Islamic civilisation. Yet, despite all that nostalgia, history of Islamic science is taught nowhere in the Muslim world; there are no departments of history of Islamic science in Muslim universities. The last research institution, with an international reputation, Institute for the History of Arabic Science, University of Aleppo, closed many years ago; the city itself now lies in ruin.

Yet, even a cursory look at the history of science in Islam reveals the reasons behind the contrast between the centrality of science and discovery in the history of Islamic societies and its marginal role today in education and in the minds of those in power.

Science cannot emerge without a scientific culture – a culture that appreciates learning and inquiry and encourages curiosity and criticism. History tells us that the Muslims of the eighth century were not only well versed with Islamic 'sciences,' which were primarily based on the teachings of Islam, but were also curious about the physical world and were keen on exploration and discoveries. They had an insatiable desire for all kinds of scientific knowledge – from mathematics and astronomy to physics and chemistry, anatomy and medicine, botany and zoology, philosophy and speculative thought. It would otherwise be difficult to imagine how an assemblage of Arab tribes from the Hijaz, who led a nomadic existence at start of the seventh century, could go on to establish a world civilisation in less than a hundred years. Early Muslims must have had the faculty and competence to master the science and art of creating a global civilisation and the science and knowledge requisite to achieve such a feat. In other words, they had developed a culture within which science and civilisation could thrive.

Science does not develop in isolation. You need to interact with the rest of the world; find out what research is being done elsewhere, join research teams, attend conferences and meetings to exchange ideas. Muslims of the classical period were not afraid of other cultures or demonised them. On the contrary, they embraced the science and learning of other cultures and civilisations – Greek, Persian, Indian. They translated scientific works from all over the then known world and imbibed them eagerly. The capacity of early Muslims to learn from others and adapt to the political realities that they became a part of, as well as the open-mindedness in their interaction with other cultures and civilisations, is truly awesome.

Science needs patronage and political support. During the golden age of Islamic science, the centre of scientific activity and creativity in the Muslim world was not fixed. During the Umayyad and Abbasid periods, the major urban centres of the Muslim world, namely Damascus, Baghdad, Cairo and Cordoba, were hubs of science. Science blossomed as a result of direct and indirect political patronage by the ruling dynasties. Umayyad rulers in Spain and Abbasid rulers in Baghdad were for the best part of two centuries in competition to capture the hearts and minds of the population.

However, science was supported not just by Caliphs and Kings, but also by wealthy patrons, *wafqs*, or charitable trusts, that provided research endowments, and a vast book and publication industry. Centres of excellent flourished at different times and different places at the generosity of patrons who loved science and learning.

Science needs openness and diversity. An idiosyncratic feature of Islamic science was that it was diverse and interdisciplinary. Polymathy was the norm; and no subject was out of bounds. Critical thought was supported and promoted by philosophy. Debate and discussion was encouraged. While dissent was not always tolerated by the rulers, it was still a major feature of the society.

The calamitous state of science in the Muslim world today is a direct result of the loss of these features in Muslim societies. The link between past and present has been destroyed. There are, as Ziauddin Sardar pointed out in his Royal Society Lecture, not one but a host of reasons for the decline of science in the Muslim civilisation – ranging from a systematic reduction in the meaning of Islamic concepts such as *ilm* (knowledge), *ijma* (consensus) and *istislah* (public interest) to colonialism. There is also a problem with putting a date: when did the decline actually start – in the fourteen, fifteenth or even in the eighteenth centuries? Controversy aside, I would emphasise two main reasons which seem obvious to me.

The first is the proliferation of dogmatism in Muslim societies. Until the end of the fifteenth century, scientific knowledge in Muslim civilisation was dominated by a few major systems. They were Aristotelian physics, Ptolemaic astronomy, Galenic medicine, and Jabirian alchemy. Science eventually reached a point where further progress became extremely difficult. It became dogmatic and static; and, by this time Muslim culture had lost its dynamism and was not vigorous enough to achieve major breakthroughs in science. A revolution in thought was necessary, but Islamic society was unable to produce such a leap. Dogmatism also made knowledge distribution within the Muslim world a problem. In 1454, one year after Sultan Mehmet II conquered Constantinople, Gutenberg printed the Bible in Mainz and the mass production of books was underway. Muslims however had to wait until 1727 to get their first printing press as the *ulama* resisted the introduction of printed books in the Muslim world. Thus, the mass dissemination of scientific knowledge via the printed word among Muslims commenced almost three centuries after it had started in Europe.

The second is the impact of colonialism. The effect of colonial interventions in the nineteenth and twentieth centuries in the Muslim world, particularly in the Middle East, compounded and aggravated the stagnation that was already underway. The colonial powers dismantled the educational and research institutions, and, in some cases, outlawed the pursuit of knowledge. The end of World War One led to the collapse of the Ottoman Empire, its science and technology in ruins, and its enemies appropriating its territories. The Middle East was carved up between Britain and France, with Britain taking control of Palestine, Jordan and Iraq and France dominating Lebanon and Syria. The colonial era resulted in the final brutal severing of ties between contemporary Islam and the golden age of scientific and technological advancement. The towering figures of the golden age in science in Islamic civilisation were now all but a distant memory. The impact was huge. It changed the way people perceived their 'ideal society'. This 'society' was no longer an extension of traditional values of culture and religion, with its emphasis on knowledge and learning. Moreover, it was not allowed, from within and without, to be in harmony with the growth of modern 'Western' civilisation. A strange mutant type of society appeared in the majority of Muslim states that was partially Muslim in tradition and values but occidental in behaviour, thought and outlook.

The period following decolonisation saw many Muslim societies embark on development programmes, establish universities and research centres despite a lack of resources and high illiteracy rates, in an effort to build a scientific infrastructure. Ziauddin Sardar's survey of *Science, Technology and Development in the Muslim World*, published way back in 1977, provides many good examples of how science development was being tackled in many countries. There were many false starts, setbacks, and wrong turns but still there was some progress. Since then, the Cold War has ended only to be replaced by the eruption of many hot wars in what is known today as the Muslim world. In the majority of Muslim societies, governance is in a state of turmoil. Many regimes are torn between upholding security, as they perceive it, on the one hand, and adopting good governance practices on the other. Military expenditures in a number of Muslim countries as a percentage of GDP remain the highest in the world.

So progress in science has come to a grinding halt. At the political level, the indifference shown by decision-makers to and the lack of political patronage of science – with a few exceptions – is truly staggering. Short-termism dominates. The oil-rich Middle Eastern states think that science can be bought like any other commodity. The arrays of multi-billion dollar educational and scientific projects that are being sprouted in Saudi Arabia and all over the Gulf are planted on a culturally arid soil. Totally dependent on expatriates, these institutions exist in a culture that is indifferent to science at best, or aggressively anti-science at worse, as demonstrated by the YouTube Saudi theologian.

There is also an assumption that if we solve the problem of illiteracy science will mushroom in Muslim societies. This is an illusion. 'Education for all' is a noble objective – but it is no guarantor for creating a culture of science or of economic development and high rates of growth in any society. Many scientists speak of the 'Sri Lankan Syndrome', where the majority of people tend to acquire a reasonable level of education and literacy is widespread, yet society seems incapable of translating the phenomenon into science development and economic well-being. For science to establish itself in a society, it must develop from the grass-roots, serve the community and enhance public good. As Omar Abdul Rahman puts it, 'science is not useful until it is seen to be useful, to be or be seen to be useful science must directly benefit the community'.

The challenges and problems faced by Muslim societies in relation to science are thus formidable. The Muslim world, made up of 57 nation states spread over four continents, occupies an area of 26.6 million square kilometres, which is equivalent to a fifth of the total global land area. It extends from Indonesia in the east to the Atlantic Ocean in the west, and from the city of Kazan in the Russian republic of Tatarstan in the north to the source of the Nile in Uganda, in the south. The OIC countries – together with Muslims in India, Russia and China – account for a population that exceeds 1.6 billion. But the OIC societies today do not have the critical mass of researchers in the majority of research disciplines because the higher education system is not producing the quantity or, more importantly, the quality of research needed. Collectively, the OIC countries are the source of just two percent of the world's science citations, and only approximately one percent of mainstream journal articles. Moreover, expenditure on science research and development is miniscule. However, in demographic terms, the Muslim world is predominantly young. This is both an opportunity and a challenge, as young populations can stimulate growth and create dynamic societies but they need good schools, universities and jobs.

The recipe for the way out of the current situation is relatively simple. The resolution of political problems that are plaguing many parts of the Muslim world could pave the way for a decrease in defence and security spending and make more resources available for science and technology. We also need a radical change in the mind-set of political leaders and those who hold economic power to put science and technology back on national agendas as a driver for social, economic and cultural advancement. Allowing citizens to enjoy basic freedoms would not only encourage a culture of questioning, criticism and discovery but would also mitigate the brain drain of scientists and intellectuals to the West. Links between universities and research centres have to be strengthened. Talented individuals have to be encouraged to pursue careers in science and technology with incentives, attractive salaries and career prospects. Admission policies of students and recruitment policies of faculty have to be based on merit; and the archaic hierarchical system of promotion, often based on political considerations and nepotism, has to be dismantled. Science education must start at school-level and continue throughout the various levels of education right up to university. To generate the public's interest in the scientific enterprise and attract bright young motivated students, universities should introduce or reintroduce courses and programmes in the History of Science, particularly in the context of Islamic heritage. High school and young university students should be encouraged to become inquirers rather than learners, and philosophy and free-thinking must make its formal entry back into school and university curricula.

Muslim societies cannot have a viable future without creating a culture of science and independent research. And educational reform, however it is defined, is not possible without making science its prime focus.

MY LIFE IN ISLAMIC ECONOMICS

Muhammad Nejatullah Siddiqi

I have been involved in Islamic economics most of my life. At school, however, I studied science subjects, but switched to economics, Arabic and English literature for my BA degree at Aligarh Muslim University (AMU), which I joined in 1949. The decision was influenced by my reading habit. I was devoted to *al-Hilal* and *al-Balagh* magazines, published under the guidance of Maulana Abul Kalam Azad (1888–1958), poet, critic, thinker and one of the great leaders of the Independence Movement. I also read *al-Tableegh*, and was influenced by the Deobandi scholar Maulana Ashraf Ali Thanawi (1863–1943), the author of the famous book on belief and correct conduct (for women), *Heavenly Ornaments*. And, as most young people of my age and time, I studied the works of Maulana Abul Ala Maududi (1903–1979). Two of Maududi's works had a deep impact on me: lectures he gave at Nadwatul Ulama, Lucknow, and a scheme he proposed to Aligarh Muslim University, both in the mid-1940s, later published in a collection titled *Taleemat*. Under the influence of these *ulamas* – religious scholars – I abandoned science and the engineering career I had planned. What I wanted now was to learn Arabic, gain direct access to Islamic sources, and discover how modern life and Islamic teachings interacted. I stuck to this mission, even though I had to take a number of detours stretching over six years – to Sanwi Darsgah e Jamaat e Islami, Rampur and Madrasatul Islah in Saraimir before I arrived eventually at Aligarh to earn a PhD in economics.

The years spent in Rampur and Saraimir were distinguished by lively interaction with Ulama. We spent most of our time discussing the Qur'an, the traditions of the Prophet, commentaries on the Qur'an, *fiqh* (jurisprudence) and *usul-e-fiqh*, or principles of jurisprudence. That this happened in the company of young men of my own age, fired by the same zeal, was an added advantage. We had each chosen a subject – political science, philosophy, economics – that we thought would enhance our understanding of modern life. We were also fired by the idea of combining modern-secular and old-religious learning to produce something that would right what was wrong with the world. We received a warm welcome from Zakir Hussain (1897–1969), the former President of India, then Vice-Chancellor of Aligarh Muslim University; Mohammad Aaqil Saheb, Professor of Economics at Jamia Milliyah Islamia, Delhi; and by eminent teachers at Osmania University in Hyderabad.

Our mission was to introduce Islamic ideas to economics. These were envisaged at three levels. A background provided by Islam's worldview, placing matters economic in a holistic framework; a set of goals to be achieved by individual behaviour and economic policy; and a set of norms and values, resulting in appropriate institutions. Maududi argued that this exercise performed in key social sciences would pave the way for progress towards an 'Islamic society'. I was fully sold to the idea. We were also influenced by the extraordinary times through which Islam and Muslims were passing all over the world. Islam was 're-emerging' after three centuries of colonisation which was preceded by another three centuries of stagnation and intellectual atrophy. The great depression had just exposed capitalism's darker side and Russian-sponsored socialism was enlisting sympathisers. Islam had a chance, if only a convincing case could be made, we thought.

In Aligarh I attended lectures by the eminent Marxian economist, D P Mukherji. Those were heady days for socialists in India. Islam and everything Islamic was perceived as anti-socialist, even pro-capitalist. That was what the faculty thought. The student body was predominantly pro-Islamic. That provided a lively environment for discussion in the class room and at the campus. The department of economics had eminent visitors like the British economist J R Hicks and post-Keynesian economist Joan Robinson. Their talks were inevitably followed by discussions along the ideological divide of that time: socialist planning versus unregulated markets. One of my earlier books, *Economic Enterprise in Islam* (1972) was influenced by this controversy. What we learn and discuss is dictated by what we feel is needed and relevant at the time. With that age gone and new challenges emerging, our focus changes and emphases shift. There must be something more enduring in the book as despite its simple language and elementary approach *Economic Enterprise in Islam* continues to inspire students. The reason: it tries to build an Islamic behavioural model and provide a framework for Islamic economic policy in the light of the Qur'an and Sunnah. Unlike other similar publications it is not focused on critiquing capitalism and socialism. It aspires to highlight divine guidance relevant for economic behaviour and policy. The book appears incomplete and a little naïve in hindsight as it seems unaware of the problems a cooperative approach would pose with respect to information. As we pass from an agricultural to industrial to service to a knowledge based economy, the information needed for meaningful cooperation among economic agents changes in nature and quantity. It is only during the last two decades that the economics profession has made meaningful progress on that front.

At a later stage I came to realise it is also important to have a new approach in identifying economic agents. Instead of placing them in the market as buyer-consumers and seller-producers why not focus on the family or the household from where they come? One advantage of doing so would be downgrading self-interest as the motivating force behind economic behaviour. We are born into a family and benefit from loving care of the mother and other members of the household. We experience gift relationship before self-interest enters the picture. Reciprocity precedes exchange relationships. By projecting the market as the premier economic institution and obliterating the roles of family and community, conventional economics wrongly projected competition as the engine of progress, relegating cooperation to the margins. A vast amount of anthropological research has debunked this understanding of our environment. I think we, those working on Islamic economics, were duped by the ruling ethos of the mid-twentieth century. We neglected the rich Islamic literature on *tadbeer e manzil* (management of the household) and missed a potential pad for launching an alternative to conventional economics, eschewing the scarcity-selfishness-competition-maximisation route, which inevitably leads to aggression and is responsible for the mess in which humanity currently finds itself.

But we pushed on. Earlier I had published *Islam's View on Ownership* (1968), which was seen by some as leaning towards socialism. I gave great emphasis to the limits within which ownership rights had to be exercised and the obligations the owner had towards others. In a long chapter, littered with quotations from the Qur'an and Sunnah and precedents from early Islamic history, I made a case for intervention by the authorities to ensure that such goals as meeting basic universal needs and keeping disparities in the distribution of income and wealth were kept in check. I think the book had some impact on the rhetoric of the Islamists.

In the Department of Economics at AMU, academics had serious reservations about mixing Islam with economics. When I expressed a desire to write my doctoral dissertation on interest-free banking I was persuaded to opt instead for 'a critical examination of the recent theories of profit' to avoid a tiff with the examiners. I went on to focus my studies on what is rightly regarded as the most significant feature of life: uncertainty. This applies to all aspects of life but its centrality for economics is beyond doubt. Even though very few in the department fully endorsed the idea of applying Islam to economics, the idea caught on. I had like-minded friends at other universities too. We came together to launch a quarterly journal, *Islamic Thought* (1954–1971), which took the idea to neighbouring countries earning patronage, among others, from Abdullah al Arabi, Professor of Economics at Cairo university. Books by other Muslim scholars including Maududi, Syed Qutb, Anwar Iqbal Quraishi, and Naiem Siddiqi started elaborating the idea – first popularised, two decades earlier, by the great philosopher and poet Mohammad Iqbal (1877–1938).

It all culminated with the First International Conference on Islamic Economics, held in Mecca in 1976. It was attended by vice chancellors from several universities. Among them was the Vice Chancellor of Aligarh, the eminent economist A M Khusro (1925–2003), who returning back home suggested the Department of Economics should take the initiative in teaching Islamic economics. Encouraged, I moved a resolution at the Board of Studies that an optional course on economic thinking in Islam should be introduced at the Master's level. I lost the motion by one vote as the chairman, supported by some senior lecturers, thought adopting it would make the department of economics look like the department of theology or Islamic studies. The course was introduced two decades later. Another decade would pass before the Academic Council of AMU would adopt a resolution to establish a post-graduate diploma in Islamic banking and finance in the department of Business Administration leading to a full-fledged department of Islamic Finance.

Several international conferences and seminars enriched the field of Islamic economics during the 1980s. Many universities were now teaching Islamic economics and doctoral dissertations and the subject proliferated even in western universities. Besides the International Centre for Research in Islamic Economics at the King Abdulaziz University, Jeddah, which publishes the *Journal of Islamic Economics*, there were now half a dozen others focusing on research and publications. I joined the Jeddah Centre in the early 1980s. It seemed that Islamic economics and Islamic Banking had come of age.

The first recorded publication on Islamic Banking is a 21-page booklet titled An Outline of Interest-less Banking by Mohammad Uzair, published from Karachi and Dacca in 1955. Maududi's *Sood* (Interest) came out in 1961; and Muhammad Abdullah al Arabi elaborated the idea of Islamic banking in a paper published in 1966. My books *Banking Without Interest* and its companion volume, *Banking Without Interest and Partnership and Profit-Sharing in Islamic Law*, came out in the late 1960s, though they had been serialised in a magazine earlier. Practitioners had meanwhile gone ahead with a number of experiments. The Malaysian Tabung Haji, pilgrim fund board, was established in 1963 and survives up to now as does the Philippine Amanah Bank, established in 1973, with a changed name. The Egyptian experiment with Islamic banking started in 1963, with the impressive saving/investment houses, named after the town where they were first established, Mit Ghamr. Launched by Ahmed el-Najjar , the pioneer of Islamic banking in Egypt, it lives on the pages of history, while the Islamic bank established in Karachi by Ahmad Irshad is almost forgotten. But a number of institutions established in the 1970s gave a boost to Islamic banking and the finance movement. Dubai Islamic Bank in the private sector and the Islamic Development Bank as an inter-governmental joint venture, both materialised in 1975. The process continued. We had many more Islamic banks by the end of the decade. There also emerged an Islamic Insurance Company (in Sudan) working on a cooperative basis and avoiding interest in its dealings. Many of these early Islamic financial institutions tried risk-sharing rather than shifting all risk to the fund users, but found the existing legal framework inhospitable to the practice. The rescue came in the idea of *Murabaha*, where the seller expressly mentions the cost he has incurred on the commodities he is selling and sells it to another person by adding some profit which is known to the buyer. The idea was first given academic prestige by the late Sami Hamoud in his PhD dissertation in the mid-1970s. The trick was to absolve the bank of all risk in 'lending' and ensure a decent return on money, irrespective of what happened at the user end. So an exploitative idea had at last been discovered and grounded in fiqh, what we call 'Islamic Law' as codified by the jurists in the first four centuries of Islamic history. Islamic banking and finance was ready to reach new heights.

Two developments gave added impetus: Changes in the power-structure in Iran, Pakistan and Sudan, where authoritarian Islamic regimes had taken power and favoured Islamic initiatives; and global banks and financial giants like Citi, Standard Chartered, ABN Amro, and HSBC, who had scented big money in Islamic Finance resulting from the hike in oil prices. A team of 'Shariah Scholars' helped anyone who was interested with financial engineering, via commodity *murabaha* and *tawarruq* (client buys X from bank on credit and sells it for a smaller amount of cash), and replicated almost every conventional financial product available on the market. You could buy a home, take a vacation, provide for your child's college education, insure your life and wife and buy health insurance. All 'enjoy now pay later' offers were now available within the framework of Islamic finance. This continued through the 1980s till the first audible voices began to be heard wondering how Islamic could be an 'Islamic finance' which operated within the comfort zone of capitalism with its consumerism, greed and increasing concentration of wealth.

Muslim minorities in Europe and the United States played a large part in establishing Islamic finance and banking. My own interaction with the west started in 1972 when I spent part of a sabbatical in the US. I found that interest in Islamic economics could be evoked, if at all, in the departments of Islamic studies or middle-eastern studies. Economists had no interest in the subject. The time was not yet ripe for the nascent (immigrant) American Muslim community to found Islamic cooperatives for facilitating home purchases or financing small businesses. But the ideas that later materialised as Muslim Saving and Investment (MSI) and American finance house, LARIBA, were already afloat. Later in 1979 when

I spent two months at the Islamic Foundation, Leicester, the Islamic economics project launched at the Mecca conference was in full swing. The two months I spent at the East West University, Chicago in 1981 also helped in mobilising talent for the project. But real progress came in the 1980s. At the initiatives of Prince Mohammad al Faisal and the Saudi businessman Sheikh Saleh Kamel a number of Islamic financial institutions were set up in Europe and the US. Meanwhile a number of Islamic financial institutions had also emerged in the Middle East and South East Asia and teaching and research in Islamic economics were spreading. These developments encouraged Muslim immigrants in the west to take similar initiatives making Islamic finance a part of their identity. Supported by Muslim money, some institutions of higher learning like Harvard, UCLA, LSE, Loughborough university and the Sorbonne started patronising the subject. Events hosted by these institutions brought together western-secular and eastern-Islamic scholarship to focus on issues of relevance to both East and West. My impression as LARIBA Senior Visiting Scholar, Center for Near Eastern Studies at the University of California, Los Angeles in 2001-02, and as a participant in Harvard and LSE events in the late 1990s, is that economists and bankers look upon Islamic economics and finance as Muslim issues at the fringe of world affairs deserving only marginal attention – they are only important as far as money can be made from them. Islamic economics is not recognised as part of the search for an alternative to capitalism. And we ourselves are partly responsible.

A main problem is that Muslim aspiration is totally out of sync with contemporary reality. Muslim aspiration to teach the world the compassionate economics preached by the Prophet Muhammad requires serious research as well as viable institution building. The International Center for Research in Islamic Economics at the King Abdulaziz University, Jeddah (now Islamic Economic Institute) was established to promote teaching and research. The Islamic Research and Training Institute of the Islamic Development Bank, the School of Islamic Economics at the Islamic University, Islamabad, and the Kulliyah of Economics at the International Islamic University, Kuala Lumpur, all share the same mission. The subject is now included in the programme of every Muslim-managed institution of higher learning. However a mist of artificiality surrounds the programmes, not to mention the superficiality of its content. There is a perception, partly thanks to the 'Islamisation of Knowledge' project, that we can simply graft the new on to the old. That the old may need to be rethought, modified or trimmed does not occur to the legions of researchers working the field. Indeed, to question the old Islamic economic norms is almost regarded as blasphemous.

Let me illustrate this with a few telling anecdotes. Of the students whose researches I supervised or examined, many belonged to the Ummul Qura University and Jami'at al Imam, both in Saudi Arabia. Many students from these universities consulted me when I was at the Jeddah Centre on a selection of subjects, research methodology and other issues related to pursing a doctorate. In one case, I suggested the concept of *israf* (extravagance) in Qur'an and Sunnah, the evolution of the concept over time and across regions and in different income strata. The research would involve textual studies as well as field work. The student would have to get questionnaires filled by selected families in selected places. But the idea was rejected out of hand by the authorities as both the subject and the field work was deemed unsuitable. Apathy towards empirical studies seems embedded in religious scholarship. I have had this impression in dealing with a number of Islamic institutions in India in the context of such subjects as the increasing incidence of divorce among Muslims. No one seems to be interested in empirical field work, or learn from ground reality or pays heed to how and why behaviour is changing.

About twenty years ago a professor giving a course at Harvard sent me some work sheets used in the context of discussing Islamic rules related to interest. All the Qur'anic verses dealing with *riba* (usury) and the main hadith on the subject were supplied asking the student to write down the rules that could be derived from them. Next the student was required to look up the appropriate sources and note down the rulings actually given by major schools of Islamic jurisprudence. Lastly the student had to comment on the differences and defend his own stand. Around the same time I sat as an examiner in the department of Islamic economics of Ummul Qura University. The student was defending his Master's thesis on labour relations in Islam. After reporting various views on employer-employee relations, he went on to say: 'I suggest ...' Immediately, the chief examiner, who was a professor of *fiqh* chided the student in harsh terms, saying: 'how dare you say I suggest. It is enough for us to learn what the great *fuqaha* (jurists) among the *salaf* (first thee generations of Muslims) have said and to transmit their opinions faithfully to posterity'.

A student who was a qualified *Aalim* (religious scholar) from Nadwah, Lucknow, and had earned a PhD in economics from AMU by writing a dissertation on murabaha in Islamic finance, took a course on *Ifta* (giving juridical opinions) conducted by a religious seminary in Hyderabad. When he completed the course I asked him how he was trained to give fatwas. 'We were given certain queries', he said, 'and asked to look up in certain classic texts to identify the rulings appropriate to the query in hand'.

This is how we have been teaching and researching Islamic economics. In view of the challenges we are facing, and are likely to face in the future, will the methodology taught to *Ifta* students at Hyderabad or the stance imposed upon students at Ummul Qura serve our purpose? Our current methods of teaching crush all independent thinking, extinguish any flicker of curiosity and kill all creativity. The absence of empirical work makes our researches hollow. We are entirely focused on texts to the total neglect of observing ground realities and learning lessons history can teach. The young minds under the tutelage of our professors and researcher are denied the benefits of a larger conversation encompassing intuition, dialogue and pragmatic considerations in dealing with their subjects of study.

Even the way we examine history is seriously flawed. A selective approach is the norm. Modern historians find serious gaps between theory and practice in the Islamic past. Muslim scholars paint an idealised picture of history where everything was rosy. Truth suffers in both cases depriving us from the real benefits of history. When I wrote the paper 'Public Borrowing in Early Islamic History' and submitted it to an Islamic economics journal it was sent to two referees. The paper reports, among other things, some cases of borrowing (during Abbasid rule in the ninth century) from non-Muslim lenders in order to pay salaries to the army on time. For paying back, the lenders were allowed to collect land revenue of a particular province. Sensing *riba* in that arrangement, one of the referees expressed great anguish insisting the story be expunged from the paper. It presented Islamic history in a bad light. We have to assume that all Muslims in history were sincere, decent and shining beacons of humanity. A variety of interpretations as well as the compulsion of circumstances cannot be recognised. Something similar to my experience with the referee happened at the Mecca Conference in 1976. One of the points vociferously made in favour of an interest-free economy was that there would be no inflation. Eminent economists participating in the conference grimaced and laughed but thought it better not to challenge the claimants. In private I confronted the late Mohammad Qutb, brother of Syed Qutb, a leading advocate of that view. I presented historical evidence refuting the absurd claim. But the Sheikh dismissed history as of no consequence when it came to the characteristics of Islamic society which must only be derived from the texts of the Qur'an and Sunnah.

A selective view of Islamic history combined with little attention to the reality around us often results in mass depression or acute frustration, which could lead to violence. This wide spread   contemporary phenomenon has roots in recent history. The Islamic Economics Center at Jeddah once had some high profile visitors from an educational institution in Peshawar, Pakistan, the city which earned the reputation of being the hatching ground for the Taliban. Most questions related to Islamic economy and what changes are expected in neighbouring Afghanistan after the departure of the Russians. One question was: 'when and how will it be possible to do what the second caliph Umar bin Khattab did, giving an annual stipend to every household?' They insisted that was the distinguishing feature of Islamic economy, whereas modern states levied taxes the Islamic state will give stipends.

Unfortunately such naivety is not confined to the piety brigade. In one of the many closed door meetings with dignitaries visiting the Jeddah Centre I attended, Najmuddin Erbakan, then Turkish Prime Minister (June 1996 to June 1997) distributed a paper titled '*al-ilaj*' (the cure). Outlining future Islamic economic policies, Erbakan suggested doing away with money in certain sectors of the economy as currency trade and speculation were at the root of many problems. Producers would deliver their crops to government which would issue them with receipts which they could use for buying what they needed. There were many other impractical utopian ideas in the paper. The researchers at the Centre prepared a rejoinder politely criticising the proposals and suggesting alternatives. We asked Muhammad Umar Zubair, a former President of the King Abdel Aziz University and a respected figure, to communicate our critique to Erbakan. He took it to Istanbul with the intention of handing it personally to the Prime Minister. But he did not, as he realised that the beloved leader accepted no criticism and tolerated no dissent. Whatever I know about the leadership of Islamic parties in the Arab world, the Indian   subcontinent and South-East Asia this is a common malaise. There is very little tolerance of dissent. Nobody invites criticism. There is no tradition of democratic decision-making. Both naivety and intolerance are wicked, but their combination has been fatal.

As a result the theory and practice of Islamic economics and banking is flawed, full of anomalies, and have basically failed as projects. All we can do is to congratulate ourselves on having re-invented capitalism by using Islamic jurisprudence! This is a far cry from the innovative creativity of jurists in the early centuries of Islam and more in line with the frozen attitudes during the colonial era.

I realised some years back that Muslims in general and the *ulema* in particular had no idea how banks functioned. The role of credit and the process of money creation in a fractional reserve system were beyond their comprehension. They could understand some institution that took people's money with the promise of doing profitable business for a share in the returns. The other possibility was a hired manager doing business on behalf of the owners of money; but they looked at financial intermediation with suspicion. My works, building on the idea of *al-mudarib yudarib* (the working partner obtaining people's money to use it profitably entering into a similar relationship with another person), argued that banking was possible by replacing fixed interest payment by a share in profit. In other words it projected profit-sharing as a possible basis of financial intermediation. I demonstrated with examples that the process involved credit creation. However, the fact that banks earned on the credit they created raises new problems. This problem is further compounded by the recent realisation that banks could increase the leverage – ratio between money advanced and cash kept in reserve to meet payment obligations – at will, in view of interbank facilities and central bank's assurances. So dealing with the issue of regulating the banking industry on the basis of analogical reasoning does not help and a consideration of consequences (*ma 'alat*) and the public interest (*masalih*) becomes necessary. Meanwhile some scholars think it will be better to do away with banks and switch over to some other institution having roots in Islamic history, like *baitulmal*, the financial institution responsible for the administration of taxes in an 'Islamic state'. The debate continues. But I am not impressed by this trend of returning back to Islamic history literally. Our Prophet retained business practices that were honest and fair. He rejected only what was harmful, like gambling and interest on loans. After all, institutions are a means for realising certain goals and operationalisation of certain values. Banking itself is not without precedents in early Islamic history. It is reported about the eminent companion of the Prophet, Zubair ibn el Awwam, that when somebody wanted to leave some money with him for safe-keeping he would say 'make it a loan to me' so he could use it and the depositor was guaranteed its return. The celebrated jurist Abu Hanifa, who had a flourishing business in silk, also acted as a banker.

The recent financial crisis has exposed the inequities and inefficiencies of the current system of money and finance initiating a world-wide rethink. Instead of promoting human felicity on a universal scale, it is enriching the top one percent and relegating most of humanity to the margins of poverty. But the discussion is focussed around the mechanics of banking and finance at the expense of the core issue: who are we creating wealth for and how can it reach them. Once again there are calls for separating investment banking from managing medium of exchange and doing away with fractional reserve in favour of hundred percent reserves. But the real issue is how risk is treated. I think no reform of the financial system would be effective until money and monetary policy are also radically changed. Debts carrying interest should not serve as money. Risks and uncertainties attending upon the human situation should be fairly distributed and shared. These characteristics call for the state to play a decisive role. They also call for universally shared perspectives. Economists of all shades must join hands and disciplines other than economics must be involved if we are to rescue humanity from its current predicament.

Creating a new vision of money and finance largely not based on debt, distributing risks fairly, in a manner that is universally acceptable is not an easy project.

Consider the last: the prospects of a new vision being adopted by all. Now given the unique characteristic of money and finance, you can't have a variety of systems in a globalised world. History is rife with wishful thinking and utopian experiments. From no money to local money to gold only money, all types of ideas are afloat, with experiments to boot. But none have any chance of universal applicability. Physical money is fast yielding to bits and bytes and the state is slowly but assuredly losing the monopoly on money creation. Current debate among economists, including Islamic economists, hovers round separating the management of payments mechanism (medium of exchange function) from profit making activities of banks and replacing fractional reserve with hundred percent reserves. But innovations and creative private initiatives may soon render all these discussions irrelevant. Nobody knows what the future has in store.

The risks associated with money centre around its purchasing power whose fluctuations cause distributional problems. The other risk relates to sharing any new wealth generated when one's money is used by another. It is very difficult to pinpoint the responsibility for changes in the purchasing power of money. It is easy to blame monetary policy but there are too many other factors which could possibly have an impact: population, tastes, technology, ecology, war and peace, for example. From the viewpoint of equity it is important to ensure all risks are not piled on the user of money. Even the owner of money who would normally bear the risks may deserve protection in certain circumstances. What is important is making life possible and its burdens bearable for everyone. Implied therein is a commitment to fairness in the framework of living as a cooperative enterprise. It is this vision that is missing from the current individualistic dispensation which fails to honour the demands of cooperative living and frees the owners of money from social obligations. Money that is debt and modes of finance that leave a trail of debts have a rigidity that militates with life's vicissitudes. Debt based money and finance does not suit the social nature of human existence.

I think it is this point which, above all, needs to be argued clearly and convincingly. Modern money is all debt. Money is created at the central bank level and injected into the economy in exchange for bonds (promises to pay later). This 'high powered money' enables commercial banks to create more money (demand deposits) as debts owed to them. All debts carry interest. Since the mere passage of time is no guarantee for growth to take place and not all money is used for productive purposes, default is built into the system and so is increasing inequality. More and more of the new wealth resulting from using money flows to the owners of money. A system that rewards enterprise more than it rewards mere ownership would be more efficient as well as more equitable. Such a system requires money that is not debt and debts that carry no interest.

So how do we move forward in this new and rapidly changing context? It is clear that the current system has passed its 'sell by' date. Teaching current textbooks in modern economics prepares the students for endorsement of capitalism. Continuing with the traditional curriculum is guaranteed to alienate the student from their environment. The confused products of our economic departments cannot make any progress towards a just and equitable society.

Economic management, especially monetary and financial arrangements, need to be put in an appropriate perspective. We have to create an environment that sustains and enhances the quality of life. First we must focus on sustenance as it makes life possible and enduring. Then comes freedom of choice and other rights without which life would be meaningless. Regulations ensuring peace and preventing exploitation, oppression and chaos are also necessary. Growth alone does not ensure that the basic and universal needs of all are fulfilled. Indeed, growth may fuel inequality, increase deprivation and foster conflict. Capitalism's failure lies in its exclusive focus on growth without any commitment to sustenance with dignity for all. An Islamic approach can avoid this by focusing on *maqasid* (purpose, intent and higher objectives) of Islam that are multi-faceted.

Maqasid impacts the human situation on a number of levels. First, every rule serves some purpose; Islamic rules are neither arbitrary nor random. Second, should a rule cease to serve its purpose due to changed conditions it has to be replaced by one designed to serve the original purpose. Third, a situation not covered by existing rules is to be handled by devising a new rule rooted in the relevant *maqasid*. Fourth, if implementation of a rule results in a perverse or an undesirable outcome, that rule has to be abandoned in favour of one suited to the relevant *maqasid*. These points are well argued in the literature on *maqasid*. Unfortunately the current approaches to economic management, especially in money and finance, fail to take cognisance of them. They remain beholden to conventional ideals and try to operate within the framework of *fiqh* or jurisprudence codified a thousand years ago under different circumstances. Classical jurists gave due weight to *manfi* (interests), *masalih 'aammah* (public interest) and *ma 'alat* (consequences), but the current generation of jurists advising decision-makers do not have the courage to do so. They are endorsing financial products that flood the market with debt documents which they allow to be traded. A commitment to maqasid would have prevented such anomalies and given us Islamic models worth emulation by the rest of the world.

Maqasid are clearly stated in the Qur'an. Sustenance has to be universally ensured based on God-given provisions (7:10). A share for the have-nots is appointed in the wealth of the haves (70:24-25). Ensuring justice and fairness in all relationships is the very purpose of God's Law (57:25 and 4:58). Chaos and disorder have to be prevented and felicity (*salah*) instituted (28:71; 30:41).

Traditional Shariah experts are suspicious of the idea of replacing old rules by rules designed to serve *maqasid* in changed situations. But this is a time-honoured methodology legitimised by numerous precedents. We could refer, as an example, to the way Umar, the second caliph, handled the conquered lands of Syria and Iraq. Despite insistence by senior companions of the Prophet like Bilal, who cited the Prophetic precedent that the conquered lands be distributed among the army responsible for the conquest, Umar let the peasants continue to operate the lands, paying *kharaj* (rent) to the state.

Another fear that prevents traditional *ulama* from direct recourse to *maqasid* is the diversity of opinion and practice that would be a natural outcome. They are bound to the idea that the divine pleasure lies in one course in every situation. But this is not supported by the Prophetic precedents, who adopted different strategies in different circumstances, the focus being the *maqasid*: communicating God's message, protecting those from harm who accepted the message, and being merciful to humanity in general. Confined to an arid valley in Mecca, he benefited from clan solidarity. Rejected by Taif, he accepted the protection of a non-Muslim resident to be able to reside in Mecca once again. He advised his followers to seek refuge in Abyssinia, cashing in on the generosity of the Christian King. Later on he emigrated to Madina on the invitation of his small band of followers. He settled the emigrants, who had left everything behind, in Medina by instituting *Muwakhat* (brotherhood) between resident *Ansars* (helpers) and *Muhajir* newcomers – a novel arrangement that lasted a couple of years. He forged a federation inclusive of Jews, Christians and people of other faiths and Muslims to administer the city – yet another novelty in a tribal culture. The truce of Hudaibiyah, the general amnesty for the vanquished Meccans after the conquest and showering Meccans with all the spoils of the battle of Hunain soon after, are some of the decisions, amongst many, that the Prophet took to suit the occasion. One fails to understand the timidity of his followers facing an entirely new world in the twenty-first century.

The future of Islamic economics and finance is tied to our efforts to rethink the entire economic system as well as in promoting criticism and self-criticism and generating new ideas. The decline of the west and the shifts in power to the East provides us with an opportunity – it may be accompanied by rejection of capitalism or at the least its radical modification. The most pernicious product that western capitalism is leaving behind is inequality and the indignity that it has visited on the bulk of humanity. Islam with its emphasis on equality, human brotherhood and sharing may well succeed in building an economy that is different. But we need new ideas suited to our time. Ideas change behaviour, give birth to institutions and change the reality on the ground. Unfortunately, our record in generating new ideas is not encouraging. But I am still hopeful, waiting and watching for the formulation and popularisation of the new and innovative ideas to emerge from Islam and Muslims.

ARTS AND LETTERS

SEEKING *ILM* ON THE SILK ROAD

Naomi Foyle

Each atom reaches here through its own gate
Each takes a different road to gain this state
And what do you know of the Way before
You now, the path you'll follow to His door?

Farid ud-Din Attar, from *The Conference of the Birds*,
translated by Afkham Darbandi and Dick Davis

Who Himself and Others Knows
Here is rightly guided;
Occident and Orient
Are no more divided

J.W. von Goethe, from *The West-Eastern Divan*,
translation on display in the Museum of the History of Islamic
Science and Technology, Istanbul

Informed in part by Farid Attar's classic twelfth century Sufi poem 'The Conference of the Birds', I am currently writing a science fantasy novel about a young warrior woman's voyage to a revolutionary commune in the desert. The third volume of *The Gaia Chronicles*, *The Blood of the Hoopoe* follows *Astra*, a *bildungsroman* in which the mixed race heroine discovers that her post-fossil fuel Mesopotamian paradise is built on lies, and *Rook Song*, in which the leaders of an uprising against her homeland decide she is the reincarnation of the goddess Istar. How did I, a white non-Muslim, come to be writing increasingly Islamic-flavoured science fiction? If I am not, in fact, guilty from the outset of cultural appropriation, how do I negotiate the minefield of my own ignorance and avoid reduplicating Orientalist stereotypes and Islamophobic tropes? May I, conversely dare to believe that my books might help create mutual understanding between cultures we are told are 'at war', even play a part in building, in place of violence and mistrust, a shared vision of a just and sustainable global society? These are questions of great ethical and aesthetic import. My responses traverse not only hotly contested political and literary debates, but spiritual beliefs and experiences that by their nature are difficult to fully express in words. What I can say with absolute certainty is that in writing these books I am educating myself, and attempting to educate others, about the richness of Muslim and other Middle Eastern cultures. Whether my novels succeed or fail in their more specific ambitions, so far writing them has given me a far greater appreciation of Islam.

I am, of course, by no means the first Western science fiction (SF) writer to take a creative interest in the Middle East. As Paul Weimer has recently explicated, so-called 'Silk Road Fantasy', or Islamic SF written by non-Muslims, is a well-established subgenre; currently dominated by Elizabeth Bear it owes historical debts to Susan Shwartz, Judith Tarr, and the early twentieth century writer Harold Lamb, whose swashbuckling tales of Cossacks and Crusaders feature many fully realised Muslim protagonists. But while it may sound smooth and flowing, this Silk Road is riddled with pitfalls. Weimer warns against 'slap-dash borrowing' to cultivate an air of 'mysticism and otherliness', while Rebecca Hankins, discussing the use of Islamic tropes in the work of Western SF authors including Brian Aldiss, Joanna Russ, and Michael Crichton, has observed that non-Muslim women writers in particular tend to take an Islamophobic approach to Muslim culture. I am the very opposite of antagonistic to Islam, but aware that cultural blind spots may lead me to get the simplest things spectacularly wrong. I am still sometimes amazed that I am attempting to walk the path at all.

Perhaps I am so conscious of the danger of cultural appropriation because I came-of-age in Canada in the eighties and nineties, at a time when First Nations people were vociferously challenging white writers' use of their traditional stories. Their objection to such practices, as I understand it, is twofold. First Nations people have been subjected to a centuries long genocide, their land stolen and way of life destroyed by European invaders; for European Canadians to use and sell First Nations stories is simply to perpetuate the plunder. In addition, as Erin Hanson explains, indigenous Canadian tales belong to complex oral traditions in which formal rules govern who can tell a story, and when: they are subject to a cultural copyright as morally binding as the legal variety. I respect that copyright, and from those formative years I have also absorbed the general principle that as a member of an oppressor group I should not attempt to write in the voice of the oppressed. But while it is not hard to abide by this prohibition in my poetry, as a novelist it is a vexing one, and to me, increasingly calls for a nuanced response.

To me the novel is a magnificent form, and the greatest of challenges for a writer because it encompasses all aspects of human existence: feeling, thought, sensation, intuition, the lyric epiphany and the inexorable epic all fall within its compass. But how can novels reflect the extraordinary diversity of human experience if writers may only write from their own cultural or individual perspective? And if one of the great values of literature is its ability to generate empathy, why should writers, of whatever background, be prevented from exercising their own empathy in the creation of characters from all sides of a conflict? In *A Thousand Splendid Suns* Khaled Hosseini demonstrates in devastating detail that a man can deeply understand the experience of brutalised women. Granted, cultural and linguistic gulfs may run deeper than gender divisions within an ethnicity, but still, with sufficient research, experience, and empathy it ought to be possible to write fiction which – even if only with gossamer – bridges those gaps in understanding and works to level those power imbalances. Politically engaged fiction, I believe, listens as much as it speaks. Rather than not attempt to write Silk Road Fantasy, I try to do so responsibly, respectfully and effectively: ultimately, to help de-Other the Other. Over time, I have developed four specific principles that guide me in this task. First, that in writing my novels I deepen my understanding of both myself and others in this complex and volatile world; second, that my research is as thorough as possible; third, that my creative writing is accompanied by activism toward the goals of a just peace in Israel-Palestine and a truly democratic, anti-racist West; and finally my books win the acceptance of at least some readers with cultural roots in the Muslim world.

My first principle is the foundation of my entire creative practice, in which I take to heart the ancient Greek dictum 'Know Thyself'. In researching and writing *The Gaia Chronicles* I inform myself about Islam, the Arab world and a wealth of other Middle Eastern cultures, and insofar as *The Gaia Chronicles* express my understanding of current conflicts and conversations between cultures and faiths, faith and science, people and power, the books represent my own intellectual, moral and emotional journey as much as my heroine's. In order to build trust and avoid shallow declarations I wish to share some of that journey with readers, but before I do, it is fitting to set those details in the context of one of the core obligations of Islam: *ilm*, the duty, as Ziauddin Sardar explains it, to pursue and disseminate knowledge. I believe that *ilm* makes of Islam and science fiction natural cohabitants. Though it is absolutely true that good fiction must be dramatic, not didactic, one thing I love about SF is the gossamer steel platform it provides to explore ideas and share knowledge – not only of bioengineering and astrophysics, but also social and political science, history, philosophy and religion. Through weaving such research into my fiction, I hope to bring the Middle East a little closer to Western readers, and though my work, which also draws on the horror genre, can be unsettling, if it is able to engage Muslim free thinkers and convince them of my respect and admiration for the intellectual and moral underpinnings of their faith, I would feel I had truly accomplished something important. At the same time, directing *ilm* inward, to illuminate the Self, is not simply an individualistic Western goal. Attar, in the Prologue to his great allegorical poem about a party of birds who set forth on the long and arduous Way to Allah, echoes the classic Greek exhortation:

> But as you haven't lost a thing, don't seek it!
> And since your formulation's wrong, don't speak it
> The things you seek and know are you, and so
> It's you, a hundred ways, you're forced to know.
>   (Lines 98-101)

I have considered deeply the question of how it is I came to be writing Middle Eastern SF and not, for example, Celtic fantasy or Tudor bodice rippers. I have realised that my journey into Islamic SF, has been years in the making, and began with almost imperceptible steps. Although I grew up without the benefit of much interaction with Muslim people, my formative experiences decisively pointed me in the direction I am now pursuing.

I was born in London in the sixties, to lapsed Christian parents: my father, a socialist and academic, is the son of a devout Anglican RAF widow, and my late mother, a poet, editor and creative writing teacher, was the great-granddaughter of a Scottish Presbyterian missionary in Calcutta (as was). I was brought up to cherish diversity; we had Hindu and Parsee family friends, my father's work involved us in a multiracial community, and when his career took us to Hong Kong, my parents adopted my Chinese sister there. That is a whole other story, but whatever the arguments over interracial adoption, I can't imagine life without my sister, and growing up with her made me as empathically aware as any white person can be, I think, of the deeply wounding nature of racism. My early years also contained one tantalising link to Muslim life: when I was four we returned to the UK to live in Liverpool, where I played on our street with a girl called Safia. But I recall very little of her, for this early attachment was not to last: when I was seven we moved to a small prairie city in Canada, and though my elementary school there is now an Islamic cultural centre, at the time I did not have Muslim schoolmates.

In Canada, though, in a move I now recognise as hugely influential upon my current interests, my parents joined the Quakers. Every Sunday I and my siblings would attend 'children's meeting', playing cooperative board games and making handicrafts to donate to charities before joining the adults for ten minutes of wiggling on our bottoms in silence, followed by a potluck meal or skiing and mulled wine in the winter. I too abandoned organised religion, I absorbed values in those meetings that have never left me: the sense that there is an undimmable light in each one of us; that not even the hardest criminal is beyond redemption; and that spirituality involves action as well as contemplation, community as well as solitude. While there are of course profound differences between Quakerism and Islam, especially the relationship to scripture, it seems to me that there are also significant similarities between Quaker values and Muslim concepts, in particular ummah, the community; *adl*, which Sardar notes is an active requirement, meaning 'distributive justice'; and above all *tawheed*, unity: for Quakers, shared silence allows communion with that divine love and truth that transcends and unites us all.

It was difficult, though, growing up in Canada, where church schools had abused First Nations pupils and robbed them of their families and language, to avoid the conclusion that Christianity was just another tool of the colonial regime. My burgeoning feminism also made traditional religious worship uncomfortable for me; visiting England in my early teens I ran sobbing from my paternal grandmother's church, unable to bear for a moment longer all the old men in black gowns telling everyone what to do. My parents eventually left the Society of Friends, and when, after their divorce in my late teens, my mother became interested in mysticism, I was ripe for conversion myself. I began to explore alternative traditions: yoga, Buddhism, Tarot, astrology, shamanism; all the usual Western escape routes. I learned a great deal from all of them. After my mother's untimely death, I had some startling experiences with psychics and mediums and, having resettled in the UK, for some years before returning to higher education I made a living as a Tarot Card reader. I became interested in my maternal Scot-Irish and paternal Norfolk heritage, and if not for Israel's bombardment of Gaza in 2008–9, I might still be working on a verse novel about Boudica written in Norfolk dialect. But the horror of watching Operation Cast Lead on television triggered all my paternal political genes and, with the force of another conversion, reawakened my dormant Quaker drive toward activism.

I credit my father for the sense of inevitability that accompanied this new direction. As well as leaving the Manchester *Guardian* and *New Internationalist* strewn about the house, he had early on instilled in me sympathies for the Palestinian cause: when I was about seven he told me that while Israel was founded to give the Jews a refuge from persecution, this was done at the expense of the Palestinians who were forced to flee their homes. It was a brief explanation to a curious child but it made a lasting impression. In high school I contributed a passionate defence of the Palestinian cause to a student newspaper. This was an isolated act of solidarity, written in response to a piece by a young Zionist; I still didn't know any Arabs or Muslims. After university, though, travelling in Greece during the first Gulf War, I was befriended by an older white South African woman and her Palestinian partner, who had recently escaped from a Syrian jail. Angela, holding court from a stool outside a clothes shop on the Acropolis, took my literary education in hand, insisting I read Jean Genet's passionate defence of the Palestinians, *Prisoner of Love*; Mohammed, with his impeccable moustache and courteous English, escorted me round

Athens to drink coffee with his Arab friends, all, like him, hoping and waiting for visas elsewhere. Later, I tried to help the couple get to Canada, and after a long hard story during which they separated, Mohammed eventually arrived in Montreal. I recalled all these experiences as, during Cast Lead I got involved in local demonstrations, and joined the Palestine Solidarity Campaign (PSC). A year later I signed up for the Gaza Freedom March, which took place in Cairo, and on my return I co-founded British Writers in Support of Palestine, whose members pledge not to accept invitations from state-funded Israeli cultural and academic institutions.

I view the Israel-Palestine conflict not as a religious or 'tribal' war, but a human rights struggle against colonialism, apartheid and ethnic cleansing, and my political activism is only quietly motivated by spiritual beliefs. Through it, however, I have positively reconnected with organised religion. Though not initially taking an interest in Islam per se, I inevitably met Muslims and became more aware of the rise of Islamophobia in the UK. Working also with anti-Zionist Jews, I read about also on this topic, learning from Mike Marqusee and others of the potent history of radical Jewish social justice movements, and from Judith Butler of the centrality of justice to Jewish teachings. Over the years I have also reconciled with my Christian heritage. My aunt, still a High Anglican, has been a great role model of compassion and social responsibility, while as my mother loved the Christmas rituals, I celebrate the winter holiday in her memory. Now, in December, though I bristle at the image of Bethlehem on the cards, I also want to engage positively with Christians about it. In recent years I have organise political street theatre with a Christmas theme, started attending Midnight Mass with a Christian friend in my local parish, rejoiced over the Bethlehem Unwrapped festival at St James Piccadilly. Though I still bridle at the gendered language of church services, and can't embrace patriarchal monotheism, increasingly I respect the good that organised religion can accomplish: creating community, preaching mercy, humility, tolerance and co-operation. My vision of a just peace in Israel-Palestine is no longer an entirely secular one: while obviously a lasting solution to the conflict must be a democratic one that respects the basic human rights of all inhabitants, to reflect the unique character of the region I increasingly believe it must also – as so many interfaith peace activists find ways to do — honour the deep attachment of all three Abrahamic faiths to the Holy Land.

Given that over six decades of Zionist oppression is currently only getting worse, Islamic fundamentalists, fuelled by the fall-out of Bush and Blair's crusade, are tearing apart the wider region, anti-Semitism is on the rise in Europe, and Western governments are still waging war on Muslims and their faith, the dream of any kind of peace in the Middle East may seem more unrealisable than ever before. But while I do not wish to create a false or glib equivalence between different cultures or religions, I am starting to believe that the Abrahamic faiths have more than sufficient common ground on which to found a lasting peace. It's a big argument, resting in part on the growing and hugely controversial argument that Zionism is itself anti-Semitic, but in essence it seems to me that the many shared narratives and motifs of Islam, Judaism and Christianity remind us not only of the religions' deeply shared historical roots but also their common values: truth, wisdom, justice, charity and love. Do not all three Abrahamic religions venerate Solomon, with his reward of the contested baby to the self-sacrificial, compassionate mother? While all religions can be guilty of sexism, xenophobia and violence against their own and others' beliefs, a strong focus on their core shared values, also central to humanist thought, can feed the potential for peaceful co-existence. Historically, this potential has been realised far more often and more profoundly in the Middle East than in Europe. Muslim majorities have accepted Jewish communities far more readily than Christians have tolerated either of their sibling faiths, while the early Israelites took some time to become purist zealots: researching *The Blood of the Hoopoe*, I was fascinated to learn that Solomon was a tolerant pluralist who erected temples to the gods and goddesses of his many wives. Solomon, whom Muslims believe spoke the language of birds and animals, had a close relationship with the hoopoe: the marvellous bird was the King's spy in the Queen of Sheba's court, and also helped him build the First Temple without defying God's stipulations, using a magic herb to cut stone without the use of iron tools — a legend thought to be the source of the magical injunction 'open sesame.' Currently echoing that call, the Open Bethlehem campaign, run by Palestinian Christian Leila Sansour, represents an invitation to people of all religions and none to help bring down the wall strangling not only the town of Jesus's birth, but all of Palestine.

Midnight Mass notwithstanding, I personally am a non-religious believer in the possibility of transcendence. But as a creative writer I aim to ignite the basic fuel of both literature and religion: stories and symbols. Working on a PhD on the warrior woman in narrative verse, in 2010 I shifted my focus from Boudica to Inanna, the ancient Sumerian goddess of love and war. Goddess also of the morning and evening star, associated with Ishtar, Esther, Venus, Aphrodite, Persephone – and by extension Christ – Inanna is Solomon's songwriter, Abraham's diva grandmother. Pieced together by scholars from fragments of cuneiform tablets, and available now in English translations by Diane Wolkstein, hers are glorious, sensual stories of self-love in date palm orchards, a bold sea voyage to get her father drunk and steal his authority, a passionate marriage to the shepherd Dumuzi, considered beneath her, and a courageous journey to the underworld, where she is murdered by her own jealous sister Ereshkigal and brought back to life by the asexual spirits of compassion. Upon her return, Inanna learns that Dumuzi has usurped her throne, and their ensuing battle ultimately results in the creation of the seasons: in order to restore balance Dumuzi and his sister Geshtinnana must each spend half the year in the underworld with Ereshkigal. While the tablets are Iraqi treasures, Innana, who birthed the story of Eden and the great descent myths of so many traditions, belongs to the human psyche. She is a 'missing archetype': not just a warrior woman, but a leader whose courage and authority were inextricable from her sensuality and vulnerability. Her myths reminds us that leadership is not a male, but a human attribute, and that leaders worth respecting must be prepared to suffer, sacrifice, and grow.

For my PhD I submitted poems about contemporary Inannas and Persephones, including the Palestinian female suicide bomber Zainab Abu Salem, and an ex-IDF soldier I'd met in India. In 2011, for the Bush Theatre's *66 Books* project, in which sixty-six writers responded to the King James Bible, I wrote a short verse drama set in contemporary Jerusalem, 'The Strange Wife', casting Ezra as an aged Zionist whose son had married a Palestinian. My poetic journey was interrupted, however, when my desk-drawer SF novel *Seoul Survivors* finally found a publisher in Jo Fletcher Books, an imprint that specialises in science fiction, fantasy and horror. My joy was tempered with panic: Jo wanted a second book, in a year. Immersed as I was in the Middle East, I couldn't imagine dropping everything to write another cyber-chiller. Rather, I wanted my science fiction to extend my quest to educate myself about the Middle East. The positive response to 'The Strange Wife' encouraged me to take a huge leap down my own personal Silk Road and set my new novel in a parallel, futuristic Middle East. Increasingly concerned about climate change, I also wanted the novel to challenge what I perceived as an insular tendency in British Green politics: to confront the possibility of eco-catastrophe but respond with the vision of a more just and sustainable global society. An image arrived, of a small girl named Astra climbing a pine tree in pursuit of a wild child named Lil, and then, hot on their grubby little heels, a whole world came into focus…

That then, is how I came to write *The Gaia Chronicles*. Doing so has involved me in myriad ethical considerations. To explore the shared mythology of the Abrahamic religions in the context of climate change, I needed to set the book on a recognisable Earth, in a recognisably Middle Eastern location – a place I have never lived in, inhabited by people whose culture, languages and religion are not my own. The last thing I want to do is commit yet another act of Orientalist imperialism, yet I must accept that no matter how good my intentions, how detailed my research, I will inevitably make errors, expose unconscious bias, display my ignorance for all to see. I feel the risks are worth taking. For one thing, how can we learn without making mistakes? Beyond that, I am not writing social realism. Though I would be horrified to peddle stereotypes or Islamophobic tropes, I do not feel I have to adhere slavishly to fact. Science Fiction and Fantasy engages the critical imagination in the task of creating alternative worlds a crucial remove from our own: *The Gaia Chronicles* are set in an imaginative space, not a geopolitically or even geographically correct one.

The series would take place, I decided, at a time when runaway climate change has led to floods, disease, and the wholesale collapse of global society. During years of chaos, libraries burn, internet servers are bombed, rising sea levels change the very maps and the planet is radically depopulated. My futuristic world has suffered a traumatic forgetting, but it has also been shocked into realising the old world order must not be resurrected. At last a new world government, the Council of New

Continents (CONC), is formed. CONC is idealistic, committed to democratic representation, enforceable international law, a fossil fuel ban and the elimination of war. But early on its members makes a fundamental error: in exchange for an invaluable nitrogen-fixing seed, they vote to allow the Gaians, an international community of radical Green eco-scientists and craftspeople, to create a 'homeland', Is-Land, in an abandoned region of Mesopotamia. In a re-greening of Eden, the Gaians clean the toxic land but then, on the grounds of protecting their own nudism and vegan lifestyles, refuse to allow the return of the original inhabitants. So far, so allegorical. As Marianne Moore said of poetry, 'imaginary gardens need real toads'. My shamanic practices and early training in acting have strengthened my imagination; research and political engagement critically inform it, while my commitment to putting my own emotional toads into my futuristic world strengthens my empathy for my fictional characters.

Research has been paramount from the very beginning, both scholarly and experiential. I had a base of knowledge from my years of activism, but travel played a catalysing role in the creation of the novels' setting. Though the pine tree in my opening image may have come straight out of the West Bank, I never wanted to re-write, or be seen to re-write, Israel-Palestine. As much as I oppose the conflation of anti-Zionism and anti-Semitism, I didn't want my work to get attention simply for becoming embroiled in that controversy. And I also didn't remotely suggest that I was putting forward some kind of visionary solution to the conflict. Quite conversely, due to rising sea levels, it was likely that in my scenario Israel-Palestine would be a Mediterranean Atlantis. Discovering that *al-jazeera* means 'island' and is not only the name of the news channel, but also the land between the northern Tigris and Euphrates, I decided, as if struck by lightning, to visit South East Anatolia. En route, I visited Istanbul's Museum of the History of Science and Technology, where long mesmerising halls of astrolabes, water clocks and constellation globes were introduced by the words of Goethe: here at the crossroads of continents it felt as though being a European seeker after *ilm* was not Orientalist appropriation but an essential intellectual quest the West had tragically lost sight of. Later, as a Canadian prairie girl wandering through Diyarbakir, I felt both a humble visitant and at home: not just in the rolling steppes, but in the daily routines of a small rural city, albeit one populated by Turks, Kurds, and Arabs and surrounded by an ancient basalt wall. Although, as the guidebook warned, I was harassed more than anywhere else I've ever been, I was also incredibly welcomed by mini-bus drivers, students, old women and a waiter who went into raptures when he saw what I was reading: the poetry of Kurdish writer Bejan Matur, who later kindly provided the epigraph to *Astra*. As I blogged at the time, the trip, followed by my first visit to Israel-Palestine, was stimulating and strangely reassuring. Upon my return I began writing *Astra*, basing the topography of Is-Land on South East Anatolia, though that soon changed.

Exploring *Astra's* warped Eden, with its multi-racial eco-community and excluded indigenous peoples, I soon realised that I was also writing about myself: a European child playing in Canada's national parks while First Nations people struggled to survive; a quarter Celt with England, Scotland and Ireland crossing swords in her veins; a great-great-granddaughter of the Raj whose interracial family is still a vector for British imperialism, and resistance to it. Both the map of Is-Land and the book's narrative trajectory evolved to reflect these more personal and more international concerns. If *The Gaia Chronicles* is an allegory, it is a multidimensional one, Astra through the looking glass, refracting psychological, personal and political realities through which I attempt, as Goethe urged, to know both myself and many others. For while Astra's eco-fascist world holds Abrahamic religions at arms-length, and nothing in *The Gaia Chronicles* is exactly as it is here, in *Rook Song* and subsequent volumes readers will recognise Muslim, Jewish, Arab Christian, Kurdish, Iranian and other Middle Eastern cultures and religions. The regional languages of Non-Land are Asfarian, Somarian, Karkish, and Farashan, for which, to evoke both the historic and mythical past, I've drawn on Arabic, Sumerian, Aramaic and ancient Persian. Learning about all these cultures is a massive, humbling task. I am taking things slowly, each book reflecting new levels of research and insight.

Take, for example, headscarves. The leader of the Non-Land Alliance, Una Dayyani, is a secular Somarian – Una means 'victory' in ancient Sumerian, Dayyani 'judge' – and doesn't cover, but her Karkish personal assistant Marti does, and encourages Una to do so to win respect in Karkish circles. Appropriating a contemporary emblem of male leadership, Una prefers a gold turban. This is by no means a scenario I could have written a decade ago. I didn't grow up surrounded by women in hijab or niqab, even as a Palestinian solidarity worker in Brighton, I don't see them frequently, and without knowing anyone who wore it, for years I felt uneasy about both garments, let alone the burqa. When I visited Dubai in 2001, staying with a New Zealander EFL teacher and reading Tarot cards to her friends in her flat, I was seriously discomforted by the niqab worn by the market stallholders: with its copper nose shield it seemed to me like a cage. Perhaps that reaction is a form of Islamophobia, but in my defence covering is a hot debate topic between Muslim feminists, and I had never generalised my qualms into any kind of ultimate dismissal of Islam – my feminist criticisms of Christianity were far stronger. And rather than feeling hostile to women who covered, I was angry at the double standard: if covering the face, in particular, was a sign of immense piety, I thought, why shouldn't male Muslims, especially those in positions of spiritual authority do it? With this resentful mindset, I couldn't even see the hijab in an entirely positive light.

Orhan Pamuk's *Snow* first began to convert me to pro-covering arguments, but it was my ten days in Egypt that completely transformed my attitude toward headscarves. Surrounded by Egyptian women in hijab I saw within a day both the euro-centricity of my discomfort – Western women generally cover our chests, after all, while men are free to go topless – and the charm and versatility of the garment: by the end of my visit I was asking a young woman in the all-female subway car to show me how to wrap my new pashmina like hers – perhaps a frivolous request, but she seemed delighted to oblige. Now, though I think it is important to see a person's face in certain situations – trials, for example – I understand that choosing to cover is a powerful way to express identity and faith, and strongly believe that when Westerners narrowly focus debate about Islam on women's dress we demean women's choices and disrespect a different cultural and spiritual tradition. Muslim women themselves are best placed to debate and improve the position of women in Islam. And surely non-Muslims can find ways to relate to the garments and customs not so far from our own? Now, reading Nnedi Okorafor, whose Afrofuturist novels feature young West African heroines moving between Muslim and magico-shamanic traditions, I can smile at her depiction of the burqa as an invisibility cloak. I think back too, to my Liverpool friend Safia. Whether because her family were Christian, or in an act of inclusivity and respect for the brown skins of the Biblical characters, she was chosen to play Mary in our school nativity, and this year when the Facebook meme 'Mary wore hijab' circulated, I fondly recalled the photograph of her in a blue headdress and robe holding the baby doll Jesus.

Overall, I try to read widely. From Shereen El Feki's *Sex and the Citadel* I learned about temporary marriage – a phrase I had heard in the context of refugee camps and had thought a euphemism for prostitution or sex slavery. It was a revelation to learn that it is in fact a sanctioned practice in Shia Islam, and though often abused, can also be beneficial to women. The *Syria* issue of *Critical Muslim*, the *Syria Speaks* anthology, news articles about the toxic waste afflicting Gaza and Fallujah, have kept me close to the multiple horrors perpetuated in Middle East, seemingly ever-escalating violence that haunts *The Gaia Chronicles*; at the same time articles on Islamic environmentalism encourage me to continue imagining a future that draws on Muslim and other traditional wisdoms. I'm still at the start of my journey into Islamic SF, indeed SF; on the whole I relate more strongly to hybrid genres, such as employed by Emil Habiby in his autobiographical fantasy *Saraya:The Ogre's Daughter*. But that means there is much to look forward to. Reading Yusuf Nuruddin discuss Ishmael Reed's *The Earth Chronicles*, it intrigued me to learn that my novels converse with that sprawling classic of urban American resistance literature. More than SF, though, right now I feel that I need to acquaint myself with Islam itself. And the more I read about the religion, here in *Critical Muslim*, in essays by Ziauddin Sardar, in Attar's spry urgings, the more beauty I find in it. I can't imagine converting, but perhaps in literature there is room for a non-Abrahamite to enter into Islam's conceptual space.

It's not enough, though, just to write. Writing from the comfort and safety of a Brighton flat about an uprising of disabled people in a futuristic Middle East, is a privilege that must be earned by work to challenge injustice and alleviate immediate suffering. Though writing novels to deadlines is time-intensive (and so far not wildly lucrative), I engage in as much political activity as I can. Activism also keeps me in touch with informed and sympathetic readers, leading to deeper discussions of the issues I am grappling with, greater leaps in my learning and renewed confidence in my project. My desire to create a Palestinian bibliography for British Writers in Support of Palestine (BWISP), for example, led me to Andy Simons, who while at the British Library contributed a magnificent article on Muslim jazz to *CM2*. Simons invited me to appear at the 2014 Tottenham Palestine Literature Festival. There, my panel discussion on Middle Eastern SFF with Rebecca Hankins (AKA Ruqayyah Kareem) and Yasmin Khan, producer of Sindbad Sci-Fi, led directly to this article while Yasmin's enthusiasm for my project got me dreaming of launching an Islamic steampunk novel at Brighton Pavilion…

I must be clear, though. I'm not setting myself the task of imagining a future for Islam – that would be arrogant and absurd. What I'm trying to do is appreciate and share Muslim culture and ideas, to educate myself and others. I am also writing fiction, not a manifesto. As fiction the novels dramatise conflict, violence and sex. My treatment of these themes make some non-Muslims uncomfortable, and the more I engage with Islamic tropes, the more I may risk offending Muslims too. That is certainly not something I intend. When I write about sex or horror I am not aiming to offend anyone. I am simply trying to present my characters as fully embodied human beings living in a world that is often violent and confusing. *Je ne suis pas Charlie*, though: I would never intentionally disrespect the Prophet. As has been argued, post-Paris, by Ziauddin Sardar and Yasmin Alibhai Brown, among other media commentators, what needs to be criticised in Islam is not the love of Muslims for Mohammed, but the abuse, distortion and manipulation of the Qur'an by power-hungry clerics, and the resultant suspicion of free thinking amongst Western Muslims as much as any other. I hope this essay conveys my excitement about my own on-going engagement with Islam. While the challenge of representing diverse global communities is immense, it feels to me that social inclusivity is one of the most important goals of our times. Silken, rocky, thorny, paved in gold or tar – our paths all cross, and beneath us the Earth is dangerously rumbling. If we are to avoid unparalleled destruction, new frameworks of knowledge must emerge, capacious and flexible enough to hold us all while respecting our differences, pragmatic and yet visionary enough to help us jointly solve the challenges we face as a species on a planet with a finite capacity to sustain us. I don't know if

Occident and Orient can become 'one', or if that is even a desirable outcome; it is my perhaps wild dream, however, that science fiction can help us envision a better future than the one to which our current global leaders are steering us, one in which humanity's collective wisdom becomes the wellspring of our moral and social evolution.

BELLS

Cheli Duran

Epimenidis opened one eye. In the flickering light of the oil lamp, a giant hand holding a needle as long as a sword crossed and recrossed the wall. Diamanda was sewing something into her mattress. The shadow grew smaller and disappeared as he drifted back to sleep.

When Epimenidis next woke up, it was dawn, and across the room the maid was waking his twin. He burrowed under the quilt. His turn came: Diamanda's cold, chapped hand passed gently over his face. 'Come, get up', she whispered. Then she was gone. His ear caught only the creak of the stairs and the click of the door at the bottom as it was unlatched.

Epimenidis struggled into his school clothes, and went out on the landing.

Diamanda had opened the shutters and lit the lantern. Both carnival costumes, their seams tacked, were neatly folded over the back of a chair – his twin's frilled and flounced blue satin gown and his black and white pantaloons, white tunic, ruff and conical hat. Epimenidis searched among the scraps by the sewing machine till his touch set off a faint jingle. Carefully, he drew out five little bells. In the bedroom, his twin had flopped back to sleep. Epimenidis climbed on the chair and managed, by stretching, to place the bells on top of the wardrobe, which was dusted only at Easter. A bell rolled, tinkling, almost to the edge.

He climbed down, and prodded his twin. 'Wake up.'

Sophia sat up, blinking. 'I heard bells.'

'No, you dreamt them.'

'Why won't Mama let me have bells on my gown?'

'Princesses wear jewels, not bells.'

Sophia let out a sigh.

Epimenidis returned to the landing. He was arranging blue and white scraps into a miniature flag when Diamanda ran up the stairs

'You leave that alone!'

Her hands were at his ribs, tucking in his shirt, then lower, buttoning his trousers. Epimenidis leaned against her to breathe in her smell of lemon and wood smoke.

'Stand up straight! I'm not a pillow.' Diamanda pushed him away, and went into the bedroom. Epimenidis heard her ask his twin why she had such a long face.

'I want bells on my costume, like Epimenidis.'

'Want. Want. Sit up... No one helped me to dress at your age.'

'Just a few bells...'

Epimenidis opened the window, and leant out. The sky was grey and starless. Down the street a rooster crowed, and the cry was echoed by other roosters from street to street, each time fainter. Epimenidis let out little breaths of mist. From his perch, he could see the snow-covered mountains. Round the corner, the first pedlar of the day called out, 'oil for your lamps, fine oooooil...'

Diamanda's arms pulled him back. 'You'll fall!'

'It won't rain, will it?'

'How would I know? I'm not a newspaper!' She shut the window.

From the master bedroom came a creaking of bedsprings and floorboards. The door opened. Epimenidis caught a glimpse of his mother pinning up her thick dark braid. His father emerged, patted him on the head, and went downstairs.

A muffled clang. From the bedroom his mother called, 'Diamanda! The gate!'

Diamanda had another voice for his mother: like a child's. 'At once, Kyria!'

Epimenidis ran downstairs after her. His father had lit the lantern over the outhouse door and it cast wavering shadows on the walls. You never knew who might be at the gate – the pots-and-pans peddlar, an Egyptian selling fish, or a relative from Diamanda's village with mountain greens and fresh cheese.

But it was only the old seamstress, in her faded mourning, come to finish the carnival costumes. She limped in, grumbling about the cold and a Turk from the market whose barrow had almost knocked her down.

'Soon there won't be a Turk on the island,' said Diamanda.

The seamstress crossed herself three times and went into the sitting room.

A pale light, filtered between branches of the lemon tree, entered the tiny kitchen. Epimenidis submitted to having his face scrubbed at the sink, then lingered to warm his chilblained hands.

The outhouse door creaked, and he ran out.

His father went to work early while it was still dark and had his morning coffee brought to him at the shop. Epimenidis often rushed out after him, wailing, 'Baba, don't go!'. Then Diamanda would give chase and drag him back and his mother would box his ears. Sometimes Epimenides would cling to the gate shouting whatever he thought might make his father return: 'Baba, you forgot your watch!' 'Baba, you forgot your handkerchief!...'

But the gate shut before he could reach it. Epimenidis went upstairs and worked on his Greek flag: the blue of his twin's ballgown was just the right colour.

'Epimenidis? Come eat!'

Epimenidis clattered downstairs, two steps down, one step up, and jumped the last two.

'...to look at the corpse,' the old seamstress was saying, hunched over her cup and saucer at the table. 'Nobody knows who he is.'

'Because he's dressed up for carnival?' asked Sophia.

'Eh? What does the girl mean? Why would anyone dress up to die?'

'Who? Who?' asked Epimenidis, his heart beating fast. He sat down.

'The man who shot himself,' said the seamstress.

'Mama, I want bells,' burst out Sophia. 'Epimenidis has bells!'

'That's enough from you...' said Mama. 'In the centre of town, and no one recognises him! Lord, remember me!' She crossed herself.

'Someone must know him,' said Epimenidis.

'The police told me they made the rounds of the refugee camps,' said the seamstress. She had only two teeth left, long, yellow and askew. 'No one is missing.'

'God must know his name!' cried Epimenidis. 'God knows everything!'

'It's a sin to kill yourself,' said Mama in a stern voice.

Diamanda's eyes were on Epimenidis' cheese, untouched on his plate.

'Stop sniffling, Sophia! Princesses don't wear bells... Why, the boy's eaten nothing!' Mama felt Epimenides' forehead. 'Are you ill?'

'I'm not hungry.'

Mama took his piece of cheese and ate it.

God could see everything, even the top of a wardrobe. Epimenidis rose from the table, grabbed his schoolbag and darted outside. The cathedral bell broke into a loud peal as his twin and Diamanda caught up with him.

Sophia was still redeyed.

'We'll go my way,' Epimenidis said. 'You can choose coming home.'

'No! Your way takes forever!' His twin loved shop windows. There were no shops on the artist's street.

'I'll draw you if you let me have your turn.'

'But you always make me look ugly. You make me look like you!'

'And if I give you blond hair?'

Sophia dabbed at her eyes. 'With curls?'

'Children, we'll be late.' Diamanda was impatient.

'Blond curls – and a blue bow.' Epimenidis knew how to get round his twin.

The artist's studio was behind the cathedral of St Minas in a street so narrow the upper stories of the wooden buildings almost touched. On their first day of school, Epimenidis had run ahead and stopped short at an open window where a small, bald man was painting a sunset. Epimenidis, on tiptoes, had followed the paintbrush as it turned the horizon to gold and spilled green and orange over a dark, swirling sea.

That first morning of school had passed in a daze. At lunch, Epimenidis had begged his father to buy him a set of paints....

Today he was in luck. The shutters were unlatched, and the studio was empty. Propped on the easel was a half finished canvas. The sky was dark and wild. A hazy, shrouded moon lit a ship that was sinking in the waves. On the prow one tiny figure was about to be engulfed in a surge of foam; another, on his knees, was embracing the broken mast; a third, his arms flung wide in despair, was staring down into the still unpainted depths.

Sophia tugged at his arm.

'Those sailors – they'll drown!' she whispered.

'No, a ship will come by and save them.'

'There's no room for another ship.'

'Children, we're late,' said Diamanda. But her eyes were on the ship.

'Of course, there's room!' cried Epimenidis.

Overhead, in the sky, a seagull drifted like a scrap of confetti. An artist could lighten or darken his work He could paint a ship sailing to the rescue. Epimenidis did not want to be a goldsmith like his father or a raisin merchant like his uncle. He would be an artist.

Diamanda dragged him away.

When they reached the school yard, the school bell was ringing. Sophia joined the line of girls. Epimenidis hung back, frightened.

'Let me stay with you, Diamanda,' he asked in a low voice.

'What – and miss school?'

'Please?' His voice rose.

Diamanda whispered, 'I'm going to view the corpse. She turned away.

Epimenidis shuffled after the other boys. In his dream, flames had shuttered the schoolroom windows, turning everything orange, while the teacher went on pointing at words on the blackboard that Epimenides could not understand. Then the door had fallen in with a bang, and his classmates were swallowed by the thick smoke. Their voices had grown fainter and fainter…

A classmate joined him. 'I'm going to dress up as a prince. And you?'

'As a pierrot,' said Epimenidis in a sad voice.

From the door of the classroom, Sophia called, just like a teacher: 'Boys! You're late!'

Gusts of salt wind from the harbour swept round the yard. Sophia, wrapped in an old shawl, sat on a stool under the lemon tree, instructing her pupils, which were three flowerpots and a faded cushion that had lost most of its stuffing. The cushion was her best pupil because you could smack it. She had a slate, a piece of chalk and a long rod. Indoors there was nowhere to play. Diamanda had driven her out of the sitting room where the table was laid for lunch, and upstairs her mother and the seamstress were busy with the costumes.

Sophia prodded the cushion. 'Now you do that sum again!'

Diamanda said it wasn't Sophia's fault – that when the three Fates knocked at the door on the day the twins were born in February, 1916, they must have heard only one baby crying. And that was why they had showered all their blessings on Epimenidis. Except for looks. Diamanda said the Fates had forgotten both twins when it came to looks.

Sophia was sure she would look much prettier if she wore spectacles, like her teacher. She prayed for spectacles.

Epimenidis ran into the yard, brandishing a stick. 'Sophia! Come be the enemy – just till lunch!'

'No,' said Sophia. She was not going to play an ancient Persian again. She always got her dress dirty when she died on the cobbles.

'She won't play?' That was Andonis' voice.

'Who cares! We'll fight the wind!' cried Epimenidis, and ran off.

Sophia went to the gate. How could you fight what you couldn't see? Epimenidis was slashing the air right and left, while the other boys cheered him on. And it wasn't windy.

She looked down the street and shrank back. 'Titos, your uncle!'

Epimenidis lowered his stick. The other boys fell silent.

Titos' uncle had arrived the week before on a hospital ship full of wounded soldiers from Smyrna. He had a bad limp, and the war had done something to his throat. 'That's right, play!' he got out in a rattling whisper.

No one moved till he turned the corner.

'My father says that was a lie your uncle told us – that our soldiers set fire to a Turkish school and all the children were burnt!' Epimenidis burst out.

'It was not a lie! My uncle was there,' said Titos.

'They were only Turkish children,' said Andonis quickly.

'But they couldn't get out! They died!' shouted Epimenidis.

'Then how could my uncle have saved them?' cried Titos.

'Epimenides' father makes his money buying gold rings cheap from the refugees!' Andonis said.

'That's because he wants to help them!' Sophia called out.

'Help them?' Andonis bellowed. 'Help them?'

Epimenidis threw down his stick and charged Andonis, who fell backwards with a soft thud like a pillow. Sophia clasped her hands in despair. Although her twin was small and thin for his age, he was a fury when he lost his temper. Nikos and Titos each grabbed a leg and tried to pull him off.

Sophia ran to the kitchen door. 'Epimenidis – fighting!'

Diamanda, her hands dripping suds, rushed out.

Sophia sat down, picked up her rod, and stared at the cobbles. She heard a couple of loud slaps as her twin, screaming that Greeks would never burn little children, was dragged into the house. When she looked up, the gate was still open and the street deserted. She went rigid with fear. What good was her rod if a stray dog entered? Sophia thought of the man who had shot himself during the night, and crossed herself three times. Baba said the Turks would never again rule Crete, but how could he be sure? In Smyrna the Turks had entered a cemetery where little Greek girls were hiding and pulled them out of the tombs and cut them into tiny pieces, that's what the teacher had told them at school, and teachers always told the truth. Sophia saw herself waiting in the tomb... She heard the sound of her own breathing....

Diamanda crossed the yard and shut the gate. 'The princess was too lazy to shut it?'

'That's your job,' murmured Sophia. She wrote busily on her slate.

'At your age I was herding goats.' Diamanda sat down hard on Sophia's favourite pupil.

Sophia tried to pull the cushion away.

But Diamanda would not budge. 'If you teach me how to write, I'll give you a present.'

Some months back, a street vendor had passed the house, pushing a cart that glittered with spectacles of all shapes and sizes. Diamanda was poor and had to save money for her dowry, or no one would marry her. Diamanda could never afford to buy her spectacles.

'Get Epimenidis to teach you,' said Sophia.

'He's too impatient. Start with my name.'

'No, you must learn the alphabet,' said Sophia. She wrote an 'A' on her slate and frowned. Her letters were not as good as her twin's.

Diamanda painstakingly copied the letter. Sophia studied it at arm's length. 'It's crooked. Rub it out and try again,' she ordered, and passed it back.

'Diamanda!' Mama had opened the landing window. 'Up here! Now!'

The slate fell out of Diamanda's hand and broke in two. With a frightened glance, she ran inside.

Sophia picked up the fragments, hid them behind a flower pot, and crept to the foot of the stairs to listen. At the far end of the sitting room, Epimenidis was drawing.

'...you lie to me!' her mother was saying.

'Kyria, why would I want bells?' Diamanda broke into sobs.

'One word to your father, and it's back to the village with you. If you think I don't have eyes to see how the cheese vanishes between the moment I unlock the cupboard and...'

'Sophia took the bells!' cried Diamanda.

Sophia could not think where to hide herself.

'Sophia, come here!'

Sophia climbed the stairs slowly, one step at a time. She was grabbed and shaken. The landing was a blur of light through her tears.

'A thief, are you?'

Sophia felt she would choke in her mother's smell of milk and wool. 'I only took a... a... one or two.... Two.'

'Where are they?' Her mother shook her again.

'In my... my... schoolbag down... stairs.'

'Your father will be very angry!'

'But, Mama, Epimenidis... Epimenidis took more than....'

'Epimenidis!' Her mother clattered downstairs.

'Truth and a cough will out,' mumbled the seamstress bent over the machine

Sophia wanted to run after her mother, but Diamanda held her back.

The seamstress glanced up. 'I never had a costume.' She twirled the wheel. 'We were too poor even to buy confetti. Bean husks... that's what we tossed at masqueraders.'

'Well, their father didn't want them to dress up this year,' said Diamanda. 'He said they should think of the poor refugees without a rag to their backs, but their mother...'

'It's not the children's fault that we lost the war,' said the seamstress.

Sophia heard what sounded like a hard slap and a scream. Her eyes swam with tears. It was all her fault that Epimenidis was being punished.

'Diamanda! The baker's lad has brought the roast!'

Diamanda ran downstairs. Sophia stole over to the basket where her baby brother lay asleep, and touched the blue glass charm pinned to his swaddling.

A moment later Epimenidis appeared and grinned at her. He shook his fists with a jingle, then opened them.

'The bells the two of you pinched, eh?' said the old seamstress, peering at him. 'Well, children are children. Put them with the others.' She bent over the ruff again.

Epimenidis added them to the pile on the table, then spun round, took a step forward and opened his fists again. Sophia stared, bewildered. He still had four bells.

The gate clanged.

'Your father,' murmured the seamstress. 'Lunch!' She rolled the stray threads into a ball, folded a scrap to make a tiny pouch, emptied the bells into it without counting them and tied it with a length of trimming.

Epimenidis, his hands in his pockets, darted into their bedroom.

Sophia started downstairs.

Epimenidis caught up with her on the third step. 'I hid them,' he whispered.

'But Mama...'

'She won't count them again.'

'Children, it's lunchtime. Do you want me to trip over you?' cried the seamstress.

'You'll get into trouble,' whispered Sophia.

'Why did you take them then?'

'I was going to put them back. But you?'

'Children, just let me by.'

Sophia flattened herself against the wall so the seamstress could pass.

'You said you wanted bells,' hissed Epimenidis.

'You took them... for me?' Sophia was touched. She loved him more than anyone, but he had always treated her like an ordinary sister, never like a twin.

At last they shared a secret, as twins should.

It was Carnival Thursday. The war in Asia Minor was over, and soon all the Greeks stranded in Turkey would return to their homeland and all the

Turks in Greece would return to theirs. Late that afternoon, after she and Epimenidis had shown off their costumes at her father's shop and visited their aunt and uncle, they would be served little pastries soaked in syrup. And then she would go up to bed, knowing that somewhere in the dark, cold room there were four gold bells, waiting for her.

Her father muttered grace and her mother began serving up the holiday roast.

'Well, Kyra Philitsa, what's the news?' asked her father.

'The American Red Cross is going to distribute beans and lard to the refugees tomorrow,' said the old seamstress.

Sophia wondered who would get the dead man's ration. 'Was he a refugee?' she asked her father.

'Who?' asked her father.

'The man who killed himself last night.'

'What put that in your head? No one knows.'

'But why does no one know?'

'Child, he might have lost his whole family.'

Sophia couldn't imagine losing her family. She would try to be good so God would keep them safe. Mama was always saying that twins should look after each other.

Epimenidis wrote his name and the date in a corner of his blank piece of paper: E. Matthioudakis, January, 1923. Across from him, Sophia struggled with her sums. The afternoon was chilly, but braziers were banned in the house because the fumes had made her faint as a baby. At the other end of the table, Diamanda was ironing the carnival costumes over a folded blanket. From the flatiron came a little waft of wood-smoke.

'You'll be the envy of the other boys,' murmured Diamanda.

Epimenidis looked up. 'Next year I'll dress as a soldier.'

'A soldier? Soldiers don't cry.'

Epimenidis scowled. 'I'm strong. I'm brave.'

'Are you! Remember that porter your father asked to teach you a lesson?'

Epimenidis drew a schoolhouse in the foreground.

'No? You'd been teasing your poor twin and getting underfoot all day.' Diamanda sprinkled water on the blue bodice. 'There was a thunder of a knock at the door...'

Epimenidis' pencil scribbled flames round the schoolhouse.

'... and there stood that cross-eyed giant from the market, roaring...' Diamanda raised her voice... '"I've come for the bad boy!" And you... ' she giggled... 'leapt into your mother's arms like a monkey, screeching, "I'll be good, Mama, I'll be good!" Oh, how we laughed!'

'They'll send that porter back to Turkey next month,' said Epimenidis. His pencil covered the schoolhouse windows with ivy. He hated Diamanda.

'I didn't laugh,' Sophia whispered.

Epimenidis pencilled the fire out. But when he turned the piece of paper over, the outline of the flames showed through...

Diamanda had only managed to peek at the old man who had killed himself, she said, the queue was so long. It was awful, his skin had gone grey, almost yellow. Thank the Lord he was no one she knew which meant she wouldn't have to mourn him. People had left her village and never returned. But after viewing the body, she had felt lighter. That was life. Everyone died. Everyone....

Epimenidis turned the paper round. 'Sophia! I'll draw you!'

Sophia sat up straight.

Epimenidis held his pencil at arm's length and closed one eye as he had seen the artist do, but this made Sophia look like the little owl that tumbled out of the lemon tree one night. He drew a long nose and round eyes, then rubbed them out with a bit of bread and started again. This time he gave his twin an oval face, a nose so tiny that it was just two dots and a small, full mouth like the one on the biscuit tin in the cupboard. Sophia had straight, dark, fine hair like a baby's, Epimenidis scribbled a mass of pencilled curls that hid the flames.

Sophia peered across. 'You said you'd give me blond hair!'

'No painting while I iron,' snapped Diamanda.

Epimenidis shut his box of box of colours.

'That's the gate!' Diamanda set the iron down, and ran out.

Epimenidis looked out the window. 'It's the priest from Diamanda's village. And her widowed aunt, oh! and the little girl, the one who can't talk.'

Mama's voice floated down through the floorboards. 'I'll be right down.'

Epimenidis watched Diamanda kneel to kiss the priest's hand, then hug her aunt and the little girl with the wide nose who moaned and dribbled.

Epimenidis had once accompanied Diamanda to her aunt's shack on the city walls. Diamanda had bought boiled sweets for the little girl because it was her name day, and the little girl had laughed and clapped her hands and Diamanda had laughed, and the floor was packed dirt, like the ones in village houses, and the tin mug he had drunk water from had not been very clean.

'You know why the girl can't talk?' whispered Sophia. 'The Three Fates cast a spell over her. Diamanda says some day a word could untie the knot.'

Their mother came bustling downstairs with the baby and led the visitors into the best room. Though it had been aired, it always smelled damp. Epimenidis never felt comfortable in the best room.

The visitors sat down stiffly. Epimenidis sat opposite, so he could gaze past them at the treasures in the glass-fronted cabinet, at the gold-embroidered cloth, the tiny silver icon from St Catherine of Sinai, the dish with Prince George's image, the silver tray.... The priest gave off wafts of goat cheese and sweat, and his eyes seemed to go right through you.

Diamanda served coffee in the little gold-rimmed cups kept for company and brought a platter of fresh cheese pastries swimming in syrup. Epimenidis' mother served two to the priest, two to the little girl's mother, and two to Diamanda, whose mouth fell open as if she couldn't believe her luck. The twins had half a pastry each, served on the same plate.

Sophia's eyes pleaded with his.

'Mama, Sophia and I want a whole pastry,' whispered Epimenidis.

'You'll be eating sweets at your aunt's later.' From his mother's voice, Epimenidis knew there was no point arguing. He ate his portion in tiny mouthfuls, to make it last.

The grown-ups talked about the war. The priest said the few Turkish families in his village were desolate at being forced to leave their homes, but the law was the law. The priest wondered whether the Kyria's husband might consider buying some of the land owned by the Turks. The miller might lease it. Perhaps the Kyria would speak to her husband. Diamanda's aunt said Greek refugees were already constructing makeshift shelters on the city walls, she could hardly see Mt Ida anymore, so who knew what they would get up to in the village.

The little girl played with the buttons on her dress while Diamanda fed her.

Epimenidis ran to the ironing board, and brought back his tunic, shaking it to make the bells ring.

'What are you doing? Your hands are sticky!' cried Mama.

'Bells to chase away evil spirits, eh?' said the priest.

Epimenidis tossed the tunic in the air. The little girl gasped, and reached out.

'Did you hear me?' Mama rose.

Epimenidis twirled, jangling the bells, and stopped short.

'B-b-b... B-b-b..' Holding on to the table, the little girl took a few steps.

'She's trying to talk!' Diamanda whispered, and crossed herself. 'Say "bells", Maria!'

'B-b-bell... B-b-bell...' The little girl stretched out her hand.

'Oh, Virgin Mary, a miracle!' cried Diamanda's aunt. 'The child's talking! She said "bells"!' The aunt bent down, kissed the girl and rocked her back and forth.

The priest made the sign of the cross and began to pray. He said it was an omen, that perhaps the church bell of the village would finally come to light.

Epimenidis had heard the story, how over a hundred years earlier the villagers had buried the church bell to keep it from being melted down by the Janissaries, and now no one knew where it was hidden. Epimenidis dug around for it every time he was taken to the village, but the soil was hard and he never picked the right spot.

Mama told Diamanda to dress the twins for carnival, it was late. They must wear woollen vests under their costumes. Epimenidis kissed the priest's hand, submitted to being kissed by the aunt, then followed Diamanda. He liked to jump up one step to the next, it made the staircase shake. His father said an earthquake could topple a whole city in a few seconds, but how could their house suddenly fall down when the walls were so thick? He thought of the hundreds of refugees camping out in tents. He thought of the man who had shot himself, and tried to jump two steps.

'Stop that!' said Diamanda, but her voice was calm.

If he kept his pocketknife, paints and pad in his satchel near the door, he could grab it and run out at the first tremor.

The wind from the harbour tugged at Diamanda's shawl, whipped Sophia's flounces and jingled the bells on his tunic. Epimenidis danced round them.

'The wind is a shepherd!' he cried, butting at Diamanda.

'Well, I'm not a sheep!' Diamanda pushed him away.

'That's my foot you're stepping on,' wailed Sophia. The holes in the mask were further apart than her eyes so she could hardly what was in front of her. When she looked back at the harbour, all she saw were lines of white froth in the dark.

Along the way they stopped to buy two packets of confetti off a pedlar. Sophia chose pink, blue and yellow. Epimenidis bought red confetti and tossed some over Diamanda.

'Don't complain when you've none left,' said Diamanda, brushing herself off.

Just before the main square, they ran into their father's friend, the notary public, who said he could not imagine who they were and recited a lot of silly names that weren't theirs. He said something under his breath to Diamanda that made her blush. As soon as they walked up the street, Diamanda got the giggles.

'Why are you laughing?' asked Sophia.

'You're the one that goes to school. You should know all the answers.'

A hurdy-gurdy was churning out snatches of song in the square. Children in masquerade drifted by. Sophia saw a boy dressed like a Pierrot and counted his bells. 'Only ten,' she said.

'No one, no one, no one has... as many... bells... as me!' cried Epimenidis.

All round the Morosini fountain people were celebrating. Diamanda held on to Epimenidis, so he wouldn't get lost in the crowd. Across the square was the coffee house where the town criers waited to be hired. Sophia felt reassured. If she was separated from her twin, her father would hire a man to shout: 'We've lost a princess in a pale-blue gown with flounces! Has anyone seen a princess in a pale-blue gown with flounces!'

'Did you ever dress up?' she asked Diamanda.

'In our village, it's the men who dress up. The wind blows and we roast chestnuts and potatoes on the stove, and suddenly bang! the door bursts open, oh... you'd wet yourself laughing if you saw my brother-in-law with bosoms squeezed into my sister's dress.' Diamanda's voice sank.

'You don't wish you were there,' said Sophia with firmness. 'You don't want to work in the fields all day.'

'Why not? My prince will find me even in a barley field.'

But Sophia knew a prince would never find Diamanda's village. Only shepherds and sheep rustlers knew where it was. Every summer Mama sent them off with Diamanda for almost a month, to fill them out, she said. It was a tiny village on a ledge, so dry and rocky and sunbaked that you didn't see it until you were there. The wind blew and blew. It howled over the windmill and round the church tower and into Diamanda's home near the edge of the cliff. Epimenidis filled his pockets with stones, so he wouldn't be blown across the sea to Turkey. Sophia did not want to live in a village. She would marry a schoolteacher, and they would both teach in a big city like Heraklion or Athens and sleep on lace-edged sheets.

In the mirror outside her father's shop, Sophia caught sight of a girl in a flounced blue satin ballgown whose hair was powdered and and piled high. She could not believe she was that girl. It was as if she had stepped out of a book.

Her father was perched on his high stool behind the counter, stringing pearls. Sophia could sit beside him quietly for hours. She loved the cabinets, the high counter of dark polished wood full of shallow drawers, the charms, earrings, chains and bracelets.

'Look! I'm a princess!' she cried.

Her father raised his eyes. 'You'll catch cold, child.'

'She's wearing a woollen vest and I have the mistress's shawl,' said Diamanda.

Behind the counter was another mirror. If Sophia looked into it from the door, she could see outside and yet not seem to be looking. In the mirror the world was the wrong way round, like a dream. Relatives, family friends, schoolmates became strangers. Diamanda's dark eyes stared past her in the mirror, and beyond Diamanda were stalls heaped with winter greens, cabbages, oranges that glowed in the dusk. Butchers waited under huge hanging carcasses. A light hail of coloured confetti pelted the window and floated above the street lamp.

The door was pushed open and their father's brother entered. He paused to stare at Sophia. 'Ah, a princess. Just arrived from Paris to have her diamonds re-set?'

Sophia could not help giggling.

'She's your niece!' cried Epimenidis. He spun to make the bells ring.

His father looked up. 'Diamanda, take the children to my sister-in-law.'

'What a beautiful dress! It'll cheer your poor aunt up to see you,' said their uncle.

Diamanda turned, and her black braids, which she had tied with red thread and wound round her head, caught the light in the mirror.

'Any news?' Sophia heard her father ask their uncle as they left.

'None.'

The door shut behind them, and Sophia, inside the world of the mirror, was once more swept up in the din and cold. Here and there she saw a red fez among the crowds. A group of sailors with red pompoms on their caps strolled by, and one of them winked at Diamanda. Sophia scowled at him, but he took no notice.

Epimenidis asked Diamanda if she thought their aunt's brother was alive.

'There's always hope.'

'Mama said they would have had some news of him by now if he was.'

'Our fate is written,' said Diamanda.

They turned into the street of bellmakers and blacksmiths. Here there were no masqueraders: the only sounds were the ring of hammers and the hiss of red-hot metal dipped in water. One of the soot-covered apprentices called to Diamanda through the sparks: 'And how are you, my lemon tree?'

Diamanda ignored him.

'Would you marry a blacksmith?' Epimenidis whispered.

'What? Sleep between sooty sheets? Not I.' But Diamanda was smiling. Epimenidis danced ahead.

'What's the surprise you'll give me if I teach you?' Sophia asked Diamanda.

Diamanda was silent for a moment. 'My little mirror,' she said.

The mirror, with its cracked frame, was among Diamanda's prized possessions. Sophia could not believe her luck. A mirror, just to teach someone to read and write!

The square beyond the market smelled of smoke, fries and roast chestnuts. Tents raised from worn blankets and sheets had been erected around the half-ruined Church of the Saviour and washing hung from the upper windows. Her father said it was unsafe to house so many families inside a tumbledown building but there was nowhere else to lodge them. Many Asia Minor refugees were camping in caves outside the city walls. Sophia was not sure how she felt about crossing the square in the dark. Though she could hardly see the refugees for the smoke that rose from their wood burners, she felt their eyes on her.

'I'm shivering,' she whispered.

'What, our princess is cold? Here you are.' Diamanda wrapped her up in the shawl.

At the fountain a line of women and girls were waiting to fill their pitchers and basins. Baba said many of them had escaped the flames of Smyrna with only the clothes on their backs. Water from an overflowing pitcher splashed on Sophia's gown, and she backed off to shake her flounces dry. When she next looked up, Diamanda and Epimenidis had vanished. Sophia peered round the fountain and spotted Diamanda talking to a young man.

Sophia ran to her. Diamanda looked startled. Sophia felt a sharp pinch that made her eyes swim, but her mask was so tight that her tears had nowhere to go. She stared at the paving stones, which rippled as if they were underwater. She tried to remove the mask and wipe her cheeks, then remembered they were rouged, Mama would be furious if she got rouge on her sleeves. Diamanda was still talking, but very low.

Sophia could not see her twin anywhere. 'Where's Epimenidis?' she whispered.

Diamanda turned on her. 'Why didn't you keep an eye on him? Epimenidis!' She stood on tiptoe, searching the crowd.

Sophia burst into noisy sobs.

'Don't scold the child,' said the apprentice.

'Epimenidis!' screeched Diamanda. 'Where is the boy? Blessed Virgin!'

'He'll turn up... Oh, there's my master, I'm off.' The apprentice strode off.

Diamanda did not seem to hear him. 'Epimenidis!'

Sophia clutched at Diamanda's skirt so she would not get lost like her twin. But Diamanda shrieked, and broke into a run, and Sophia lost her hold.

'Wait, wait!' she wailed. She tore off her mask, gathered up her flounces and ran after Diamanda. Everyone was bigger and taller, and Sophia was shoved one way and another, till she found herself on the edge of the crowd.

Epimenidis stood alone on the cobbles. His mask dangled from one ear. His tunic was split open, exposing his woollen vest and pale skin. His pointed cap lay at his feet, and his thin, fine hair stuck straight up. He was shivering and looked tiny.

Diamanda flung herself at him. 'What have they done to you?' she shrieked.

Epimenidis opened his mouth but Sophia could not hear a word.

'And you let them!' yelled Diamanda. 'You just stood there and let these Turks steal your bells!' Her voice was piercing.

'But they're not Turks, Diamanda, they're Greeks, like us!' cried Sophia, afraid the refugees might turn on her too.

'Turks!' screamed Diamanda wildly. She tried to pull Epimenidis away but he kicked at her and twisted out of her grasp. All round her, Sophia heard the Greek refugees asking one another what was going on, what had the boy done, who was he, what was happening. Fluttering strips of Epimenidis' costume trailed after him as he tried to escape Diamanda.

'Wait, wait!' cried Sophia. She could hardly see for tears. She remembered the mirror Diamanda had promised her. She would give it to Epimenidis. And she would let him choose the way to school every day. She prayed to the Virgin to protect her.

As she ran, Sophia spotted one of the glittering bells. But she did not dare stop.

THREE POEMS

Ilona Yusuf

retribution
i

prologue

the neighbour's children —

the little girl who sings
sweet voiced with wonder
and her brothers who play cricket
keep dogs feed street cats

today
they are lined up
with two friends and a servant
in front of their alsatian

tied and seated upright
he has their pet parrot
clamped in his jaws —
the open cage
beside him —

snapping over
his mouthful
of feather and bone

…scarlet flash of beak

alarmed squawk
stiff folding flutter of green
cracking wing feathers
vainly outstretching
as the dog
gags to swallow

meanwhile the children
shriek and goad
a rhythmic chant

come blackie, go, yes
come blackie, go

rocking
back and forth
gleeful in
fixated
horror

ii
retribution

monsoon morning

whispers
sibilant electric
along air
heavy with heat
and damp

thieves thieves
dacoits
we are
robbed looted
destroyed

lost lost
after them

space tightens
tight-alleyed houses
spew a crowd

that surges into open ground
whispers swell to shouts

meets
two boys
fresh-bathed
cricket bats
shining oiled
out to play

blood boils
righteous
through mile
on red-coiled mile
pumps air
through muscle
bulging
strength

confluence –
time place
traps two
in a pool of
beating bodies

elation a
high roar at the
satisfying snap of
splintering limb

meeting staff rod stone

spattering faces as
roses flower
on pulped skin

oozing rivulets
pooling dust*

lynching of two boys in the city of Sialkot, 2010

two voices and a postcard from pakistan
i

our land
hallowed pure
by the grace of god
by muslims
for muslims

thanks be to him
our land is a bastion
of our faith
protected by our lord

by the grace of god
all that happens is by his will
if fire and bombing
suicide and death
surround us
it is the work of our enemies
those who envy our faith
so strong
thanks be to him,
most beneficent, most merciful

if sons and daughters
mothers and fathers go hungry
this is by his will
their sufferings will be rewarded
for all that happens is by his will
those who would destroy
our fastness of faith

god forbid
god protect us from evil
those who would speak against our faith
those who would question his decree
those who would speak against us

god forbid
god protect us from evil
must be chastised
for defiling god's own laws

god forbid
we must turn
the sharpened knife
to flesh of their flesh
blood of our blood

ii

that's all there is
television run amok
debris from bomb blasts
scraps of bloodied metal
prostrate bodies
smoke

waves of people
walking

infants the infirm the old
held on their shoulders

and nameless men
muffled to the eyes
machine guns slung
across their arms
like satchels

iii

roadblocks manned by bullet vested policemen
piled sandbags pointed barrels of
safeguarding guns
winding lines of cars and trucks
tight-packed delivery vans
motorcycles the high open jeeps of
booted men in black shirts that say 'no fear'
automatics resting easy
pointed down and out towards us
custodians of smooth convoys
swinging swiftly past

a motorcycle couple
she in a suit that's a green field
strewn with red roses
twirling a single long stemmed red rose
as he wheels round the roundabout
face lifted to the sky

at the roadblock
in the car before me
a young woman in the back seat
leans sideways

with tender grace
touches her cheek
to the face of
the passenger
beside her

untitled

william lipton conquered
the great subcontinent
of india
at the turn of the
twentieth century

tea from his gardens
crossing the umpteen miles
through village past dusty village
boxed on the backs of men

'two paisas for a cup of tea'
hawked at the station
from kettles on pushcarts
'magical beverage!
that cures fatigue and pain'

at truck stops
drivers order
tea and cake

the frontiersman
abandons spiced sweet kava
that washes down fat meat

the buttermilk drinking farmer
grows to the brew

simmered in great cauldrons
milk-thick, sweet

the motorbike family
kids astride the gas tank
the littlest in front
eyes closed tight against
the air stream
have come out after chai
poured milky from a thermos

the cook in the rich man's kitchen
with his simmering saucepan
served to the sundry
staff in his command

begums fling down shopping
for tea! tea!
delicately perfumed
in porcelain cups

it's tea and parley for
generals and functionaries
tycoons and statesmen
partisans and chieftains

hooded gunmen
bonded farmhands

for
youths and children
watching chanting
chanting waiting
watching waiting
chanting

THREE POEMS

Marilyn Hacker

Room

Sudden reflection,
leaf-shadows cast on the shades
the night bus' headlights

the dictionary
open on a Coran stand
notebook and pencils

three in the morning,
noise in the street, parch of thirst
glass of water, sleep

recedes as heart-beats,
decided jurors, pace in
with avid faces.

Chapter

Bending down to gather the scattered Lego
Jan recalled a moment, another childhood,
scooping up a ball in a sunlit courtyard
before her name changed.
Who was she in consonants that her children
mispronounced, or did on the rare occasions
that they tried. Her grandmother used a pet name
almost forgotten.

Hidden child, perpetually a virgin,

learned to make love in an adopted language:
twelve years old, her mother tongue blushed though she herself was a mother.

... But in things

A zinc bucket with roses from last week
infused with sugar-water, fading fast.
The summer solstice is a fortnight past,
light on the cusp of evening is oblique.
A photocopied page in Arabic
graffitied with French/English pencil scrawl,
not a testimony, just a tale
that I can translate better than I speak.
Beside a blue placemat from Monoprix
Le Monde des Livres and the LRB,
an earthenware pitcher from Tripoli.
As in that shop bead-curtained from the street
the statement in a shaft of alien light
questions an object and its history.

Question an object and its history :
this dark red silk scarf, lightweight, lightly shirred,
whose tiny label says that it was made
in Halab. Ordinary luxury
to roam the ancient caravanserai
then everybody's market, where I played
at haggling with a wisecracking, yes, almond-eyed
merchant of twenty whose job-skill was repartee,
and two girl students loitering near the stall
praised me for speaking Arabic at all.
You've read the same damn headlines. Ubi sunt
the multi-coloured silks, the girl students?
The fourteenth-century wooden arcades
burned first. The boy, what choice on fire, what words?

REVIEWS

REVISITING DEOBAND

Iftikhar H. Malik

The madrasa system evolved over the centuries in the early Islamic period. During the Fatimid and Abbasid reigns Muslims felt an earnest demand to seek out critical answers to several new and old questions emerging from philosophy, theology, mysticism and philology. The Sufi, Asha'ari, Mutazilla and Ismaili discourses emerged during this period, as did the various strands within the Sunni and Shia schools of thought. The madrasas were a product of the struggle between legal traditionalism and theological rationalism. They developed more in the spirit of a tutorial tradition with a know-all teacher and a group of committed but immensely deferential students and became the main conduit of ecclesiastic and secular knowledge. Their main purpose was to ensure a continuous supply of clerics to meet the basic needs of community such as leading the prayers and teaching the Qur'an to the future generation. Several madrasas, with established scholars and self-sufficient libraries evolved as residential seminaries often in a charitable sector or with the nod from the sultans. For example, the Seljuk Sultans in Persia and the Asia Minor, the Ghanzanvids in Southwestern Asia, Fatimids in Cairo, the Samanids in Khorasan and the Delhi Sultans in India ensured a proper upkeep of eminent madrasas through the *waqf* system where land grants ensured self-sufficiency to these seminaries. In Konya, Delhi, Lahore, Nishapur, Qairawan, Fez, Isfahan and the Hejaz, madrasas attracted leading scholars and jurists to undertake residential tutoring. Arabic remained the supreme language of instruction, soon to be joined by Persian until the early modern era when religious literati become more receptive to 'vernacular' languages followed by a reluctant exposure to European languages.

The madrasa tradition began to be challenged following the Mongol invasions that led to the further pluralisation of Muslim communities. Theologians such as al-Ghazali (1058–1111) and Ibn Tamayyiah (1263–1328) looked at philosophy and rational theology with suspicion and critical questioning as mere hair-splitting which could have serious consequences for the Muslim community. However the greatest challenge to the Muslim seminary system came from European colonialism that not only exposed the acute structural weaknesses of the land-based empires but also raised serious issues about the exclusive writ and usage of the madrasa system. A grave sense of loss, growing acceptance of Western scholarship and its resultant trajectories in the forms of powerful philological traditions, scientific discoveries, modern judicial and the educational system unleashed a deep sense of insecurity among the Muslim elite. Even at the time of Emperor Aurangzeb (1658–1707), the inefficiencies of 'eastern' knowledge and its institutional frameworks were apparent. But no serious attempts

Ebrahim Moosa, *What is a Madrasa?*, University of North Carolina Press, Chapel Hill; Edinburgh University Press, 2015.

were made, either by the Mughals or the Ottomans or the Safawids to redress imbalances and undertake ameliorative efforts. European printing presses, greater usage of a robust knowledge of geography, western historiography and, most of all, a well-endowed missionary enterprise on the back of an assertive capitalism exposed multiple inherent weaknesses in the venues and output of traditional scholarship. In the Indian Subcontinent, the failure of the Revolt of 1857 propelled the ulama, religious scholars, to launch an emphatic and systematic attempt to reform and re-energise the madrasa tradition. Printed books were introduced, greater use of Urdu was made, and a gradual diversification of the curricula started to feature more prominently. The ulama were compelled to change their erstwhile politics of armed resistance and began using religious instruction and activism as 'politics by other means'.

Madrasas such as Farangi Mahall, created during the reign of Aurangzeb in a house formerly owned by a European (Farangi) in Lucknow, and its future successors such as the madrasas of Deoband and Nadwah, made valuable efforts to meet new challenges – there was much soul searching but, on the whole, their curriculum, remained biased towards the older prescribed texts. In sharp contrast to Syed Ahmed Khan's (1817–1898) Mohammedan Anglo-Oriental College at Aligarh and its modern companions, madrasas have largely remained rooted in the texts and commentaries of the early classical period both in Arabic and Persian though Urdu was adopted as the medium of instruction.

Ebrahim Moosa does not tell us much about the evolution of the madrasa networks in classical Islam. His focus is the madrasa system in the Subcontinent. He spent six years studying at seminaries in India – away from his native South Africa. The book, 'my own complicated life story', is partly personal but largely a sympathetic but no less objective study of the South Asian madrasa system. He focuses only on Deobandi revivalists and admits that he is not covering Tablighi, Brelvi, Sufi and Shia seminaries. The madrasa he deals with include Deoband, Farangi Mahall and Nadwah, which came into being during the nineteenth century. Moosa visited these madrasas and some of their branches in Pakistan between 2004 and 2007, and studied their curriculum, traditional tutoring system and overall attitudes towards modern education including the growing demands for female madrasas. His insider-outsider comments on this age-old tradition avoid being totally judgemental, though towards the end of his volume he invites his former teachers at these seminaries to rise to the dire challenges of the multi-directional assault on the entire madrasa tradition since 9/11. The treatise is a homecoming for someone who taught at Duke and now teaches at Notre Dame University. It offers copious details on the traditional texts used in these madrasas while avoiding unnecessary negativity towards the syllabus, which has sadly become the hallmark of rushed works often penned by Western scholars, or Muslim researchers working for Euro-American think tanks. Moosa is annoyed by the stigmatisation of madrasas which he sees as a 'larger post-Cold War security firewall erected against Islamdom'.

His initiation into madrasa education began in apartheid-infested South Africa. During his school days a class fellow, who was a Jehovah's Witness, tried to insinuate that the prophet of Islam was an imposter who had allegedly borrowed his precepts from the other Abrahamic traditions. The school library only contained books on Islam by authors such as William Muir and Montgomery Watt with their own specific slants. An encounter with the local Tablighi Jamaat intensified his urge to gain Islamic knowledge within a traditional Muslim locale. Thus began his journey to Gujarat, which then took him to Deoband after a sojourn at Bangalore, and subsequently to Nadwah in Lucknow. He was deeply impressed by the scholarly commitment of Deobandi luminaries such as Sheikh Mahmud Hasan (d.1920), Ubaidullah Sindhi (d. 1944), and Husain Ahmad Madani (d. 1957) and admired their anti-colonialism in the tradition of their great spiritual mentor, Shah Wali Allah (1703–1762). Despite his devotion to Nizamuddin (1677–1748), the founder of Nizamia syllabus taught at all these seminaries, Moosa idealises Nadwah, perhaps because in its original incarnation in 1899, Nadwah aimed at synthesising Islamic and Western scholarly traditions.

Moosa discovers a greater sense of continuity at all these institutions with even more funds, students and technical facilities. Yet he desires some vital changes in what they teach and how they teach. Despite their historic and ongoing significant role in preserving and transferring classical knowledge of Islam, he sees them as isolated islands dotting the entire South Asian expanse. One gathers an impression that he is quite reticent in evaluating the work, thought and pursuits of his former teachers. Perhaps it is due to the traditional adab, the student-teacher relationship, he acquired from his madrasa education. However, without spelling it out clearly, Moosa does detect 'china walls' around this prestigious system. They need to be more self-critical, he suggests; and not just as a defence mechanism to forestall accusations as incubators of militancy. He has no problems with the quality and devotion of the teachers and pupils, who are there out of genuine commitment, yet finds their curriculum and emphasis out of step with the times. He highlights the need for knowledge of Islam which is geared towards moral regeneration. Despite the apparent tensions between Sufism and Sunni puritanism as epitomised by the Deobandis, he sees a consensus among these scholars to foster social change and usher in political activism. 'Deobandi piety', he writes, 'can range from the cerebral and intellectually stunning version of Ashraaf 'Ali Thanvi's Sufi teaching and Muhammad Ilyas's model of popular Sufi piety in order to advance social reforms in the guise of the Tabligh Movement to the politically active Deobandi scholars who joined Mahatma Gandhi in a nonviolent anticolonial struggle against British colonialism'.

The most vivid section of his study is devoted to the texts studied at these madrasas. South Asian madrasa students learn and debate texts written during the early period in Egypt, Spain, Persia and Greater Syria as prescribed by Nizamuddin. They study the Arabic primer by Abul Ikhlas Shurrunbulali (d.1659), an Egyptian jurist, and _Guide to Wisdom_ by Athir al-Din al-Ahbari (d. 1263), both supplemented by *Commentary on the Guide to Wisdom* by Husayn al-Maybudhi (1408–1504). The latter was a Persian scholar who lived near Yazd and because of his Sunni teachings faced Safawid wrath. Other noted volumes would include *The Ladder* by an Indian scholar, Fazl-i-Imam Khairabadi (d.1829), and classical works on Arabic grammar by Sibawayhi (d.796), and by Abul Qasim Mahmud al-Zamakshari (d. 1144). Another prized author is Sayyid Sharif al-Jurjani (d. 1413), who was the intellectual ancestor of Nizamuddin's own father, Qutbuddin, whose scholarship was duly acknowledged by Aurangzeb. Certainly, these classical works reaffirm a greater sense of Islam's intellectual internationalism since the authors belonged to various parts of the Muslim world. Moosa asserts that 'the contemporary South Asian madrasa retains some features of an ancient scholastic tradition that blurs the role of a master-teacher, embraces didactic texts, fosters hermeneutical skills, and impart core of knowledge of foundational teachings in every discipline'. He eulogises the days of old when education was more varied and universal: 'while Europeans studied what in Latin was known as the *trivium* – grammar, logic, and rhetoric – Muslim students in addition studied mathematics, philosophy, astronomy, literature, and a dizzying array of subjects related to specialised learning in theology and exegesis of scriptural sources'. However, the polymath of the early medieval times has been shrunk to mere theology-centred pursuit with a rather bleak indifference to recent philosophical and scientific heritage along with a pervasive negativity towards arts. 'Teaching antique texts seem to yield a diminishing harvest for students today given the gap between the style and presentation of classical authors and the contemporary sensibilities of readers'.

In Lahore, Moosa has discussions with tutors at Jamia-i-Naeemia, and recalls an encounter with the late Mawlana Sarfaraz Naeemi, who was murdered by the Pakistani Taliban for his criticism of suicide bombings. At Madrasa Aisha, a women's madrasa, he notices a parallel tradition which Nizamuddin, Muhammad Ilyas, Hussain Madani, Abul Hasan Nadvi and others might have not foreseen. Indeed, South Asia has witnessed a steady growth in women's madrasas allowing female jurists to come to the fore. Interestingly, Moosa has little to say about the 2007 siege of the Red Mosque in Lahore. The students of the Mosque, including the female students of the adjacent Madrasa Jamia Hafsa, openly called for the overthrow of the government and the imposition of the Sharia. Heavily armed, they engaged in violent demonstrations, kidnapped women and policemen, and demanded that women must wear the burqa. The siege ended in a bloodbath. One feels that Moosa is deliberately side stepping the more nefarious dimensions of the madrasa system. At one level, he aims to cover a wider terrain, but at another, he confines himself to just a few relatively safe case studies from the Deobandi strand. Neither does he offer a comparison between Deobandi madrasas and their Shia, Bohra, Ismaili and even Ahmadi counterparts. No attempt is made to explore the madrasas on the Frontier – Khyber Pakhtunkhwa – responsible, rightly or wrongly, for earning such an ignoble reputation for the institution.

Moreover, we hear little about the scholastic attributes of the teaching faculty at these places. They are facetiously presented, on the whole, as one-man organisations often falling victim to personality cults. Are we to assume that the faculty members are mere instructors working as human medium for transferring received knowledge without any input on their part? Can we also assume that the selected curriculum disallows any consideration of parallel systems and both the faculty and students are stuck in a monolithic mode with an ingrained irreverence not only towards modern scholarship but also towards diverse Muslim pedagogies? Is there a kind of super-imposed and even authoritarian consensus that remains the order of the day hushing up any intellectual questioning? Better organisation and a more comparative approach would have answered these question and improved the narrative considerably. Moosa also fails to adequately tackle allegations that the madrasa system is misogynistic. And one remains rather uninformed on the true nature of learning at these madrasas since the pervasive image is of young men pursuing rote-based acquisition and not attempting scholarly debates both through written assignments and within the purview of group-based seminars.

These quibbles aside this is an engaging and wonderful book. Moosa provides an enlightened corrective to the demonisation of madrasas in the wake of 9/11. Far from being defensive, he invites a more informed analysis based on his own experience and exploration of the madrasa system, its core texts, and teaching methodology. There is a rationale in devoting seven to nine years specialising in an area without seeking mundane inducements.

THANK YOU, *MAWLANA*

Shanon Shah

I have always been slightly envious of people with a madrasa education. In Malaysia in the 1980s, I understood attending madrasa as spending a few hours after school every day in the local mosque with the other kids and learning Qur'anic recitation. These neighbourhood madrasas were not the equivalent of full-time *sekolah agama*, or state-funded religious schools. My elder sister and brother attended madrasa for a while. When my father learnt that they spent only a sliver of time reciting the Qur'an in front of the teacher – the remainder playing hide and seek or tag – he hired a gentle, diligent *ustaz* (religious instructor) to teach us at home. As much as I respected my *ustaz*, I never shared the experiences of my madrasa-going friends – especially those taught under more structured syllabi. Of course we all had to take compulsory Islamic Studies throughout primary and secondary school, but that was not really the same thing. I felt I had missed out on a combination of after-school fun and proper Islamic tutelage.

In the wake of the 11 September 2001 attacks, I was bemused by reports on CNN and other news outlets insinuating that madrasas bred terrorists. I was guilty of harbouring similar assumptions in the past, too, becoming suspicious and contemptuous of *sekolah agama* graduates. I imagined that conversations with them would involve interminable debates about what is haram (forbidden) and halal (permitted), conduct and impromptu inquisitions about prayers and other minutiae of worship. So I laughed when at university I found out that a religiously educated friend studied with a cigarette in hand and Metallica blasting in the background, while others memorised the lyrics to Paula Abdul's greatest hits. They were pious, though, observing obligatory Islamic worship steadfastly but without fuss. Still I wondered, like so many CNN anchors after 9/11, if the madrasas in Pakistan and Afghanistan were different and really did churn out bloodthirsty fanatics.

Ebrahim Moosa has therefore done me and others like me a huge favour with *What is a Madrasa?*. He focuses mainly on South Asian madrasas, including those he attended in India in the late 1970s. The book is meant as a 'primer about the role the madrasas play in the cultural, intellectual, and religious experiences of Muslims in the present and past'. Within the current geopolitical context, it is also a dual critique of post-9/11 stereotypes that madrasas breed militancy and the rigid, anti-Western orthodoxy espoused by many Islamic authorities. The book is particularly valuable because Moosa attempts to include his own insights as a madrasa-educated South African Muslim who is now a professor of Islamic Studies in the US. In fact, it concludes with Moosa's two open letters to Western policy makers and his former teachers, containing constructive criticisms for revitalising madrasas and improving relations between the West and the Muslim world.

The book combines succinct introductions of core Islamic concepts – mostly through user-friendly information boxes – and a larger critique of South Asian madrasas as producers of Islamic knowledge. Part of Moosa's narrative is that two 'streams' informed the growth of modern madrasas – a relatively 'tolerant cosmopolitan tradition' espoused by the Farangi Mahall school and nineteenth-century reformism eventually dominated by the Deoband school. These inter-madrasa differences have developed into multiple bitter divisions, although rival madrasas seem to share a common 'fear and loathing of a materialistic West'.

These inter-madrasa rivalries have also turned more expansive views of knowledge among earlier generations of Muslims into an emphasis on religious dogma above all other sources of learning. Moosa argues that twentieth-century madrasas commit a 'category mistake' in holding that knowledge of/for 'individual salvation' is enough for social advancement. This 'faith-based' hegemony has also been exacerbated by experiences of colonialism which have transformed madrasas into 'cultural barricades' against Westernisation. So where madrasa graduates were once equipped to contribute and find employment in various social spheres, they are now mostly confined to becoming imams at mosques. For many, transitioning to non-religious spheres of employment or further education would be tantamount to mini-apostasy.

Moosa gathers these different threads to contend that madrasas 'have been turned into scapegoats by Western governments with the aid of despotic Muslim governments' in the War on Terror. For him, the way forward is a 'Faustian bargain' – the *ulama* (religious specialists) and *mawlanas* (religious graduates) must risk opening up the madrasa curriculum and incorporate a wider view of knowledge, including from the humanities and social sciences.

However, Moosa is not going to change the minds of the most hardened ulama or the rankest of Islamophobes – but that is not his goal anyway. The book is meant as a resource for intelligent lay Muslims and non-Muslims to engage more meaningfully with public debates about Islam. Moosa is also frank about trying to reach 'the voices at the margins of the madrasa tradition' that understand the necessity of providing an enlightened orthodoxy for Muslims today.

In that sense, Moosa could have done more with how the book opens, specifically in the early section devoted to 'lived experiences'. He acknowledges that the book combines the 'observations of a participant... mingled with an interpreter's insights'. So he includes, for example, notes on a typical day in madrasa life – worship, academic study, communal meals and sporting activities. He also sketches the concerns of current madrasa students based on his more recent visits to South Asia, who were mostly curious about the 'condition' of Muslims in the West. But, surprisingly given his background in journalism, Moosa is not a good story teller. A captivating story shows rather than simply recounts an incident. His anecdotes amount more to a telling rather than showing of the lived experiences within the madrasa, including his personal recollections. Moosa's fluctuating insider-outsider status could have produced a more engaging account of the diverse experiences of madrasa administrators, teachers and students. A brief example. Moosa writes early on that he and his fellow students would sometimes 'lampoon' what they were taught and question its 'utility'. This is a valuable observation because while many of Moosa's target readers might not be able to envision madrasa life, they could certainly imagine rebellious teenagers giving lip to teachers or parents. But the question then would be how exactly this 'lampooning' takes place. Do students challenge their teachers outright? Do they gang up and gossip behind a teacher's back? What are the consequences of such 'lampooning'?

In *Telling About Society* (2007), the sociologist Howard Becker relates how he discovered the meaning of the term 'crock' when he was studying medical students and the medical education system. Not understanding medical jargon or the details of medical training, Becker hung around during the students' daily rounds examining patients, and noticed one day that the students were not very interested in a particular patient, with one of them later referring to her as a 'crock'. The comment was meant to be self-evident, but Becker became interested in what criteria students applied when they decided that some patients were 'crocks'. Was someone a crock for exaggerating symptoms or whinging a bit too much? Not really, students told Becker. By openly engaging them in discussion, Becker eventually discerned that 'crock' usually referred to a patient presenting 'no medical puzzles to be solved'. For example, students could 'learn nothing about cardiac disease from a patient who is sure he's having heart attacks every day but has no murmurs to listen to, no unusual EKG findings, no heart disease'. 'Crocks' were thus not useful cases for medical students primarily interested in real-life clinical experience to advance in their studies. In Moosa's context, did 'lampooning' a particular topic or even a particular teacher involve the use of a label equivalent to 'crock'? Such details would have enriched an unfamiliar reader's insights into madrasa life.

Moosa certainly understands the importance of such details, and there are many attractive photographs accompanying his discussions and reflections. But we need more engaging stories to be able to visualise the various madrasa actors as flesh-and-blood human beings, hearing their voices and understanding their cares and concerns. Storytelling, even using pseudonyms for recurring characters, would have animated the 'lived experiences' section and hooked readers into engaging with the more conceptual content of the remaining chapters.

Misunderstandings and stereotypes abound when we do not make the effort to get to know the Other out of mutual respect and beyond trivial niceties. How many madrasa-educated Muslims actually have deep and meaningful friendships with Hindus, Jains and non-Muslim Westerners, or even non-traditional Muslims? For that matter, do anti-Muslim ideologues in the West actually know any Muslims in any profound way? Works such as these therefore facilitate such encounters with the Other for the rest of us, especially when the Other remains physically and geographically remote and inaccessible. But the Other's experiences need to be demonstrated through more concrete scenarios and characterisations to engage the minds and hearts of a wider audience.

More vivid storytelling would have also added dimension and depth to Moosa's confession about his frustrating attempts to convince various *ulama* that for Islamic tradition to thrive, it needs to be updated. Moosa argues compellingly that the absence of a 'credible orthodox tradition' will only enable more manifestations of 'do-it-yourself Islam that jettison tradition', particularly those promoting intolerance and violence. And yes, we are bombarded with vivid media images of Boko Haram in northern Nigeria and the so-called Islamic State in Iraq and Syria (ISIS) as well as draconian, supposedly Islamic regimes such as Saudi Arabia. But if Moosa's goal is to demystify and de-link madrasas from stereotypes of Islamic terrorism, his readers will need stronger counter-images of madrasa life.

Like so many other Islamic concepts and references, the word 'madrasa' has become a polarising and politicised symbol – either of everything wrong with Islam or everything wrong with the West. In polemics that pit the two as mutually incompatible, it represents the supposedly inherent divide between Islamic and Western worldviews. As Moosa argues, there is nothing inherent or inevitable about this alleged divide. Rather, it is constructed and maintained by multiple authorities – whether in the West or the Muslim world – that benefit from stoking suspicions of the Other. Here lies the book's ultimate strength – as a madrasa-educated Muslim who now teaches Islam in the West, Moosa is a good example of how the two can and do meet. He does not trumpet his experiences or insights as representative or authoritative but generously offers them as an invitation for more informed dialogue.

So, thank you Mawlana. But your readers would have benefited with a more evolved style of storytelling, and a more in-depth exposure to your rich experiences and those of other madrasa students and teachers.

BY THE GRACE OF GOD

Mohammed Moussa

Knowledge is not a fragile glass lamp wherein its flame can be snuffed out in a single breath. Centuries of the interweaving of various insights and scholarships in the case of the Islamic tradition simultaneously demonstrate the durability and malleability of the production, transmission and reception of knowledge. The challenge of reform, variously associated with *islah*, *tajdid*, *ihya* and *nahda* in the Arabo-Islamic milieu, is thus not an existential threat to the body of beliefs, rituals, acts, norms, practices and institutions under the umbrella of Islam in the age of (post)modernity. In his tersely titled book *What is a Madrasa?* Ebrahim Moosa has intervened in a stormy debate about the very institutions which transmitted to him the multifaceted corpus of the Islamic tradition. Reform punctuates the pages of a critical and calm meditation on the relatively recent emergence of the madrasa system on the Indian subcontinent.

The title of Moosa's book is taken verbatim from the opening line of Mohammad Akram Nadwi's book about Dar ul-Uloom Nadwatul Ulema (Nadwa, for short), published and translated in English in 2007 (Turath, London). A question which Akram Nadwi, a protégé of Nadwa's late well-known rector Abul Hasan Ali Nadwi, answers in a string of comments and reflections documenting a typical day of his student life in the Indian city of Lucknow. Although eight years separate the publication of the two books, both authors graduates of Nadwa, a forthright dialogue about reform within the madrasa is clearly in the offing. Intimate snapshots of the inner workings of the world of the madrasa on the subcontinent do not reveal sword-brandishing or gun-toting hordes of fanatics, so-called 'jihadis' seeking to overwhelm *Dar al-Harb* (the Abode of War) or *Dar al-Kufr* (the Abode of Disbelief). A vast repertoire of acts beginning prior to the break of dawn to after midnight inspired by a meticulously cultivated piety instead comes to the foreground.

However, Moosa goes beyond the spiritual meditations of the enquiring student committed to the Islamic tradition as religious piety, disputative practice and literary grace. His account is that of both insider ('gatekeeper') and outsider ('sojourner') to a contested geography of knowledge, power, ritual and authority. The twin roles of the author of *What is a Madrasa?* emphatically blur the lines between the construction of objectivity and the formation of subjectivity to render both problematic (and on an epistemological plane meaningless) in the search for a new Islamic vista. I would like to offer a reading of Moosa's reflections through the lens of two interrelated and important facets which are, at the same time, potential weaknesses and strengths of the Islamic tradition: the process of manufacturing authority through the madrasa and the laborious task of reforming tradition.

A corporate identity based on the scholarly proficiency and widespread recognition to interpret God's law, embodied in the Shari'ah, is filled with authoritative presence. General claims by religious scholars to authority tend to be rooted in the notion of the supremacy of texts considered to be sacred in origin. Each interpretation is more or less authoritative according to its distance to these texts and proximity of meaning to other interpretations, from theological to mystic to jurisprudential. Thus, the Islamic tradition developed in tandem with a notion of textual orthodoxy. The overarching corporate identity of interpreters of the Islamic sacred texts acquired an institutional backbone. Madrasas expressed the trend towards the consolidation of Islamic law during the medieval period. These institutions were first established by ruling dynasties such as the Fatimids, al-Azhar in Cairo, and the Abbasids, Nizamiyya in Baghdad, dedicated to serve the stability of the state through the training of religious missionaries and government bureaucrats. On the Indian subcontinent, the belated introduction of the Muslim religious sciences was blended with influences from Persia and the local milieu. Particular expressions of the Islamic tradition embodied the age-old dichotomy between *manqulat* or *naql* and *ma'qulat* or *aql* with the former referring to transmitted knowledge and the latter connoting rational disciplines.

Various combinations of this dynamic found a tour de force in the curriculum of Mullah Nizamuddin Sihalwi (1677–1748) in his privileging of the rational in Islamic education while it was not taught by members of his cohort in the form of a madrasa at Farangi Mahall until 1905. This curriculum was fittingly named *Dars-i nizami* after its founder. For Moosa, the content of instruction revived a community of like-minded scholars on the subcontinent contributing to a 'Muslim Republic of Letters'. A peer group of the learned situated in a local place, east to the former heartlands of Islam, was connected to a multifarious web of authors and tracts in other places and stretching into the very distant past. The written word was the vehicle for ideas, laws and scholarly etiquette. In all likelihood, the paideia of the learned Muslim was one steeped in knowledge, not strictly religious, centred on the cultivation of a pious and intellectual subjectivity. One reading of Islamic education proposes the cultivation of the mind and the soul of the Muslim demonstrating the connection of the mundane to the sacred in what became known as *ta'lim* and *tarbiyah*. Strong emphasis on the rational facets of the Islamic tradition, namely logic and philosophy, in the *Dars-i nizami* was originally envisaged to train government bureaucrats in India during the Mughal period paying little heed to Qur'anic commentary. Those instructed in the curriculum seem not to have wielded religious authority in the guise of a 'cleric' but rather utilised their education for the purpose of running a state.

Ironically, the curriculum of Nizamuddin Sihalwi experienced a gradual shift towards the study of hadith epitomised by the notion of orthodoxy formulated by Shah Waliyullah al-Dihlawi (1703–1762) and his descendants. No longer geared towards the churning out of bureaucrats suited for government service, increasing study of hadith, to ascertain the sunnah of the Prophet Muhammad, radically changed the spirit and objective of the Dars-i nizami in the institutions where it was taught. The madrasa system on the subcontinent appears to have adopted, with varying modifications, the circumscribed version of this curriculum. Knowledge is synonymous with piety of a specific type. Ascetic poverty appears to be the lifestyle of the ideal Muslim putatively inspired by the Prophet Muhammad's example recorded in the literature of hadith taught at the madrasa. Only *din*, translated by

Moosa as 'salvation practices' with just cause, ought to be the utmost concern to Muslims without unwarranted distractions of the *dunya* or world. Soteriology pervades the ritual acts and bodily practices associated with worship. Salvation of the soul through the body accompanied by knowledge of religion narrowly defines the Islamic tradition's contents. The life of the mind occupies no importance in its own right except to arm faith with weapons to vanquish disbelief and to tread on the path towards knowledge, albeit religious, a light received by the grace of God.

Pervasive change upsets the status quo. An ostensible platitude this may seem but upon closer scrutiny the weighty edifice that is conservatism in religious traditions is a matter not of reactionary clerics or conservatism for the sake of conservatism. Put simply: the very survival of a peculiar notion and practice of authority, of the *ulema* (religious scholars) or mullahs, is at stake. However, the web of authority binding interpreters, texts and 'lay' Muslims has undergone drastic changes in the last two centuries. Previously, on the cusp of the arrival of modernity in the Muslim world, the rise of revivalist scholars and movements loudly proclaiming a 'return to the sources', principally the hadith, was an internal challenge to tradition. The founder of Wahhabism, Muhammad ibn Abdul Wahab (1703–1792), was merely a furious example, in a broad and varied spectrum, who disputed the authority of the madrasa-based curriculum immersed in the classical schools of jurisprudence and Sufism in the Arabian Peninsula. Farther east, Shah Waliyullah sought to shore up the study of hadith without sacrificing, in a certain sense inspired by, Sufism in an expansive syncretism including philosophy. Conservatism on the subcontinent, however, rallied around the hadith in a bid to preserve tradition and the privileges, not necessarily material, accompanying the role of gatekeepers of Islamic knowledge. During the nineteenth century, the waning of the Mughal Empire and the feeling that Muslim power was receding created the conditions for a madrasa system independent from the state, particularly colonialism.

A major stake in the transmission of tradition as hadith and other classical treatises to the next generation of scholars is holding together a 'Republic of Piety'. Extant knowledge of the Muslim religious sciences was transmitted in face-to-face encounters binding discipline to teacher, leading to an *ijaza* (authorisation). This in turn allowed the further transmission of the acquired knowledge to others which has been replaced with the *alamiyyah* (diploma certificate) within the madrasa setting. Deference to the *ulema* is underpinned by the creation and maintenance of a 'clerical' class mediating between God and the individual conscience of the believer. More importantly, obedience to God's law is a matter of conforming to the norms, rules and practices considered to be orthodox by a 'clerical' class trained in madrasas. More recently, higher education institutions teaching Islamic Studies such as Islamic University of Medina and the modern university system of al-Azhar in Cairo offering degrees and postgraduate studies in religious subjects have made claims to promote and defend Islamic orthodoxy.

Tradition can be lived through in a variety of ways. From being a burden on the present or cultural resources for liberation in the here-and-now, the past is filled with numerous possibilities. Demystifying the Islamic tradition in the latter scenario can be an act of internal reform. Rifa'a Rafi al-Tahtaw (1801–1873) was a decisive figure in the attempt to graft Western thought onto an Islamic repertoire. He was grounded in the Muslim religious sciences in addition to Sufism obtaining *ijazas* (authorisations) from his teachers. Five years in France, a member of the study mission sent by Muhammad Ali Pasha's (1762–1849) autocratic yet modernising government, for al-Tahtawi was instrumental in his acquisition of the French language, ideas and knowledge. The reform of the Islamic tradition was conceived to be a transcultural admixture of the past and the present, both Muslim and non-Muslim, in a context of the increasing power of the state. The search for knowledge in European sources led al-Tahtawi to argue that travel to other lands, the religion of its people being immaterial, to be essential quoting the Prophetic hadith 'seek knowledge, even if it is in China.'

Any proposed reform of the Islamic tradition, including madrasas, must confront the thorny question of what is knowledge. Rational considerations are not defied by the seeming primacy of salvation and piety over all other forms of knowledge in the madrasa and other religious institutions. Even soteriological doctrines can be subject to questioning through the interpretive methods of hermeneutics, discourse and narrative. *Din* versus *dunya* and the more latterly *din* and *dunya* binaries are amenable to a demystification of categories. Simultaneous expansion of the definition of knowledge and the reinterpretation of the religious knowledge of Muslim life, *dunya* and *akhirah* (the Afterlife), open the door for reforming tradition in an unruly and changing world. Redrawing the boundary demarcating the authority of the *ulema* is partly a critique of the conservatism presiding over the definition of mandatory and praiseworthy knowledge to be essentially religious. The *Dars-i nizami* had been moulded into a pious development of the Muslim subject, while the political fortunes of the Mughals were overtaken by British colonialism. Paradoxically, the colonial environment engendered the notion of 'useful' knowledge that has been adopted by champions of reform of an outdated madrasa syllabus not in step with the demands of time. Institutions such as Nadwa founded for the express purpose 'to combine the useful past with the beneficial modern' appear to have retained, in large part, the principal texts of the *Dars-i nizami* in law, theology and the study of Qur'an.

Far-reaching changes to this syllabus are tied to the broader promise of reform within the Islamic tradition which has not yet been realised. The 'historicity' of texts, authors and social contexts is proposed by Moosa to enable students to bridge the past and the present in order to better comprehend the landscape of Islamic scholarship. And moreover, the transformation of *Dars-i nizami* into a postgraduate programme is more apt for would-be students after preparatory study equipping them with the skills needed to navigate treatises and tracts going back a thousand years. Another proposal includes teaching the lingua franca of the globalised world, English, and other languages alongside Arabic and Urdu in a serious and concerted fashion rather than a mere afterthought. The original focus on the training of government bureaucrats replaced by the formation of clerics, mainly prayer leaders and preachers, can perhaps be restored within the madrasas' very precincts. Another possibility for the reform of the *Dars-i nizami*, admittedly unfeasible at present, is the formation of Muslim subjects with the skills, knowledge and competence suited to the bureaucracy of the modern state. Political science, sociology and anthropology provide a sense of the new subjectivities emerging in a world less and less governed by the nation-state and more and more by globalising forces. However, different schools of thought from Barelvi to Deoband to Ahl-i Hadith to Nadwatul Ulema dwell in a shared, disputed and fragmented terrain of authority which presents a major obstacle to any wholesale project of reform in India. Competing visions of reform are not lacking. The achievement of a consensus on what reform would look like remains problematic in the madrasa system on the subcontinent and outside of its walls among Muslim communities.

The writings of Ebrahim Moosa, especially his monograph on Abu Hamid al-Ghazali, embody the creative synthesis between two traditions of learning. He is both a scholar from within the Islamic tradition and an academic in the American, perhaps also global, public sphere. Certainly, the unshackling of tradition from the institutional monopoly of the madrasa has contributed to the reforming of knowledge purportedly Islamic. Historicising the Islamic tradition opens up a myriad of opportunities for reforming not only the *Dars-i nizami* but also how Islam can be known through a variety of modes of reasoning. The Muslim self (or selves) is locked into an interdependent relationship with the other, neither monolithic nor alien, thereby opening the door to a new threshold of knowledge and insights. New realities present themselves as risks and opportunities, a looming 'Faustian bargain', in the age of postmodernity and globalisation. Human life appears to be increasingly rootless thanks to the emergence of new spaces of social relations through the Internet. Transcultural encounters have become common currency.

Constant changes are a hallmark feature of the wider world of the apparently conservative, rather than static, environment of the madrasa almost two decades after the millennium. Texts and experience can be deployed as formidable tools to carve out space within the Islamic tradition for reform on pressing issues such as gender equality. At Nadwa, visiting his alma mater, Moosa audited a class of an erstwhile teacher, Mawlana Sayyid Salman Husyani Nadvi, who highlighted the egalitarianism inspiring the public role of women in early Islam recorded in the canonical *Sahih Bukhari* in direct contrast to their seclusion proffered by so many scholars of the madrasa system. The mantle of gatekeeper to the Islamic tradition provides Moosa with two conflicting dispositions or 'tensions', the 'romantic' and the 'realist', in preserving a tradition of rich texts or adapting it to the present. Hybridity of cultural forms are by no means precluded in an Islamic tradition reflecting the multiple subjectivities of Muslims in dialogue among themselves and the other.

WHAT'S LOVE GOT TO DO WITH IT?

Merryl Wyn Davies

Love is complex and complicates things. However, contrary to the old adage love is not blind. Who knows the beloved so well as the lover? To know the beloved's true nature is to see and accept the whole gamut of their beauties and strengths as well as fallibilities and foibles. In which case, it could be argued that there is no genuine criticism without love. Telling criticism, the just point that cuts to the quick is most resonant when it comes from true love, the kind that can balance knowledge, the honesty of informed insight with a measured passionate intensity. However, it is just as possible for love to let the beloved off the hook.

The madrasa is seldom cast as beloved these days, although it is undoubtedly a centre of passionate controversy. As an institution it has acquired a menacing reputation in popular punditry. In the west it is perennially cited for blame as a causal factor in the rise of terrorism. Despite the frequency of its demonisation what madrasas actually do, what they teach, their history, and place in the intellectual and religious heritage of Muslim civilisation past and present, is much less known or understood. As a product of a traditional madrasa education and now a distinguished Islamic scholar at a leading American university Ebrahim Moosa is ideally placed to offer a detailed answer and telling critique of the basic question 'what is a madrasa?'

It is evident that Moosa is a lover. He is enamoured of the scholarship that constitutes the intellectual heritage of the madrasa. He is an ardent advocate urging appreciation of the historic context from which this distinctive system of education derives. Training in rational humanistic ways of thought were necessary and by no means inimical skills to be acquired alongside and to facilitate understanding of the textual tradition of religious knowledge. What stimulates the heart strings for Moosa is the approach to knowledge characterised by the great historian and sociologist Ibn Khaldun (1332–1406). As Moosa says, 'without a critical apparatus that includes "a good speculative mind and thoroughness" as well as knowledge of custom, political realities, the nature of civilisation, sociology (what he calls 'human social organisation') and comparative studies a historian is doomed to err, wrote Ibn Khaldun. And if one did not explore historical contexts with the aid of philosophy and science, what Ibn Khaldun called "knowledge of the nature of things" then one can stray "from the truth and (find oneself) lost in the desert of baseless assumptions and errors'.

The Nizami curriculum, which remains the basis of education in thousands of madrasas throughout South Asia and beyond was devised in a compatible mould. Contemporaneous with the Enlightenment in Europe, Mulla Nizamuddin (d.1748), who was given the honorific Teacher of Hindustan, showed a rare ability to select classical texts for a syllabus that produced highly skilled and literate scholars, bureaucrats, writers and intellectuals. The texts he included while terse and enigmatic were designed to help the student grasp the essentials of a subject and instil 'forensic skills – the ability to analyse and solve textual and literary puzzles'. Nizamuddin believed in grounding students in the rational disciplines. His goal was to produce graduates who could think logically, acquire excellent writing and linguistic skills and above all know enough about Islam as religious tradition to address issues beyond basic questions of religious practice. In effect his syllabus was equivalent to today's basic college education: the grounding upon which higher specialisations could be pursued.

We are not offered eulogies to the past by this lover of his intellectual heritage but we are given clear evidence that in South Asia it was critically adept, nuanced and capable. Most of all it was capable of being relevant to the social realities of its time. For example giving support for the first Indian war of independence (the Indian Mutiny to the uninitiated), while during India's second struggle for freedom from colonial rule key figures in the madrasa networks supported Gandhi.

Moosa's passion for and facility in elucidating the intellectual gems that crown a genuine engagement with the classical texts is abundantly evident. His detailed history of the protean nature of the growth of the networks of madrasas across South Asia illuminated by the life stories of their funders and leading personalities is a significant contribution to understanding. The arcane points of religious differences between Deobandis and Brelevis which have constructed major fissures that are social as well as theological are lucidly explained. The communal rifts produced are analogous to the denominational disputes that were/are familiar enough fare in other religious traditions. Yet all this glorious context and detail is in its way the critical stiletto by which his subject is eviscerated. The truth is Ebrahim Moosa did not learn to love nor to reason with his beloved intellectual heritage in the madrasas where it was first encountered and taught to him. His epiphany of understanding that produces his subtle and important insights and erudition was acquired thanks to his studies in secular western educational establishments!

Moosa finds his own experience is not unique; now it is the norm. In short he shows how tradition is no longer safe in the hands of traditionalists. Whatever their claims to preservation and continuity, how the madrasas operate in our day and age represents a contractive diminution – a belittling – from what Moosa terms the republic of letters to the republic of piety. It is a contraction not only of the texts studied but of the reasoning faculties inculcated in students who no longer acquire the skills, logical, linguistic or analytical, to comprehend the import of such classical texts as they are taught: 'A tradition of scholasticism and learning whose beauty is lost on those who dedicate themselves to study this monument to the intellectual past' says Moosa. And one hears his anguish: 'if only the advice of Ibn Khaldun was heeded and the madrasas taught the history of Muslim disciplines, especially the biographies and histories of the texts and authors studied in the Nizami curriculum, then the beauty and complexity of this tradition of learning might be appreciated'.

Like a lover spurned, Moosa can be cutting about the operation of the republic of piety. He bemoans the way the madrasa that once prized reason now 'yields defenders who take refuge in debilitating dogmatism.' Or even more tartly the generalised barb: 'many critics question whether the current madrasa does not recycle intellectual mediocrity and portray it as piety.'

The historic transition to a republic of piety over the course of the twentieth century is founded on retention of historic modes of pedagogy epitomised by the importance attached to the master/student relationship. This system promotes monastic introspection, asserts the primacy of asceticism, and a desire to acquire right knowledge that is only that knowledge which leads to salvation and comes from a concentration on the study of Quranic exegesis, the prophetic tradition and adherence to the rule based principles of the discipline of law (*fiqh*). The result is an impressive and powerful sharia mindedness and piety. The madrasa student now has a narrower training, much of which is received opinion that is often difficult to comprehend. 'Madrasa communities adopt a narrow account of the meaning and end of knowledge while ignoring an inclusive account of what knowledge is.' Graduates therefore are suitable only for a vocation as a Muslim religious functionary or a cleric.

If the graduates of madrasas cannot reason with tradition, or indeed accept that tradition is to be reasoned with rather than re-enacted as received opinions, they can keep alive only a rotting hulk that once had relevance. It is not difficult to see how their narrow sharia-mindedness operated without reasoning ends with ways of doing Islam that in operation and effect can be called 'unIslamic' – one has only to think of and look at the implementation of the *zina* (adultery) laws in Pakistan to see how the spirit and meaning of the religion can be lost through addiction to unthinking rule-based legalistic practice dressed up as piety.

The madrasas have 'avoided a tryst with modernity' repeatedly and consistently on the evidence offered by Moosa. It has been no accident of history but matters of choice and design. Meanwhile experiments to integrate multiple knowledge traditions to enhance the study of religious discourses 'have been shockingly incompetent' with little tangible outcome. Which is not to say they are oblivious of modern technology. The narrow sharia and fatwa issuing mindedness as well as the rhetorical fulmination of sermonising has found a home in cyberspace. Forget reviving intellectual heritage; computer skills on the other hand are keenly adopted. Indeed cyberspace has become a major growth area and lucrative outlet for madrasas and their graduates – to the dismay of many.

Moosa yearns to see the madrasa reformed. He wants them to broaden their curriculum and recommit themselves to the spirit of inclusive knowledge and inquiry. 'There is a fundamental absence of grasping the fact that knowledge of science, maths, civics, sociology, politics, economics and history in addition to languages and skills is all part of one's basic equipment and literacy in today's world.' So the question what is a madrasa and what are its problems are set in context and the agenda of change that has repeatedly failed and been spurned is, once again, politely offered. Critics are asked to understand where the institution is coming from and accept its essentially benign nature. Here Moosa misses out any mention of the efforts made by Darul Uloom Deoband to address the question of terrorism. In May of 2008 they organised a major conference on 'Anti -Terrorism and Global Peace' attended by representatives of all major madrasa networks. It culminated with Deoband issuing what amounts to an institutional fatwa condemning terrorism and stating that Muslims should not cooperate with people who spread the lie of terrorism; those who do are 'committing sin or oppression'.

The trouble is Moosa's often withering critique fails to pursue the very perspective by which he wants to rescue the madrasa from its own inadequacies and decline. He wants the curriculum to adopt a more rationalist trend with the inclusion of sociology, history, philosophy and economics – a modern version of ibn Khaldun's study of the way of things. As Moosa notes, such developments are already underway elsewhere in the Muslim world. However, what he does not consider is the wider impact of the production line of students produced by the republic of piety who are only fit for work as religious functionaries yet are fitted with nothing but a truncated, traditionalised narrow mindedness and ascetic outlook and who have little or no acquaintance with the way of things and the way things are in wider society. These are the adepts of limited understanding of Qur'anic exegesis, prophetic tradition and rule based practice of law. They have been groomed to promote piety as 'a lowest common denominator'. The emphasis of their education is 'cultural preservation and to entrench Muslim identity through a stripped down version of traditional learning'. What effect do they have in increasing conservatism in society across the subcontinent? What impact do they have on attitudes to women? What is their importance in communities where 'secular' educational provision is withering on the vine? What is the cumulative consequence of the pernickety fatwa minded approach they bring to radically changing social circumstances? How do we calculate the effect of their abhorrence of modernity and their visceral dislike of western materialism? What is their impact on societies where a majority of the population are young, often languishing without fulfilling prospects, disaffected by the multiple disadvantages that afflict them and yet exposed to and aware of the blatant injustices of the global order? What part have the madrasas to play in the cultivation of victimhood, the sense of having been done injustice, as the general stance of Muslim consciousness to modernity? Are we calculating the impact of the rhetoric of fighting in the cause of Allah from the mouths of unsophisticated religious functionaries on impressionable and under-informed minds? These questions are the Khaldunian agenda of inquiry which Moosa does not intimate and yet which are a legitimate part of understanding 'what is a madrasa' in contemporary times.

Moosa's analysis raises questions not just about context and consequences inside the madrasa but for its impact on society in our changing and testing times. Madrasas must be assessed by their product which is religious functionaries. Can we really ignore the synergy by which the ideological agenda of extremism feeds off so many of the retrograde attitudes and implications of what is taught in the madrasa? The direct and overt institutional denouncing of terrorism by the madrasa networks is an important initiative. However, the piety the madrasas promote has so far proved itself incapable of deterring or derailing those whose perversions are practiced in the name of tradition. It is not merely a stereotypical response and function of demonisation to ask how the mind-set taught by contemporary madrasa impacts on radicalisation and extremism. If madrasa networks are a franchise they are also loose associations of institutions of variable quality with little or no oversight. It is not by eastern windows only that when daylight comes, comes in the light.

It is the duality of his own relationship, his then and now perspective, which brings out Moosa's most devastating criticism. Yet as a lover of what he has learnt since leaving the madrasa world his tender heart cannot bear to contemplate what follows from and is enabled by the critique he has made. The madrasa networks may be contingent elements in the threads of causation that produce fragmentation, friction, conflict and ultimately terrorism but they are part and parcel of the wider context of the problems of Muslim society. Their contingency and agency should not be immune from consideration. We need to ask how and in what way the truncated pietistic, legalistic approach they have cultivated disseminates and popularises attitudes that seed the path to extreme ideologies. Pondering these wider questions is where the lover fears to tread.

Some years ago I travelled around northern Nigeria with a group of local Muslim activists talking about the problems of the post 9/11 world. One part of the programme was a documentary film the Nigerians had made designed to explain what is a madrasa to non-Muslims. In Nigeria the boys who travel from far and wide to attend madrasas, which is the only free education available to them, are often seen as a social problem. To many they are feral youths suspected of criminality who seem to have a great deal of free time to roam around and of course have no links to the local community in which they reside. The film explained the benign and necessary purpose the education the madrasa provided. It had artistic sequences of that stock image, youths squatting and swaying behind low benches as they intoned the Qur'an. Every time I watched the film just one thought struck me. It was presented to the audience by a man who was an educationalist, a high ranking lecturer at a university who designed courses for the training of teachers and was affiliated to the Ministry of Education. So one day I mustered the courage to ask the nagging question: would you adopt this system of teaching in your courses? Do you think this madrasa syllabus constitutes of sound education? What can I tell you, he was not a lover, but he was dedicated to his Muslim identity. Therefore, my question had never occurred to him before. He was dumbfounded because he suddenly realised that as an expert educationalist he would never dream of doing things the madrasa way in this day and age.

Like the inertia that has gripped the institution of the madrasa in South Asia the inertia of Muslim critique leaves tradition in the unsafe hands of traditionalists. Think about it. Tradition is too important for that. I would feel safer, more invigorated, better informed, and served if tradition was left to a lover who understands its meaning and spirit, who is enlightened and enlivened to positive constructive purpose by what he knows. It is the classic dilemma we all need to resolve. Just because they are old does not make institutions venerable and worth preserving. Tradition is not tradition if it cannot change. If tradition will not change we need the critical acumen to recognise its time to move on by and let dead branches wither away. I would rather read a book by Ebrahim Moosa than a madrasa full of pamphlets by a whole gaggle of traditionalists because I know I would learn more from the former than the latter could possibly imagine. My problem is that Moosa is in love with something that has been, an institution that was once great in history, but cannot be redeemed. We know the humane way to reduce the agony of a much loved race horse when the unfortunate animal breaks its leg is to shoot it!

ET CETERA

ON EDUCATING ONESELF

Ebrahim Moosa

It dawned on me, very late in life, that one must value the role of education in one's life. Yes, I did attend school in South Africa, did my homework, got decent grades, but for the most part it was a perfunctory performance and drudgery. My education made no connection to my surroundings or my psychological state as a teenager. Occasionally, the literature classes titillated my curiosity as did the history and geography lessons, about events a long time ago and places far away. All this made me yearn for adventures of my own. Mathematics and physics remained a black hole of incoherence: more truthfully, the physics did make sense. But trigonometry and solving for x, made no real-life connections for me.

On reflection, I was clueless about habits I ought to have cultivated within me. I did not realise how important it was to develop excellence in skills such as punctuality, reading, writing, arithmetic and thinking as life-long assets. I missed the importance of a proper sensibility of morality: to have a heart, a conscience and take an uncompromising stance on human dignity. I am not libelling my parents, for I was not a feral child who was raised by wolves. I was taught to respect others and to care for them, to be truthful and be good, the basics of morality. My point is, I never found a compelling moral narrative coming from within me, what philosophers call personal virtues that would make me acutely aware of the importance of the hallowed things in life. I think it had something to do with gutter 'apartheid' education. Or so I like to think.

Graciously, I did not entirely miss out on the vital lessons worthy of pursuit in life. What really set my mind and heart on fire as a youth, was my six-year sojourn in India's madrasas, Islamic seminaries, as chronicled in my book *What is a Madrasa?* a subject of a symposium in this issue. The madrasas taught me a great deal not only about Islam as a faith-practice and an intellectual tradition, but more: about life, religion, politics and values. And later, my modest role in South Africa's anti-apartheid struggle as a Muslim theologian, activist and as a professor of religion, clarified some lessons for me. I realised in hindsight, that these were values and meanings I should have craved for much earlier.

In some ways I am a latecomer to the complexities of life, but a fortunate person in many ways, gifts for which I give thanks. Yet, many like me, have to defy the aphorism of some idealistic and exacting Muslim sage whose linear imaginary of time made him write: 'one whose beginning is not red hot, cannot anticipate a luminous ending.' I will not feign modesty and say I am not seeking a 'luminous ending.' But I find the sage's wisdom too cut and dry, two-toned and implying that if you missed the first boat, then you are a loser. I prefer the wisdom imparted by literary critics and artists like Edward Said who explained this lateness, not as a chronological delay, but as an allegory: the recovery of an aesthetic sensibility that has the double burden of being simultaneously enchanted by new insights of the recoverability of the past, and the anguish of the shortness of time.

Completing *What is a Madrasa?* and the contemporary debates, politics and controversies surrounding this institution, I realised that I was actually both enchanted with the madrasa-tradition after a period of disenchantment and, that I was also trying to say something more. If I was trying to create harmony and resolution between the rhythms and traditions of the madrasa with that of the modern tradition, then it was a misguided attempt on my part. That assumes I have ready-made answers. More honestly, I was possibly thinking more ambitiously of Islamic education as a state of intransigence and difficulty; where the old and the new jostle in unresolved contradictions but posing so many questions that it promises a new wave of creativity. Yes, I yearn to recover the madrasa as a knowledge tradition in all its glorious complexity in order to render it an institution that makes a meaningful contribution in our age.

Proponents of madrasa education have regrettably not put enough daylight between themselves and those brutal groups who often trade on the legacies of the madrasas in pursuit of their violence, such as the Taliban and other groups. Hence, the monstrous severities perpetrated by some extremist groups blackball all of 'Islamic education.'

Yet, having witnessed a few revolutions in my lifetime and the frightening aftermath of each, I always surprised myself to be an optimist, to believe in the human capacity to do good. But now, I must confess, the voices of scepticism rise disturbingly in my head more often than I would welcome. The ugly consequences of the Iranian revolution, the contradictions and paradoxes produced by the Arab spring, the dehumanising civil wars – all only reinforce a gnawing pessimism. One day millions of Egyptians protest in the streets for change and some eighteen months later, these same millions beg for the return of a military dictatorship. Syrians prayed for change and their society spawned revolutionaries, some of whom have since morphed into humans who commit unspeakable acts on their fellow beings in the name of Islam and in pursuit of a craven idea of a caliphate.

Conditions of death and destruction force us to ask the question: what is wrong with human beings? What is the human condition? In other words, what dehumanises our souls, minds and sensibilities to commit such unspeakable acts to each other? Why do some of these muscular devotees of Islam produce teachings that violate human dignity at every turn? I need not be reminded that their super power adversaries are equally craven. But I also often wonder why Muslims who live inside and beyond the West always use the West as the benchmark of morality. Does the West's use of unbounded violence mean unbounded violence in return? Is that what a religious sensibility teaches? Is it not time that conscientious Muslims produce what can be called the 'violence critique?' Have we failed to provide people an education that produces decent human beings? I have seen decency in shantytowns and in spaces of grinding poverty around the world: so I am not so sure about the bread and butter causes of violence.

These days I find myself frequently murmuring the comment made by Immanuel Kant and popularised by the political philosopher, Sir Isaiah Berlin, 'Out of the crooked timber of humanity no straight thing was ever made.' Yet I also hear another message. 'Hope,' I hear the novelist Annie Lamott pushing against my cynicism preach, 'is a revolutionary patience.'

So I often ask myself how did I and countless others dodge internalising the slogan, 'Islam is the solution,' a meaningless refrain made popular by well-intentioned but utterly misguided Islamists? While I concede my education was imperfect, but from somewhere I acquired the sensibility to question the unquestionable. The example of the hierodules, those slaves who served the ancient Greek temples come to mind. The hierodules had the advantage over the priests when it came to the secrets of the cult. They were surely no less knowledgeable than the priests, but because they were servants they were prepared to take risks and were more willing to expose, question and explore the secrets of the cult. I too behaved like the hierodules.

As I was becoming more religiously literate in my teens, I always found the idea of corporal penalties propounded by Shari'a jarring to my human nature even though all the learned scholars of Islam fiercely threatened with their constructed dogmas that such questioning is tantamount to unbelief. But once I was skilled enough to read my madrasa texts as well as other texts of the Muslim intellectual tradition, I began to think of Islam as both a faith tradition as well as a world civilisation. Both were subject to the vicissitudes of culture and complex historical processes. Even the loftiest religious proclamations, I discovered in the madrasa, were constructions produced by human intelligence and subject to refashioning. That discovery became my shield against craven ideological constructions peddled in the name of Islam. Questioning opened the way for greater awareness and served to be my best teacher. 'Is not to question the best remedy for ignorance?' the Prophet Muhammad was reported to have asked.

Yet asking the right questions in order to educate the next generation of Muslims has been elusive for generations of modern Muslims. Conferences held in holy cities like Mecca, universities brandishing 'Islamic' qualifiers, knowledge baptised as 'Islamic' and the 'islamisation' of everything under the sun, have yet to even yield mediocrity. Rather the harvest has been to produce closed minds and even worse: dangerous minds whose ugly deeds carry the imprimatur of a distorted faith. If the mindset were inward looking and defensive it would be a consolation. Instead, it has produced a pandemic of destructive behaviour. How to make human beings out of the crooked timber of humanity remains our challenge. Perhaps if serious questioning displaces the trumpets of hollow triumphalism there is hope for a future.

Is it because I, and perhaps some of the readers, have seen too much and have now become sceptics, given the state of the world? I, perhaps we, have now painfully realised that if the human soul is not sufficiently tempered and formed by education, then the best intentions and the most precious opportunities given to our species are guaranteed oblivion. This is hardly any major discovery: it's only a brutally painful realisation I reluctantly admit.

I think of the enormous human sacrifices made in the twentieth century in pursuit of revolutionary change. And then most hopes were dashed into nightmares because the human condition was never nurtured. Think of the revolutions – Bolshevik, Cuban, chairman Mao's cultural revolution, the wars of independence against colonialism and the Iranian revolution. All were instances of great hope claiming to heal humanity but alas, they left many corpses along the road. We are passing through another stage of world history where both the powerful and the powerless have the potential to leave only utter destruction on the world stage.

As a teacher I often wonder whether I am educating a generation that will reproduce the errors that the previous generation had committed. I hope not. In order to secure a better future, the priority is not to stuff heads with facts and information. These are resources even a machine can be fed. It is to create human beings who can feel for their fellow beings.

And yet I cannot afford to accommodate the darkness of the pessimist and thus have to turn to the light of optimism. I have to believe that we do have gems within us. Therefore, a real education must of necessity instil a sensibility to care for all of humanity and treat all wisdom as our own. In the words of the invincible Muslim mystic Ibn 'Arabi, one must hope for an audacious pluralistic future. He claimed and wished for others to see the 'other' within the self, when he sang the following lines:

'My heart can take on
any form:

for gazelles a meadow,
a cloister for monks,

For the idols, a sacred ground,
Ka'ba for the circling pilgrim
the tables of the Torah,
the scrolls of the Qur'an.

I profess the religion of love.
Wherever its caravan turns
along the way, that is the belief
the faith I keep...

TEN KEY TEXTS ON ISLAMIC EDUCATION

You want to be happy, educated and true to the spirit of Islam? Well, good fortune smiles on you: there is no lack of great thinkers eager to walk you through to your destination. The issue of knowledge and education has preoccupied Muslims right from the inception of Islam. There is a vast body of Islamic literature on how young minds should be nurtured, how critical insight can be inculcated, and how to be happy and virtuous. It all starts with the first word of the revelation we call the Qur'an – 'Read', and the Prophet's injunction that 'seeking knowledge is a duty of all Muslims', and moves forward with a plethora of classical scholars, philosophers and thinkers exploring and delineating what a good education ought to be. A good education, they thought, is not simply about transmission of knowledge but also includes emotional, social and physical well-being of the student. It is about creating a well-rounded moderate person with passion for thought and learning. The kind of individuals who ended up pursuing higher education at al-Azhar University in Cairo and al-Karaouine in Fes, established in 970 and 859 respectively.

The Islamic literature on education and knowledge is as fresh and relevant today as it was in the classical period. Of course, the world has moved on. But just as we still study Plato and Aristotle, so we ought to be reading works such as *The Treatise on Matters Concerning Learners and Guidelines for Teachers* by al-Qabisi (936–1012) and *Exposition of Knowledge and Its Excellence* by ibn Abd al-Barr (978–1070). Or exploring the classification schemes of al-Kindi (801–873), al-Farabi (d.950) and Fakhr al-Din al-Razi (864–925) to see how knowledge was organised in the classical period. Or scrutinising the *Fihrist* (Catalogue) of al-Nadim (d.995–998) to determine what the young folks of the tenth century were reading and studying. The legacy of classical Islam only has meaning as a living heritage; only as a dynamic tradition can it provide us with a sense of continuity and identity, and tell us not only where we have been but also where we ought to be.

So begin your great learning adventure by discovering the works of some prodigious minds, classical and modern, Muslim and non-Muslim. Here are ten key texts everyone concerned with education and knowledge should know intimately.

1. The Refinement of Character by Miskawayh

Miskawayh (932–1030) began as a librarian before moving on to philosophy, logic, history and pedagogy. *The Refinement of Character* is his most famous book, and is amongst the first works on Islamic ethics. It consists of six discourses: principles of ethics, character and refinement, the good and its divisions, justice, love and friendship and the health of the soul – the sort of things that enhance our humanity and young Muslims yearn for today. For Miskawayh, the only happiness worthy of its name is 'moral happiness'. Everyone can be changed; and everyone can change things for the better. The young should be praised for the good things they do, encouraged to rise above basic desires and trained to admire moderation and generosity. 'When the activity of the rational soul is moderate, when it seeks true knowledge, not what is presumed to be knowledge but is in reality ignorance, it achieves the virtue of knowledge followed by that of wisdom'. What better advice can one give?

2. The Memoire of the Listener and the Speaker in the Training of Teacher and Student by ibn Jammah

Ibn Jammah (1241–1332) was a highly respected jurist and teacher. A guide both for teachers and students, *The Memoire* describes the qualities needed in a teacher and the etiquette required from a student so both work as equal partners in the pursuit of knowledge. The 'Listener' and 'Speaker' in the title emphasises the fact that ibn Jammah favours discussion as the basic instrument of teaching and learning. Ask questions fearlessly, ibn Jammah tells the students; encourage students to ask questions, and where necessary help them formulate critical questions, teachers are told. And both should observe the etiquette of handling books and treat them with grace and dignity!

3. Instruction for the Student: The Method of Learning by al-Zarnuji

Al-Zarnuji (d.1223), who flourished in Turkistan, was amongst the first to write on the theory and practice of professional education. *Instruction for the Student* was used as a standard text for over six centuries; and was translated into Latin in 1838. Al-Zarnuji distinguishes between education and knowledge and is concerned with 'whole education' rather than mere academic attainment. You could have a PhD, he seems to be saying, and yet still be uneducated – a common currency in contemporary Muslim societies. Education is acquired through effort, aspiration, pursuit and persistence; knowledge is about moral and ethical acumen.

4. The Book of Knowledge by al-Ghazali

Al-Ghazali (1058–111) begins his monumental forty-volume *Ihya Ulum al-Din* ('The Revival of Religious Knowledge') with *The Book of Knowledge*. It is the first book of the first quarter on the Acts of Worship – preceding 'The Articles of Faith' and 'The Mysteries of Purity'. In other words, knowledge is supreme worship for al-Ghazali. Peppered with hadith (not all particularly authentic it has to be said), aphorisms, and pearls of wisdoms from pious sages, *The Book of Knowledge* offers a discussion on the value of knowledge, the praiseworthy and objectionable branches of knowledge, the qualities needed in teachers and students and ends with a blistering praise of the 'noble nature' of the intellect. Al-Ghazali was perhaps the first to note that knowledge has a downside too – it could be 'evil' designed to perpetuate injustice and suffering. And there is nothing worse than the 'learned hypocrite'. 'Knowledge is not the prolific retention of tradition, but the fear of God'.

5. Knowledge Triumphant by Franz Rosenthal

It would be reasonable to assume that thinkers and scholars such as al-Ghazali, ibn Jammah, al-Zarnuji and Miskawayh were obsessed by the concept of knowledge. Or, more appropriately, *ilm*, which is normally translated as knowledge. But the term 'knowledge' does not fully express the factual and emotional content of *ilm*, which has a deeper and wider meaning. Given that it was a central concept for Muslim civilisation, the delineation of its full meaning was seen as paramount. At the zenith of Muslim civilisation, over 500 definitions of *ilm* were being discussed and debated; and most are explored in this meticulously researched classic by Franz Rosenthal (1914–2003), a renowned German scholar of Islam and Arabic literature, who taught at Yale University for some decades. There is no branch of intellectual, religious, political and daily life of the 'average Muslim' that remained untouched by the all-pervasive concept of *ilm*, notes Rosenthal. 'What does it mean for a civilisation, and beyond it, for the history of mankind, if knowledge is made its central concern'? he asks. His answer: 'a great deal can be achieved by the fusion of intellectual and spiritual values in one dominant concept'; but there are 'drawbacks' – most notably, the danger of the spiritual subsuming the intellectual.

6. The Rise of Colleges by George Makdisi

What use is knowledge if it cannot be transmitted to the next generation? Institutions devoted to thought, learning and education were needed to perform this task. *The Rise of Colleges*, subtitled 'Institutions of Learning in Islam and the West', tells us everything we need to know about the emergence of colleges and universities in the Muslim world, from their organisational and administrative structure to how they were funded, their curriculum, the methods of teaching and learning, the designation of professors and the classification of students, the intellectual ferment of the scholastic community to how the Muslim system of education was transmitted to the West. George Makdisi (1920–2002), who was Professor of Arabic and Islamic Studies at University of Pennsylvania, is rightly acknowledged as one of the greatest Arabists of his generation – *The Rise of Colleges* provides ample evidence of this fact.

7. *The Arabic Book by Johannes Pedersen*

Students and professors needed books. During the time of al-Ghazali, over a million books were published every year in Baghdad. How did such a prodigious book publishing industry evolve? How were books actually published and distributed? How were they protected from plagiarism and forgery? In this classical text, Johannes Pedersen (1883–1977), Danish theologian and scholar of the old school of European orientalists, provides detailed, and often surprising answers to these questions, including what went on in the margins! It was a truly phenomenal industry with no rival in the Middle Ages.

8. *The Fihrist of al-Nadim*

Then, as now (or at least before the arrival of Amazon), you went to a bookshop to buy your books. And if you lived in Baghdad, you would, more than likely, end up in the bookshop of Al-Nadim (d.995 or 998). The bookseller was also an accomplished calligrapher and a *warraq* – that is, someone who copied manuscripts for sale, at the speed of sound. His celebrated bookshop, spread over several floors, was a favourite haunt for the scholars, students and the literati. The *Fihrist* is a catalogue of books that he sold. Each manuscript could be copied within a day or two, if not hours, by a string of *warraqs* who worked in unison. A testimony to the thriving book culture in classical Islam, al-Nadim's bookshop had everything that a seeker after education and knowledge of this period could wish for. Not just the sacred texts of Jews, Christians and Muslims, and countless commentaries on them, but also studies on the doctrines of Hindus, Chinese and Buddhists. Not just texts on hadith, law, grammar, philology, history and philosophy, but also biography, poetry and literature, fiction and fables (from as far afield as Persia, Byzantium and India), discourses on ethics, morality, pedagogy, as well as sports and sex and – let us not forget – the study of pigeon droppings (very important for young men and women looking for a hot date). The *Fihrist* is the ideal double tome that you should keep by your bedside and dip into from time to time; and weep at what you are missing in contemporary times.

9. Islamic Education by A L Tibawi

Before Edward Said, and the Said industry, there was Abdul Latif Tibawi (1910–1981): historian, educationalist and critic of Orientalism. Born in Palestine, Tibawi lectured in Arab Education at the Institute of Education, University of London. His *English Speaking Orientalists*, published in 1964, is a landmark study offering a masterly dissection of the techniques and methodology of Orientalism. *Islamic Education: Its Traditions and Modernisation into the Arab National System*, provides a concise history of Islamic education from its origins in the seventh century to early attempts at modernisation in the nineteenth century, explores the educational theory of Islam, and analyses the problems of modernisation by looking at specific cases – the modern national systems of Iraq, Egypt, Algeria, Morocco, Saudi Arabia and a host of other Middle Eastern states. It is perhaps the first comprehensive study of educational problems in the Arab world. The changes, Tibawi laments, are not good for 'stimulating thought'.

10. The Venture of Islam by Marshall Hodgson

The pedagogical texts, educational system, colleges and universities, and the book publishing industry were all major ingredients that shaped the Muslim civilisation of the classical period. But the Islamic civilisation was not simply 'Islamic': it was a world civilisation, a point aptly demonstrated by the monumental four-volume *The Venture of Islam* by historian Marshall Hodgson (1922–1968). Hodgson, a Quaker who taught at the University of Chicago, and tragically died young, differentiates between 'Islamic', meaning religious and pious, and 'Islamicate', the cultural products of Muslim societies. *The Venture of Islam* presents Islamic history as world history – and no Muslim intellectual can maintain his or her self-respect without reading it.

CITATIONS

Introduction: The Integration We Seek
by Jeremy Henzell-Thomas

Ziauddin Sardar's 'Reinventing Ourselves: From Islamisation of Knowledge to Integration of Knowledge' will be published by IIIT, Washington; his critical quote on Islamization is from *Desperately Seeking Paradise: Journeys of a Sceptical Muslim* (Granta Books, London, 2004), 194–203. The words of the spokesman for the Indians of the Six Nations were reported by Benjamin Franklin, 'Remarks concerning the savages of North America', London, 1784; the version related in this essay is taken from Roland Barth's *Learning by Heart* (Jossey-Bass, San Francisco, 2001), 49–50. The story told by Joe Couture about the educational value of story-telling is related by F. David Peat in his *Blackfoot Physics: A Journey into the Native American Worldview* (Fourth Estate, London 1994), 57. My paper on 'The Power of Education' appeared in *Critical Muslim: 14 Power* (Hurst, London, 2015), 65–86.

On the problem of 'narrative fallacies' see Nassim Nicholas Taleb, *The Black Swan: The Impact of the Highly Improbable* (Random House, New York, 2007). On the benefits and drawbacks of rapid thinking, see Daniel Kahneman, *Thinking, Fast and Slow* (Penguin Books, London, 2012). The doctrine of the 'Clash of Civilisations' is the subject of Samuel Huntington's *The Clash of Civilisations and the Making of the New World Order* (Simon and Schuster, New York, 1966). Fred Halliday's critique of Huntington appeared in 'A new world myth', *New Statesman*, 4 April (1997), 42–43. Other influential examples of ethnocentric, supremacist polemics include Niall Ferguson, *Civilisation: The West and the Rest* (Penguin Books, New York, 2011) and Dinesh D'Souza, *The End of Racism* (The Free Press, New York City, 1995). The misuse of the term 'relativism' is highlighted by Jacques Barzun in his monumental survey *From Dawn to Decadence. 1500 to the Present: 500 Years of Western Civilisation* (HarperCollins, London, 2001), 760–61. Abu Ishaq Al-Shatibi's ideas on supra-historical principles and moral values are from his *Al-Muwafaqat*, published by Dawlat Al-Tunisia in four volumes in

1882. Muhammad Asad's eloquent affirmation of the legacy of the culture of learning and inquiry derived from the Qur'an on the development of Western civilisation is from his Foreword to *The Message of the Qur'an* (Bath: The Book Foundation, 2004), vi. On 'civilisational bankruptcy', see Malik Bennabi, *The Question of Culture* (1954, republished by the Islamic Book Trust in 2003) and on 'archaism' as one of the symptoms of a declining civilisation, see Arnold Toynbee, *A Study of History* in 12 volumes (Oxford University Press, 1934-1961) and D.C. Somervell, *Abridgement of Volumes 1-X* (Oxford University Press, 1960). Harry Lewis's critique of the loss of meaning, purpose and ethical compass in modern liberal education in America is in his *Excellence Without A Soul: Does Liberal Education Have a Future?* (PublicAffairs, 2007). For he multi-layered meaning of the term *'aql*, see the entry for Al-'Aql, in Cyril Glassé, *The Concise Encyclopaedia of Islam* (Stacey International, London, 2001), 55, and Karim Douglas Crow, 'Between Wisdom and Reason: Aspects of 'Aql (Mind-Cognition) in Early Islam', *Islamica*, 3:1 (1999). For Jalaluddin Rumi's distinction between the two types of intelligence, see *Mathnawi* III, 2527-2528 and IV, 1960–1968. On 'd-mode' and 'practical intelligence', see Guy Claxton, *Hare Brain Tortoise Mind: Why Intelligence Increases When you Think Less* (Fourth Estate, London, 1997).

On multiple intelligences, see Howard Gardner, *Multiple Intelligences: New Horizons in Theory and Practice* (Basic Books, 2006), on emotional intelligence see Daniel Goldman, *Emotional Intelligence* (Bantam, New York, 1995), and see also: S.J. Ceci and J. Liker, 'A day at the races: a study of IQ, expertise and cognitive complexity', *Journal of Experimental Psychology: General*, Vol. 115 (1986), 255-266.

Rowan Williams's comments on British society are from his article 'Is our society broken? Yes, I think it is', *Daily Telegraph*, 17 September, 2007. For the development, organisational structure and decline of Muslim learning institutions see George Makdisi in *The Rise of Colleges: Institutions of Learning in Islam and the West* (Edinburgh University Press, Edinburgh, 1981.

What is a University? by Richard Pring

John Henry Newman's *The Idea of a University*, first published in 1852, can be downloaded from: http://newmanreader.org/works/idea/

Marod Muborkshoeva's *Islam and Higher Education: Concepts, Challenges and Opportunities* is published by Routledge (London, 2012) and Thomas Pickety's *Capital in the Twenty-First Century*, is published by Harvard University Press (Mass., 2014)

Richard Peters' books include *Ethics and Education* (Allen & Unwin, London 1968), *The Philosophy of Education* (Oxford University Press, London 1973), and *Moral Development and Moral Education* (Allen & Unwin, London 1981). Cabinet Office publications can be obtained from: https://www.gov.uk/government/publications

Universities in Muslim Contexts
by Marodsilton Muborakshoeva

The bulk of my research, on which this essay is based, is published in Marodsilton Muborakshoeva, *Islam and Higher Education: Concepts, Challenges and Opportunities* (Routledge, London, 2013). I have also referred to my article 'Islamic Scholasticism and Traditional Education and their Links with Modern Higher Education and Societies', *The International Journal of Religion and Spirituality in Society*, 3:1 (2013), 37-51. In describing the development of European universities from the early Middle Ages to modern times, including those features borrowed from Muslim institutions of higher learning, I have drawn on the following works: George Makdisi, *The Rise of Colleges: Institutions of Learning in Islam and the West* (Edinburgh University Press, Edinburgh (1981); Alan Cobban, *Medieval Universities: Their Development and Organisation* (Methuen, London, 1975); Jose Ignacio Cabezón, *Buddhism and Language: a Study of Indo-Tibetan Scholasticism* (SUNY Press, New York, 1994); and Alasdair McIntyre, *God, Philosophy, Universities: A Selective History of the Catholic Philosophical Tradition* (Rowman and Littlefield, London, 2009). In discussing the 'Islamisation of Knowledge' movement and other aspects of Islamic education I have referred to the following: Syed Muhammad Naquib Al-Attas, *The Concept of Education in Islam: A Framework for an Islamic Philosophy of Education* (BM3 Synergy Corporation, Kuala Lumpur, 1980); Seyyed Hossein Nasr (ed.), *Philosophy, Literature and Fine Arts* (Hodder and Stoughton, Jeddah, 1982); and Aziz Talbani, 'Pedagogy, Power, and Discourse: Transformation of Islamic Education', *Comparative Education Review*, 40:1 (1996), 66–82.

Thinking of Reconfiguration by Abdelwahab El-Affendi

The quotes are from R. Chan, G. T. Brown & L. Ludlow, 'What is the purpose of higher education?: A comparison of institutional and student perspectives on the goals and purposes of completing a bachelor's degree in the 21st century', Roundtable paper presented at the American Education Research Association(AERA) Annual Conference. Philadelphia, PA: April 7, 2014, p2 and Steven Schwartz, 'The higher purpose', *The Times Higher Education*, 16 May 2003, http://www.timeshighereducation. co.uk/176727.article.

Reforming Self and Other by Abdulkader Tayob

This essay is based on the research supported by the South African Research Chairs Initiative of the Department of Science and Technology and National Research Foundation (NRF) of South Africa.

The quotations from Ashraf Ali Thanvi are from his 'Archives: The Raison D'Etre of Madrasah.' *Islamic Studies* 43 (4): 653–7, p667; and the quotes from Ismail Raji al-Faruqi are from 'Islamization of Knowledge: The General Principles and Workplan' in *Knowledge for What? Being the Proceedings and Papers of the Seminar on Islamization of Knowledge, Organized Jointly By the National Hijra Centenary Committee, Pakistan, the Institute of Education, Islamic University, Islamabad, and International Institute of Islamic Thought, Wyncote, Pennsylvania, USA* (National Hijra Council, Islamabad, 1406 AH), 1-49, p22-23 and p14; and quotes from Jalal al-Din Rumi are from Rumi *Discourses of Rumi* (Ames, Iowa: Omphaloskepsis, 2000), which can be downloaded from: http://topiel.info/rumi.pdf

See also: Muhammad Abduh, 'The Necessity of Religious Reform' in *Contemporary Debates in Islam: an Anthology of Modernist and Fundamentalist Thought*, Mansoor Moaddel and Kamran Talattof (eds), 45–51 (Palgrave Macmillan, New York, 2000); Khayr al-Din al-Tunisi, Aqwam al-Masalik fi Ma'rifat ahwal al-mamalik (al-Dar al-Tunisiyyah li 'l-nashr, Tunis, 1986); Zygmunt Baumann, 'From Pilgrim to Tourist – or a Short History of Identity' in *Questions of Cultural Identity*, Stuart Hall and Paul du Gay (eds), 18–36 (Sage, London, 1996); Stuart Hall, 'Introduction: Who Needs "Identity"?' in the same anthology; Fazlur Rahman, *Islam and Modernity: Transformation of an Intellectual Tradition* (University of Chicago Press, 1982);

Yoginder Sikand, *Bastions of the Believers: Madrasahs and Islamic Education in India* (Penguin, Delhi, 2005); Charles Taylor, *The Ethics of Authenticity* (Harvard University Press, Cambridge, 1991); Syed Farid Alatas, 'The Sacralisation of the Social Sciences: a Critique of an Emerging Theme in Academic Discourse' *Archives de sciences sociales des religions* 40 (91): 89–111 1995; Suleman Dangor, 'Islamisation of Disciplines: Towards an Indigenous Educational System.' *Educational Philosophy and Theory* 37 (4): 519–31 2005.

The Sheepskin Effect by Martin Rose

The following works have been cited or used in researching this article: Barduk, Ummahun, 'Labour Market and Education: Youth and Unemployment in the Spotlight', *IEMed Mediterranean Yearbook*, 2014; Bohlander, Margaret, 'The Youth Unemployment Crisis in Tunisia', http://www.cipe.org/blog/2013/11/18/the-youth-unemployment-crisis-in-tunisia/#.VDu-4fldXuJ; Enterprise Surveys, www.enterprisesurveys.org, data cited in World Bank, *Breaking Even or Breaking Through*, 2011, p5; ERF, *Egypt Labour Panel Survey* (Economic Research Forum and CAPMAS), 2006; Furceri, David, IMF Working Paper WP/12/99, *Unemployment and Labour Market Issues in Algeria*; Guerraoui, Driss, Le chômage des jeunes et l'expérience de recrutement dans la fonction publique, *L'Observateur du Maroc*, no. 235, 1–7 November 2013; King Mohamed VI, HM The King Delivers Speech To Nation On Occasion Of 60th Anniversary Of Revolution Of King And People, 20 August 2013, full text: *Agence Marocaine de Presse* http://www.map.ma/en/activites-royales/hm-king-delivers-speech-nation-occasion-60th-anniversary-revolution-king-and-peopl; Knoema, http://knoema.com/WBWDIGDF2014Sep/world-development-indicators-wdi-september-2014; Loveluck, Louisa, Education in Egypt: Key Challenges, a Chatham House background paper, March 2012, citing Tarek Osman, *Egypt on the Brink*, New Haven and London (Yale UP) 2011; Lynch School of Education, Boston College, http://timssandpirls.bc.edu/; OECD, Integrity of Public Education in Tunisia: Restoring Trust: Results of a Preliminary Integrity Scan, *(PRINTS) of Tunisian Education* – OECD 2013 – http://www.oecd.org/cleangovbiz/Tunisia-Integrity-Education.pdf; OECD, http://www.oecd.org/pisa/pisaproducts/48852548.pdf; OECD, *Gender Inequality and entrepreneurship in the Middle East and North Africa*, OECD 2013 http://www.oecd.org/mena/investment/Statistical%20Portrait.pdf; Roudi, Farzana, Youth Population and

Unemployment in the Middle East and North Africa, PRB, 2011 http://www. un.org/esa/population/meetings/egm-adolescents/roudi.pdf; Ryan, Yasmin, The Tragic Life of a Street-Vendor, http://www.aljazeera.com/indepth/ features/2011/01/201111684242518839.html; Segalla, Spencer, *The Moroccan Soul: French Education, Colonial Ethnology and Muslim Resistance 1912-1956*, Lincoln, Nebraska, 2009; United Nations, Millennum Development Goal Report 2014, New York (UN) 2014; Egypt Human Development Report 2010, UNDP; Arab Human Development Report 2003, Building a Knowledge Society, New York (UNDP), 2003; Vermeren, Pierre, *Ecole, Elite et Pouvoir au Maroc et en Tunisie au XX Siècle*, Rabat 2002; Vermeren, Pierre, The North African Educational Challenge: From Colonisation to the Current Alleged Islamist Threat, *Mediterranean Journal of Educational Studies*, Vol 14(2), pp 49-64, 2009; World Economic Forum, Global Competitiveness Survey 2014-15, World Economic Forum 2014, http://www3.weforum.org/docs/WEF_Africa_ Competitiveness_Report_2013.pdf; World Bank, The Road Not Travelled: Education Reform in the Middle East and North Africa, Washington DC (World Bank), 2008; World Bank, www.data.worldbank.org; World Bank, http://data. worldbank.org/indicator/SE.ADT.1524.LT.ZS; World Bank, http://www. worldbank.org/content/dam/Worldbank/document/MNA/ QEBissue2January2014FINAL.pdf; World Bank, Jobs for Shared Prosperity, World Bank 2012

Measuring Quality by Paul Ashwin

For the research on which this article is based see: Paul Ashwin, Andrea Abbas and Monica McLean, 'How do students' accounts of sociology change over the course of their undergraduate degrees? *Higher Education*, 67: 219-234 2014; 'Representations of a high-quality system of undergraduate education in English higher education policy documents. *Studies in Higher Education* 40: 610-623 2015; Neoliberal policy, quality and inequality in undergraduate degrees' in P Whitehead and P Crawshaw (eds), *Institutionalizing Neoliberalism: Analysis, Impacts and Effects* (Anthem Press, London, 2011); 'Teaching through Biographical Methods', Special Edition of *Enhancing Learning in the Social Sciences* Vol 3. No. 3 2011 (available: http://www.eliss.org.uk/CurrentIssue Vol3No3/Biographical methods/tabid/336/Default.aspx); and 'The pedagogic device: sociology, knowledge practices and teaching-learning processes' in P Trowler et al (eds), *Tribes and Territories in the21st-Century: Rethinking the Significance of Disciplines in Higher Education* (Routledge, London, 2012); and M McLean, M Abbas and P Ashwin, 'University knowledge, human development and pedagogic rights' in A Boni and M Walker (eds), *Human development and capabilities: re-imagining the university of the twenty-first century* (Routledge, London, 2013, pp. 30-43)

See also: G Gibbs, *Dimensions of Quality* (Higher Education Academy, York, 2010), which is available from: www.heacademy.ac.uk/assets/documents/evidence_informed_practice/Dimensions_of_Quality.pdf; E Hazelkorn, *Rankings and the reshaping of higher education: the battle for world-class excellence,* Palgrave Macmillan, London, 2011; W Locke et al, *Counting What Is Measured or Measuring What Counts? League Tables and Their Impact on Higher Education Institutions in England*, Higher Education Funding Council for England, Bristol, 2008, which is available at: www.hefce.ac.uk/pubs/hefce/2008/08_14; and S Marginson, 'Global university rankings: Implications in general and for Australia' *Journal of Higher Education Policy and Management* 29: 131-142 2007.

Researching Islamophobia by Sindre Bangstad

For the House of Literature series on public anthropology, see the forthcoming edited volume S. Bangstad, *Anthropology in Our Times: A Series in Public Anthropology,* Palgrave MacMillan, New York, 2016. For the work of Matti and John Bunzl, see M. Bunzl, 'Between Anti-Semitism and Islamophobia: Some thoughts on the New Europe', *American Ethnologist* 32 (4) 499-508 2005; M. Bunzl, *Anti-Semitism and Islamophobia: Hatreds New And Old in Europe,* Prickly Paradigm Press/University of Chicago Press, Chicago 2007; J. Bunzl and A. Senfft (eds), *Zwischen Antisemitismus und Islamophobie: Vorteile und Projektionen in Europa und Nahost*, VSA Verlag, Hamburg; P S. Bangstad and M. Bunzl, 'Anthropologists Are Talking About Islamophobia and Antisemitism in the New Europe', *Ethnos* 75 (2) 213-228 2010. For John R. Bowen's response to Matti Bunzl's article, see J. Bowen, 'Commentary on Bunzl', *American Ethnologist* 32 (4): 84-85. For the limits to the analogy between Islamophobia and anti-Semitism, see B. Klug, 'The limits of analogy: comparing Islamophobia and antisemitism', *Patterns of Prejudice* 48 (5) 442-459 2014 and E. Bleich, 'What is Islamophobia, and

How Much Is There? Theorising and measuring an emerging comparative concept', *American Behavioural Scientist* 55 (12) 1581-1600 2011.

On 'Eurabia', see B. Ye'or, *Eurabia: The Euro-Arab Axis* (Farleigh Dickenson University Press, Madison, 2005), and for a Norwegian adaptation, see H. Berg, *Letter to Lady Liberty: Europe in Danger* (Koloritt Forlag, Oslo). For my analyses of the 'Eurabia' literature see S. Bangstad, 'Eurabia Comes To Norway', *Islam and Christian-Muslim Relations* 24 (3) 1-23 1-23, and for Matt Carr's early and prescient analysis of this literature and analogies with The Protocols see M. Carr, 'You are now entering Eurabia', *Race & Class* 48 (1): 1-22. For a good essay on conspiracy theories, see C. Sunstein and A. Vermeule, 'Conspiracy theories: causes and cures', *Journal of Political Philosophy* 17 (2): 202-27. For detailed analyses of the Progress Party's Islamophobic discourses in Norway in the period 2001 to 2011, see S. Bangstad, *Anders Breivik and The Rise of Islamophobia* (Zed, London, 2014). For the concept of 'stealth jihad', see R. Spencer, *Stealth Jihad: How Radical Islam Is Subverting America Without Guns or Bombs* (Regency, Washington, D. C. 2008). On liberalism and Islam, see J. Massad, *Islam in Liberalism* (Chicago University Press, 2015). On the TV2 documentary 'Freedom, Equality and The Muslim Brothers', see S. Bangstad, 'Terror in Norway', *American Anthropologist* 114 (2) 351-52 2012.

For Fernando Bravo López fine essay about the genealogy of the term Islamophobia, see F. B. López, 'Towards a definition of Islamophobia: approximations of the twentieth-century', *Ethnic and Racial Studies* 34 (4): 556-73. For the 'coming of age' of the term Islamophobia, see B. Klug, 'Islamophobia – a concept comes of age', *Ethnicities* 12 (5): 665-81. For the recommendation of moving towards measuring Islamophobia, see E. Bleich, 'What is Islamophobia, and How Much Is There? Theorizing and measuring an emerging comparative concept', *American Behavioural Scientist* 55 (12) 2011: 1581-1600. Finally, S. Collini's *What are Universities for?* is published by Penguin (London, 2011).

The Case for Fictional Islam by Ruqayyah A. Kareem

The novels mentioned in this article include: Saladin Ahmed, *Throne of the Crescent Moon* (DAW Books, New York, 2012); Steven Barnes, *Lion's Blood: A Novel of Slavery and Freedom in an Alternate America and Zulu Heart* (Warner

Books, New York, 2002, 2003); Ian Dallas, *The Book of Strangers* (Pantheon, New York, 1972); Yasser Bahjatt and Ibraheem Abbas, *Hawjan* (Yatakhayaloon, Riyadh, 2014); Roquia Sakhawat Hussain, *Sultana's Dream* (Tara Books, Chennai, 2015, original 1908); Ahmad Saadawi, *Frankenstein in Baghdad* (in Arabic, 2013); and G Willow Wilson, *Cairo* (D C Comics, 2007) and *Ms Marvel* Volume 1: No Normal (Marvel 2014).

See also: Shahizah Hamdan, 'Ideas in Science Fiction: Probing Contemporary Contexts through Science Fiction Texts', *Asian Social Science*, Vol. 8, No. 4; April 2012; Yusuf Nuruddin, 'Ancient Black Astronauts and Extraterrestrial Jihads: Islamic Science Fiction as Urban Mythology', *Socialism and Democracy* 20.3 (2006), pp. 127-65; and Anas Al-Shaikh, 'The Need for Education', *Islamica Magazine*, 20 2008, which can be accessed at: www.islamicamagazine.com/issue-20/the-need-for-education.html; Kate Fossett, 'Can Science Fiction Survive in Saudi Arabia?' *Foreign Policy* 10 December 2013, which can be accessed at: http://foreignpolicy.com/2013/12/10/can-science-fiction-survive-in-saudi-arabia; and interview with Yasser Bahjatt http://www.aresmagazine.com/?page_id=240.

Some useful resources include: Muhammad Aurangzeb Ahmad, Islamic Science Fiction website; http://www.islamscifi.com; Sindbad Sci-Fi www.sindbadscifi.com/ and Yatakhayaloon at: http://yatakhayaloon.com/EN/HWJN_English.html

Facing Muslim History by Farid Panjwani

The quotation from John Stuart Mill is from *On Liberty* (Penguin, London, 1974), p121-122; from W Kymlicka is from *Liberalism, community, and culture* (Oxford University Press, 1989), p52; and from H Alexander from 'What is common about common schooling? Rational autonomy and moral agency in liberal democratic education' *Journal of Philosophy of Education*, 41(4) (2007), pp. 609-624 2007, p612 and 618; from A K Soroush is from *Reason, freedom, & democracy in Islam: Essential writings of Abdolkarim Soroush* (Oxford University Press, 2000), p96; that of C Bailey is from *Beyond the present and the particular: A theory of liberal education* (Routledge, London, 1984), p181; Khalid Abou El-Fadl quote is from *Speaking in God's name: Islamic law, authority and women* (OneWorld, Oxford, 2006), pp. 9-10; from Syed Muhammed Naguib Al-Attas is from *Aims and Objectives of Islamic Education*

(Hodder and Stoughton, London, 1979), p19; the Abdullah Sahin quote is from *New directions in Islamic education: Pedagogy and identity formation* (Kube, Leicester 2013), p238; Jacques Waardenburg's topology of Muslim position is from 'The medieval period: 650–1500' in J. Waardenburg, ed., *Muslim Perceptions of Other Religions* (Oxford: Oxford University Press, 1999), p21; and Tinker and Smart quotes are from their paper 'Constructions of collective Muslim identity by advocates of Muslim schools in Britain', *Ethnic and Racial Studies*, 35(4) (2012), pp. 643-663. The conversation with the teacher of a Muslim school is taken from Farid Panjwani, 'Faith-schools and the religious other: the case of Muslim schools', in J. Chapman et al (eds), *International Handbook of Learning, Teaching and Leading in Faith-Based Schools* (Springer, London, 2014), p.139.

See also: al-Ghazali, *The faith and practice of al-Ghazali*, translated by W. M. Watt (Allen and Unwin, London, 1953); Tahir Abbas, *Islam and education* (Routledge, London, 2011); C Tan, *Reforms in Islamic Education: International perspectives* (Bloomsbury Academic, London, 2014); Y Waghid, *Conceptions of Islamic education: Pedagogical Framings* (Peter Lang, New York, 2011); and Matthew J Nelson, 'Dealing with difference: Religious education and the challenge of democracy in Pakistan' *Modern Asian Studies* 43 (3) (2009), pp 591 – 618.

What about Science? by Moneef R. Zou'bi

On the decline of science in the Muslim civilisation see A Y Al-Hassa et al (eds), *Factors behind the Decline of Islamic Science after the Sixteenth Century* (Unesco, Paris, 2007, Part II), which is available online at: http:// queriesonislam.wordpress.com/2010/12/24/factors-behind-the-decline-of-islamic-science-part-2/; M Golshani, 'The Rise and Decline of Science in the Muslim World' in the *Proceeding of Sixteenth Conference of the Muslim world Academy of Sciences on Science, Technology and Innovation for Sustainable Development in the Muslim world: The Policies and Politics Rapprochement* (Kazan, Tatarstan, 25 – 28 August 2008); George Saliba, 'Unravelling the Mystery of the Decline of Islamic Science: Key Projections on Today's World' in the *Proceedings of the Eighteenth Conference of the Muslim world Academy of Sciences on The Muslim world and the West: Rebuilding Bridges through Science and Technology* (Doha, 22-24 October 2011); an edited version of Ziauddin

Sardar's Royal Society Lecture, 'Islam and Science: Beyond the Troubled Relationship', delivered on 12 December 2006, was published in *Nature* 448 131-133 11 July 2007.

The quote from Omar Abdul Rahman is from 'Forging Creativity and Technopreneurship Agenda for OIC Countries', in M Ergin and M R Zou'bi (eds), *Science, Technology and Innovation for Socioeconomic Development: Towards Vision 1441* (Muslim world Academy of Sciences, Amman, 2008). See also: Pierre Léna, 'Much More is Required: Science Education in the 21st Century: A Challenge' in the *Proceedings of the Pontifical Academy of Sciences*, Rome, 2004, p. 142; M Ergin, M Doruk, and M R Zou'bi (eds), *Science and Technology Education for Development in the Muslim world* (Muslim world Academy of Sciences, Amman, 2000);

Ziauddin Sardar, *Sardar, Science, Technology and Development in the Muslim World* (Croom Helm, London, 1977); and 'Islam and Science' Nature 444, 2 November 2006.

On the *ijaz* literature, see Nidhal Guessoum, *Islam's Quantum Question: Reconciling Muslim Tradition and Modern Science* (I B Tauris, London, 2011). The pronouncements of the Saudi Sheikh Bandar al-Khaibari on a stationary Earth are widely available on YouTube; search for 'Saudi cleric rejects that Earth revolves around the Sun'.

My Life in Islamic Economics by Muhammad Nejatullah Siddiqi

My early works are in Urdu: Mohammad Nejatullah Siddiqi, *Islam ka Nazariyah e Milkiyat* (Lahore, 1968); *Ghair Soodi Bank Kari* (Lahore, 1969); *Shirket aur Mudarabat ke Shar 'I Usul* (Lahore, 1969). The English titles include: *A Critical Examination of Recent Theories of Profit* (Bombay, Asia House, 1971); *Economic Enterprise in Islam* (Islamic Publications, Lahore, 1972); *Banking Without Interest* (Islamic Foundation, Leicester, 1983); *Partnership and Profit-sharing in Islamic Law* (Islamic Publications, Lahore, 1985); and *Role of the State in the Economy: An Islamic Perspective* (Islamic Foundation, Leicester, 1996). My critique of 'Islamization of Knowledge' appears as 'Islamization of Knowledge: Reflections on Priorities', *American Journal of Islamic Social Sciences* vol.8,issue#3 pp 15-35 2011.

Authors and books mentioned in this article include: Muhammad Abdullah Al-Arabi, *Al-Iqtisad al Islami wa'l Iqtisad al Mu 'asir* (Al-Azhar, Cairo, 1966); Ahmad Muhammad Abdulaziz Al-Najjar, *Bunuk Bila Fawaid ka Istratijiyah li'l Tanmiyah al-Iqtisadiyah li'l Duwal al Islamiyah* (Jamiat Malik Abdulaziz, Jeddah, 1972); Sami Hasan Ahmad Hamoud, *Tatwir al A 'mal al Masrafiyah be ma yettafequ wa'l Shariet* (Amman, al Islamiyah, 1976); Syed Abul Ala Maududi, *Sood* (Islamic Publications, Lahore, 1961) and *Ta 'leemat* (Islamic Publications, Lahore, 1963); Naiem Siddiqi, *Islami Usool per Banking* (Banking according to Islamic Principles) Chiragh e Rah, Karachi, 1(11) Nov.48:60-64; Dec 48:24-28 1948; Anwar Iqbal Quraishi, *Islam and the Theory of Interest* (Ashraf, Lahore, 1946); Syed Qutb, *Social Justice in Islam* (Dar AlShorouk, Cairo, 1993; orginal 1967); and Mohammad Uzair, *An Outline of Interless Banking* (Karachi, 1955).

See also: Irfan Harris, *Heaven's Bankers: Inside the Hidden World of Islamic Finance* (Constable, London, 2014); Joseph Stiglitz, *The Price of Inequality* (Penguin, 2013) and *Freefall: Free Markets and the Sinking of the Global Economy* (Penguin, 2010).

Seeking *Ilm* on the Silk Road by Naomi Foyle

On the Gaia Chronicles, see Naomi Foyle, *Astra* and *Rook Song* (Jo Fletcher Books, London, 2014 and 2015, respectively). The novels and books mentioned in this essay include:

Farid ud-Din Attar, *The Conference of the Birds*, translated by Afkham Darbandi and Dick Davis (Penguin Books, London, 2011, second edition); Mark Cocker, *Birds and People* (Jonathan Cape, London, 2013); Jean Genet, *The Prisoner of Love* (Picador, London, 1989); Shreen El Feki, *Sex and the Citadel: Intimate Life in a Changing ArabWorld* (Vintage, London, 2014); Emile Habiby, *Saraya:The Ogre's Daughter:A Palestinian Fairy Tale*, translated by Peter Theroux (Ibis Editions, Jerusalem, 2006); Malu Halasa et al (eds), *Syria Speaks: Art and Culture from the Frontline* (Saqi, London, 2014); Khaled Hosseini, *A Thousand Splendid Suns* (Bloomsbury, London, 2009); Mike Marqusee, *If I Am Not For Myself: Journey of an anti-Zionist Jew* (Verso, London, 2010); Bejan Matur, *How Abraham Abandoned Me* (Arc Publications, Lancs, 2012); Nnedi Okorafor-Mbachi, *The Shadow Speaker* (Hyperion, NewYork, 2006);

Nnedi Okorafor, *Who Fears Death* (DAW Books, New York, 2014); Orhan Pamuk, *Snow*, translated by Guneli Gun (Faber & Faber, London, 2005); Ziauddin Sardar, *How Do You Know? Reading Ziauddin Sardar on Islam, Science and Cultural Relations* (Pluto Press, London, 2006); Ziauddin Sardar and Robin Yassin-Kassab (eds), *Critical Muslim 11: Syria* (Hurst, London, 2014); and Diana Wolkstein et al, *Inanna, Queen of Heaven and Earth: Her Stories and Hymns from Sumer* (Harper, New York, 1983).

Papers are articles mention are: Naomi Foyle, 'The Strange Wife' [play] in *66 Books: 21st Century Writers Speak to the King James Bible* (Oberon, London, 2011); Rebecca Hankins, 'Fictional Islam: A Literary Review and Comparative Essay on Islam in Science Fiction and Fantasy', *Foundation: The International Review of Science Fiction*, Vol 38 No. 105, pp73-92 2009; Yusuf Nuruddin (2006) Ancient black astronauts and extra-terrestrial Jihads: Islamic science fiction as urban mythology, *Socialism and Democracy*, 20:3 127-165 2006.

See also: Alibhai Brown, Yasmin (Jan 11 2015). 'Far Too Many Western Muslims Speak of Freedom as a Sin', which can be retrieved from http://www.independent.co.uk/voices/comment/far-too-many-western-muslims-speak-of-freedom-as-a-sin-9971118.html; Judith Butler (Feb 24 2010). [Interview.], http://www.haaretz.com/news/judith-butler-as-a-jew-i-was-taught-it-was-ethically-imperative-to-speak-up-1.266243; Erin Hanson, 'Oral Traditions': http://indigenousfoundations.arts.ubc.ca/home/culture/oral-traditions.html; Leila Sansour, (n.d). 'The campaign' can be retrieved from http://www.openbethlehem.org/the-campaign/; and Paul Weimer's (July 14 2014) 'Writing in Ink to Samarkand' can be retrieved from http://aidanmoher.com/blog/featured-article/2014/07/writing-ink-samarkand-silk-road-fantasy-paul-weimer/

The List: Ten Key Texts on Islamic Education

Constantine Zurayk's translation of *The Refinement of Character* by Miskawayh, originally published by American University of Beirut (1968), has been reprinted by Kazi Publications (Chicago, 2002). An English translation of Ibn Jammah's *The Memoire of the Listener and the Speaker in the Training of Teacher and Student* is published by the Pakistan Hijra Council (Islamabad, 1991), in its lists of 'One Hundred Great Books of Islamic

Civilisation'. *Instruction for the Student: The Method of Learning* by al-Zarnuji is available from Starlatch Press (Chicago, 2003). Al-Ghazali's *The Book of Knowledge*, translated by Nabih Amin Faris, is widely available in various editions, including Muhammad Ashraf (Lahore, 1962). *The Fihrist of al-Nadim*, translated and edited by Bayard Dodge, is published in two volumes by Colombia University Press (New York, 1970). F Rosenthal's *Knowledge Triumphant: The Concept of Knowledge in Medieval Islam* is published by Brill (Leiden, 19670); *The Arabic Book* by Johannes Pedersen, translated from the original Danish by Geoffrey French, is published by Princeton University Press (Princeton, 1984); *The Rise of Colleges: Institutions of Learning in Islam and the West* by George Makdisi is published by Edinburgh University Press (Edinburgh, 1981); *Islamic Education* by A L Tibawi, sadly out of print, was originally published by Luzac & Co (London, 1972); and the four-volume *The Venture of Islam: Consensus and History in a World Civilisation* by Marshall Hodgson is available in paperback from Chicago University Press (Chicago, 1974).

A L Tibawi's *English Speaking Orientalists* was published by Luzac & Co (London, 1964). See also *A Philosophy Reader from the Circle of Miskawayh: Text, Translation and Commentary*, translated by Elvira Wakeinig (Cambridge University Press, 2014); and Bruce Lawrence, 'Genius Denied and Reclaimed: a 40-Year Retrospect on Marshall G S Hodgon's The Venture of Islam', which can be read at: http://marginalia.lareviewofbooks.org/retrospect-hodgson-venture-islam/

CONTRIBUTORS

Paul Ashwin is Professor and Head of Department of Educational Research at Lancaster University ● **Sindre Bangstad** is a researcher in the Faculty of Theology, University of Oslo, Norway ● **Merryl Wyn Davies** is Co-Director of the Muslim Institute ● **Cheli Duran**, who grew up in Cuba, works in London and is a Greek citizen, and a well-known writer of children's books ● **Abdelwahab El-Affendi** is co-ordinator of the Democracy and Islam Programme at the Centre for the Study of Democracy, University of Westminster ● **Naomi Foyle**, a lecturer at Chichester University, is a science fiction writer ● **Marilyn Hacker** is a celebrated poet ● **Jeremy Henzell-Thomas** is a research associate and former visiting fellow at the Centre of Islamic Studies, University of Cambridge ● **Ruqayyah A. Kareem (Rebecca Hankins)** is Africana Resource Librarian and Associate Professor at Texas A&M University ● **Iftikhar H. Malik** is Professor of History at Bath Spa University, Bath ● **Ebrahim Moosa** is Professor of Islamic Studies at the University of Notre Dame in the Department of History and the Kroc Institute for International Studies ● **Mohammed Moussa** is a postdoctoral fellow at Tokyo University of Foreign Studies, Japan ● **Marodsilton Muborakshoeva**, Lecturer, Department of Graduate Studies, Institute of Ismaili Studies, London, is the author of *Islam and Higher Education* ● **Farid Panjwani** is Assistant Professor at the Aga Khan University's Institute for the Study of Muslim Civilisations, London ● **Richard Pring**, who was Director of the Department of Educational Studies at Oxford University, is now at Green Templeton College, Oxford ● **Martin Rose**, who is a visiting fellow at the Prince Walid bin Talal Centre for Islamic Studies at Cambridge, has worked in the Middle East and North Africa for many years, most recently as Director of the British Council in Morocco ● **Shanon Shah** has just obtained his doctorate from the Department of Theology and Religious Studies, King's College London ● **Mohammad Nejatullah Siddiqi**, regarded by many as the grandfather of Islamic economics, is Professor Emeritus in the Department of Management Studies, Aligarh Muslim University ● **Abdulkader Tayob** is Professor in the Department of Religious Studies, University of Cape Town, South Africa ● **Ilona Yusuf** is a British Pakistani poet ● **Moneef R Zou'bi** is Director General of Islamic World Academy of Science, Amman, Jordan.